HUMAN DEVELOPMENT IN CULTURAL
AND HISTORICAL CONTEXTS

Adolescent mothers in later life

HUMAN DEVELOPMENT IN CULTURAL
AND HISTORICAL CONTEXTS

General Editor: Urie Bronfenbrenner
Associate Editor: Glen H. Elder, Jr.

Adolescent mothers in later life

FRANK F. FURSTENBERG, JR.

University of Pennsylvania

J. BROOKS-GUNN

Educational Testing Service

S. PHILIP MORGAN

University of Pennsylvania

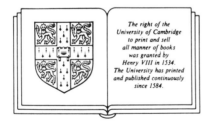

The right of the
University of Cambridge
to print and sell
all manner of books
was granted by
Henry VIII in 1534.
The University has printed
and published continuously
since 1584.

CAMBRIDGE UNIVERSITY PRESS

Cambridge
New York   Port Chester   Melbourne   Sydney

Published by the Press Syndicate of the University of Cambridge
The Pitt Building, Trumpington Street, Cambridge CB2 1RP
40 West 20th Street, New York, NY 10011, USA
10 Stamford Road, Oakleigh, Melbourne 3166, Australia

First published 1987
Reprinted 1988
First time paperback 1989
Reprinted with corrections 1990

Printed in the United States of America

Library of Congress Cataloging-in-Publication Data

Furstenberg, Frank F., 1940–
Adolescent mothers in later life.
(Human development in cultural and historical contexts)
Bibliography: P.
Includes index.
1. Adolescent mothers – Maryland – Baltimore –
Longitudinal studies.   2. Mother and child – Maryland –
Baltimore – Longitudinal studies.   1. Brooks – Gunn, J.
II. Morgan, S. Philip.   III. Title.
IV. Series
HQ759.4.F86   1987   306.8′743′088055   87-709
ISBN 0-521-33417-9
ISBN 0-521-37968-7

British Library Cataloging-in-Publication Data Applied for

Contents

v

Tables and figures

Tables

Figures

Preface

A great many debts are incurred in a research project that spans 20 years. Some were gratefully acknowledged in the preface to *Unplanned Parenthood: The Social Consequences of Teenage Childbearing* (1976), which described the earlier phase of this study. Our gratitude to the many individuals who helped launch the Baltimore research has only increased over time because the quality of the data collected in the early years of the project provided the foundation for this volume.

We are able to date rather precisely when the idea of a 17-year follow-up occurred to us. In the summer of 1981, J. Brooks-Gunn and Frank Furstenberg first met at an Aspen Institute conference on "The First 20 Years of Life" sponsored by the Foundation for Child Development and organized by Orville (Bert) Brim and Jessie Emmett. We discovered a mutual interest in longitudinal research on families, a mutual concern about the intellectual chasm between studies of family socialization produced by sociologists and developmental psychologists, and a mutual commitment to improving the link between research on disadvantaged families and social policy aimed at improving the lot of the poor.

Over the years, Furstenberg had thought of revisiting the Baltimore mothers when their children reached puberty. He lacked the courage for such an undertaking. But a collaboration with Brooks-Gunn seemed just the thing. Fantasies of this sort rarely go any further than conversation over drinks. Many people deserve credit for making this fantasy a reality.

Bert Brim, who brought Furstenberg and Brooks-Gunn together at the Aspen Institute conference, is the intellectual godparent of this study. We are no less indebted to Margaret Mahoney and Thomas Moloney of the Commonwealth Fund for providing the material and psychological support to carry out the study. Maloney encouraged us at an early stage to conduct the follow-up and provoked us to produce results that would be useful to policymakers and practitioners. Mohoney was unstinting in her willingness to marshal the necessary resources to conduct the study.

The Commonwealth Fund solicited excellent advice in planning the research design and data-collection procedures from an ad hoc committee consisting of Howard Freedman, Beatrix Hamburg, Lorraine Klerman, and Kristin Moore. Many of their helpful suggestions improved the quality of our research.

Anyone who has been through the process of fielding a study knows that a project such as this one ultimately can fall into the hands of what Julius Roth once called "hired hands," who may not share the same vision or lofty research standards as those who manage the study. We feel fortunate that our "hired hands" were no less committed to high-quality research than we. Ellin Spector, who supervised the data collection, and Carolyn Jenne and Ann Roth, who oversaw the coding and data reduction, were genuine collaborators in the study, as was the entire staff of the Institute of Survey Research at Temple University. Without Ellin Spector's persistence, we most certainly would not have been as successful as we were in relocating the participants in our study. We were also ably assisted by Vivian Washington, the Baltimore community leader who took a special interest in this project.

S. Philip Morgan joined us as we began the formidable task of organizing and analyzing the life courses of over 300 families and three generations. Longitudinal studies often inadequately address the timing and sequencing of life events. In addition, no study (at least of which we were aware) had tackled the problem of looking at the *interconnection* between the mother's life decisions and her child's life-course trajectories. Morgan's intellectual contribution to unraveling these puzzles was so great that he inevitably became our collaborator. From the point he joined the study, we formed a truly interdisciplinary team: sociology, demography, and developmental psychology.

The individuals with whom we worked at the Educational Testing Service and the University of Pennsylvania were no less committed to the success of the study than we were. They repeatedly gave extra time and effort to improve the quality of the research and the quality of life within the research project. Our early work in developing the survey instruments was greatly facilitated by Deborah Ward and Lorraine Luciano. Later on, Kathleen Mullan Harris, Mary Elizabeth Hughes, Laura Blakesley, and James Rosso patiently ran, and reran, the many computer analyses necessary to describe the lives of the Baltimore study women. Others gave generously of their time during the data collection and analyses phases: Susan Zuravin, Connaught Meagher, and Christine Winquist Nord.

A description of life courses would be quite sterile if the voices of the respondents were not heard. We were extremely fortunate to have a skilled ethnographer interview 25 of the Baltimore mothers. From these rich transcripts, the portraits of three of the Baltimore mothers were painted. Carolyn Zinsser's sensitivity in capturing the more elusive qualities of the families was a great gift to us.

Perhaps most critical to the smooth functioning of the study, and to everyone's frame of mind, were Julia Robinson and Rosemary Deibler. Not only did they decipher our sometimes unreadable handwriting and act as unofficial editors, but they also coordinated activities between Princeton and Philadelphia. Their competence, patience, and sense of humor were indispensable to the wellbeing of the study and to us.

The Baltimore study touches on issues about which all of us have strong beliefs, especially with regard to stereotypes about the teenage mother and the existence and maintenance of an underclass in society today. Many of our colleagues gave thought to the policy implications for the Baltimore study; Andrew Cherlin, Anne Petersen, Jane Menken, Susan Watkins, Eugene Bardach, Kay Pyle, Richard Lincoln, Marie McCormick, David Featherman, George Valliant, and Urie Bronfenbrenner deserve special mention.

A first draft of this manuscript was reviewed by the Panel on Adolescent Pregnancy set up by the National Research Council to review current research and public policy related to teenage pregnancy and childbearing. We appreciate the encouraging and constructive comments of the panel members and staff: Daniel Federman (chair), Wendy H. Baldwin, Ezra C. Davidson, Jr., Joy G. Dryfoos, Jacqueline D. Forrest, Beatrix A. Hamburg, Cheryl D. Hayes, Sandra L. Hofferth, Richard Jessor, Judith E. Jones, Frank Levy, Robert H. Mnookin, Kristin A. Moore, Ross D. Parke, Harold A. Richman, and Maris Vinovskis.

The Commonwealth Fund solicited reviews of the initial draft report from Blanche Bernstein, Charles Murray, and Gilbert Steiner. Their comments regarding the manuscript were both generous and provocative.

Glen Elder's thoughtful reading of an early draft of the manuscript was welcome; many of his comments have been incorporated into the book, as have been his methods of analysis as exemplified by his work on the Great Depression.

It is standard in such statements to acknowledge the support provided by families, most particularly forbearing spouses. Because it is standard, it is no less heartfelt. Our spouses, Nina Segre, Robert Gunn, and Susan Evans, provided more than support. Along the way, they provided advice, sound judgment, and, not least of all, loving care.

The Baltimore study continues into the next generation. Through the generous support of the Robert Wood Johnson and Ford Foundations, we are now studying the transition from late adolescence to adulthood among the firstborn children of the adolescent mothers. Our attention has turned to the enduring effects of poverty on this generation. The Office of Adolescent Pregnancy Programs is supporting a detailed study of those adolescents who have become teenage parents and their offspring – the fourth generation in the Baltimore study. The Dodge Foundation and the Commonwealth Fund have provided the support to interview again the first generation – the parents of the original teen mothers. We would like to thank Oscar Harkavy, Prudence Brown, and Shelby Miller from the Ford Foundation; Ruby Hearn, Linda Aiken, and Paul Jellinek of the Robert Wood Johnson Foundation; and Scott McVay and Valerie Peed of the Dodge Foundation for their help in monitoring this new phase of the Baltimore project.

Our most important debt is to the families in the Baltimore study who have given so generously of their time and have provided such thoughtful responses to our queries. This is really their story, and we are only the storytellers.

1 Reassessing adolescent parenthood

The emergence of teenage childbearing as a social problem

Unlike most of Western Europe, where family formation traditionally occurred at older ages, teenage childbearing has never been uncommon in the United States (Wattenberg, 1976, p. 54). However, not until the middle of the twentieth century did a substantial proportion of teenagers ever marry and have children. At the height of the baby boom, close to half of all women wed in their teens, and well over a quarter of all women had their first birth before age 20 (Cherlin, 1981). Curiously, in the 1950s, the prevalence of early parenthood hardly received public notice, and it certainly escaped public opprobrium when it was far more common than today.

By the following decade, adolescent pregnancy and childbearing seemed to emerge suddenly as a social problem. Teenage pregnancy first appears in 1970 as a distinct category in the *Reader's Guide to Periodical Literature,* marking its cultural debut as a public issue. By the early 1980s, teenage pregnancy was "the problem that hasn't gone away" (Alan Guttmacher Institute, 1981). And in 1985, a pregnant teenager appeared on the cover of *Time.*

At the root of this shift in public attitudes is a series of longstanding demographic changes dating back to the end of the baby boom, when adult fertility rates began their dramatic plunge. As Table 1.1 shows, the adolescent birthrate also declines consistently across recent decades, though it was more gradual than for older women. Especially among the younger teens, rates of childbearing hardly declined at all. This differential decline in birthrates was magnified by the huge number of young adolescents reaching childbearing ages as the large postwar cohort entered their early teens. Between 1955 and 1970, the number of births among 15- to 19-year-olds rose by a third, climbing from 484,000 to 645,000 (see Table 1.1), and lifted the relative share of all births born to teenage mothers from 12% to 18% during the same 15-year period (Baldwin, 1976; Furstenberg, Lincoln, and Menken, 1981; Vinovskis, 1981).

These trends might have gone unnoticed, except to demographers, were it not for the fact that a growing percentage of teenage births occurred to unmarried

1

Table 1.1. *Adolescent fertility by race, 1955–1984*

Age/race	1955	1960	1970	1980	1983	1984
			Number of births (in thousands)			
15–19						
Total	484	587	645	552	489	470
White	373	459	464	388	338	321
Black	111[a]	129[a]	172	150	137	134
18–19						
Total	334	405	421	354	317	303
White	269	329	320	260	229	216
Black	65[a]	76[a]	95	84	79	77
15–17						
Total	150	182	224	198	173	167
White	104	130	144	128	110	105
Black	46[a]	53[a]	77	66	58	57
<15						
Total	6	7	12	10	10	10
White	2	3	4	4	4	4
Black	4[a]	4[a]	7	6	5	6
			Birthrates (per thousand women)			
15–19						
Total	90.3	89.1	68.3	53.0	51.7	50.9
White	79.1	79.4	57.4	44.7	43.6	42.5
Black	167.2[a]	156.1	147.7	100.0	95.5	95.7
18–19						
Total	—	—	114.7	82.1	78.1	78.3
White	—	—	101.5	72.1	68.3	68.1
Black	—	—	204.9	138.8	130.4	132.0
15–17						
Total	—	—	38.8	32.5	32.0	31.1
White	—	—	29.2	25.2	24.8	23.9
Black	—	—	101.4	73.6	70.1	69.7
<15						
Total	0.9	0.8	1.2	1.1	1.1	1.2
White	0.3	0.4	0.5	0.6	0.6	0.6
Black	4.8[a]	4.3	5.2	4.3	4.1	4.3

Table 1.1. *(cont.)*

Age/race	1955	1960	1970	1980	1983	1984
		Rates of out-of-wedlock births (per thousand unmarried women)				
15–19						
Total	15.1	15.3	22.4	27.6	29.8	30.2
White	6.0	6.6	10.9	16.2	18.5	19.0
Black	77.6[a]	76.5[a]	96.9	89.2	86.4	87.1
		Ratios of out-of-wedlock births (per thousand births)				
15–19						
Total	143	148	295	476	534	556
White	64	72	171	330	391	415
Black	407[a]	421[a]	628	851	883	891
18–19						
Total	102	107	224	398	457	481
White	49	54	135	270	323	349
Black	324[a]	337[a]	521	792	835	848
15–17						
Total	232	240	430	615	676	692
White	102	116	252	452	527	552
Black	524[a]	543[a]	760	928	948	950
<15						
Total	663	679	808	887	904	910
White	421	475	579	754	799	807
Black	801[a]	822[a]	935	985	984	985

Note: All totals include whites and all nonwhites, which is somewhat more than the sum of whites pius blacks. Dashes indicate data are unavailable.
[a] Includes all nonwhites, not only blacks.
Sources: Moore et al. (1986); Collaborative Perinatal Study (1984); U.S. Department of Commerce, Bureau of the Census (1984); National Center for Health Statistics (1985, 1986).

women. The relatively early marriages, characteristic of the period following World War II, had concealed a high rate of premarital sexual activity. In the late 1950s, close to one-half of all women married before they reached 20, and perhaps as many as half of these women were pregnant at the time (Cutright, 1972; O'Connell and Moore, 1980). As marriage age ascended in the 1960s, early sexual activity and premarital pregnancy became more visible. Table 1.1 shows that the rate of out-of-wedlock childbearing, which had been rising slowly in the preceding decade, soared in the period from 1960 to the mid-1970s. (Since then, it has continued to rise steadily for whites while declining among blacks.) In the face of an overall drop in the teenage birthrate, the rise in out-of-wedlock fertility had the effect of dramatically increasing the proportion of births to single teenagers. The trends documented in Table 1.1 indicate that the percentage of all births to teenagers out-of-wedlock jumped from 14% in 1955 to 56% in 1984.

The population changes described above had profound political ramifications. For the first time in American history, the link between marriage and sexual activity was severed. Premarital sex, not uncommon in early epochs, had become prevalent by the middle of the twentieth century. However, until the 1970s, premarital sex remained a part of the courtship sequence. During the 1970s, large numbers of teens initiated sexual intercourse with no prospect of marriage in mind. The proportion of sexually active teens rose by two-thirds, so that by the end of the decade 49% of all 17-year-olds and 69% of all 19-year-olds living in metropolitan areas were nonvirgins (Zelnik and Kantner, 1980). These trends, documented by social science researchers and effectively publicized by family-planning advocates, helped to create a sense of social crisis (Hayes, 1987).

The legalization of abortion contributed to the mounting perception that the traditional pattern of family formation was breaking down. After the 1973 Supreme Court case, Roe v. Wade, abortion became more accessible. Large numbers of pregnant teens, who might otherwise have chosen early marriage, opted instead to terminate their pregnancy. From 1974 to 1979, the number of teenage abortions rose by nearly two-thirds, while the proportion of pregnancies ended by abortion climbed from 29% to 43% (Henshaw and O'Reilly, 1983). Large numbers of abortions, especially among young unmarried women, heated up what was already a politically volatile issue.

Sexual activity and resulting patterns of abortion and out-of-wedlock childbearing became part of a new constellation of family patterns. Demographers and sociologists do not fully understand why the shift from an early to a later marriage pattern was so abrupt in the period from 1965 to 1980, but the rapid disappearance of early family formation reflected in part changing economic opportunities for youth (Fuchs, 1983; Thornton and Freedman, 1983). Unemployment rates among teenagers doubled from the mid-1960s to the mid-1970s, no doubt limiting the economic viability of early marriage.

Education became increasingly important as an admission ticket to the labor market and to eventual occupational mobility. High school graduation and post-secondary schooling, prevalent in the 1950s, became almost mandatory in the decades following. Women, to a greater degree than ever before, were reluctant to move directly from school into marriage and childbearing without spending some time in the labor force (Masnick and Bane, 1980). Given the mounting costs of supporting a family, the high rates of unemployment of young adult males, and the growing prevalence of marital disruption, women's decision to invest more in work and defer marriage seemed prudent, even imperative. Deferring marriage had the consequence of reinforcing the need for further schooling in order to obtain employment, which in turn drove the marriage age up even further, fostering a kind of inflationary spiral. Early family formation, which may have been ill advised in the 1950s, seemed all-the-more misguided by the end of the 1970s.

Students of the life-course perspective have argued that the timing of marriage and childbearing is determined by a delicate interplay between individual decisions, based on personal and economic considerations, and prevailing social norms, reflecting general cultural or subcultural beliefs about age-appropriate behavior (Elder, 1984a, b; Modell et al., 1976, 1978). Age norms in turn are structured by the availability of economic and social opportunities. Early marriage and childbearing occur when individuals have the resources to establish and maintain a family and to set up a new household. The social timetable for family formation is continually being revised by individuals in light of the availability of resources as well as prevailing age norms governing the transition to adulthood.

Such a process of adjustment may have occurred during the 1960s when marriage age rose in response to increasing educational demands and declining economic opportunities for teenagers. The deferral of marriage made it increasingly difficult to maintain the traditional courtship pattern, a pattern that placed sexual activity in the context of probable marriage. When the link between sexual intercourse and marriage was broken, the likelihood of abortion and out-of-wedlock childbearing greatly increased. These behaviors in turn underscored the prevailing view that the family was in a state of crisis (Furstenberg et al., 1981; Petchesky, 1984).

Attention was initially focused on the black family in part because it experienced the most dramatic changes in the last quarter century (Cherlin, 1981; Rainwater and Yancey, 1967; Ross and Sawhill, 1975). Marriage among teenage blacks virtually disappeared over the past two decades. Close to a third of all 18- and 19-year-old black women were married in 1960 compared to less than 3% in 1984 (U.S. Bureau of the Census, 1985). By the mid-1980s, almost all children of black teenage mothers were born out-of-wedlock (89%; see Table 1.1). These dramatic changes helped create the belief that teenage childbearing is primarily a black issue. But recent trends suggest that blacks may simply have been pacesetters for the population at large. Marriage rates among whites have been declining rapidly, and both the rate and ratio of out-of-wedlock childbearing have risen sharply. Recent international data collected by the Alan Guttmacher Institute indicate that U.S. whites have the highest rates of teenage pregnancy and childbearing of any Western nation (Jones et al., 1985; Westoff, Calot, and Foster, 1983). Indeed, white teenagers in America are more than twice as likely to become pregnant as Canadians and more than four times as likely as Swedish youth. These international trends do not take into account the fact that U.S. teens, white and black alike, have traditionally started families earlier than their European and Canadian counterparts. What is different today is that teenage fertility typically occurs outside marriage. And early marriages, when they do occur, are unlikely to survive. Thus, children born to teenage mothers have an extremely high probability of living in a single-parent family.

Research on teenage childbearing

The wave of public concern about teenage childbearing sweeping the country during the past decade was fueled by social scientific data providing evidence that early childbearing was hazardous to adolescent parents. Aside from a modest concern in the 1950s about the ill effects of very early marriage, virtually no research had been carried out on early parenthood prior to the late 1960s. At that time, changes in family formation led a few social scientists to recognize the potentially adverse effects of early childbearing. Arthur Cambell's 1968 statement was one of the earliest.

The girl who has an illegitimate child at the age of 16 suddenly has 90 percent of her life's script written for her. She will probably drop out of school; even if someone else in her family helps to take care of the baby, she will probably not be able to find a steady job that pays enough to provide for herself and her child; she may feel impelled to marry someone she might not otherwise have chosen. Her life choices are few, and most of them are bad. (p. 238)

Cambell's observation was really a conjecture since almost no data were available at the time to substantiate his claim about the deleterious consequences of early parenthood. However, his assertion acknowledged the changing structure of the life course for young people by the late 1960s. School dropout and hasty marriage, common patterns for dealing with premarital pregnancy a decade earlier, were already being described as possibly undesirable in 1968. The costs of entering marriage and parenthood without adequate schooling and employment experience were becoming abundantly clear.

In the following decade, close attention was given to the impact of early and out-of-wedlock childbearing on the life chances of adolescent parents and their offspring (Alan Guttmacher Institute, 1981; Chilman, 1983; Furstenberg et al., 1981; Hofferth and Hayes, 1987; McAnarney and Schreider, 1984; Moore and Burt, 1982). Much of this work implicitly or explicitly drew upon theoretical insights derived from the life-course perspective simultaneously developed in sociology, demography, history, and psychology (Baltes and Brim, 1978–1981, vols. 1–4; Demos and Boocock, 1978; Elder, 1974; Hareven, 1978; Hogan, 1978, 1980; also Modell et al., 1976; Riley, Johnson, and Foner, 1972). Although it is difficult to summarize this extensive literature briefly, it is fair to say that in many respects Cambell's hypothesis has been substantiated. Using a variety of study designs and data-collection strategies, investigators have discovered that early childbearers are much more likely to experience economic hardship and family disruption in later life than later childbearers (Chilman, 1983; McAnarney and Schreider, 1984; Moore and Burt, 1982). First, early childbearing appears to be linked to school dropout among adolescent mothers and, to a lesser extent, among teenage fathers (Card and Wise, 1978; Haggstrom, Kanouse, and Morrison, 1983; Mott and Maxwell, 1981; for further references see Hofferth and Hayes, 1987, ch. 7). Although disagreements exist over the strength of this link and the precise causal connection between pregnancy and the interruption of schooling, virtually all social scientists agree that teenage mothers do not achieve as much education as women who delay childbearing. Many reasons have been advanced to explain the connection. Teenagers who have children are pressured to leave school; adolescent mothers find it difficult to perform their schoolwork; and poor students are disproportionately likely to become pregnant and to drop out when they do bear children (Rindfuss, St. John, and Bumpass, 1984). In general, pregnancy usually precedes dropout, but a substantial minority of young mothers drop out before conception (Hofferth and Hayes, 1987).

Low educational attainment foreshadows difficulties in the job market. Teenage mothers are less likely to find stable and remunerative employment than are women who delay childbearing. Accordingly, they are more likely to receive public assistance at the entry to parenthood, to become reliant on public assistance, and to end up in poverty (Card and Wise, 1978; Hofferth and Moore, 1979). Unfortunately, most existing studies of economic status are short-term. It is not as clear whether economic disadvantage continues beyond the childbearing years or, if teenage mothers do reduce the gap, how much they are able to catch up (Hofferth and Hayes, 1987).

The creation of economic disadvantage – temporary or permanent – results in large measure from high rates of marital disruption and instability often following a teenage birth. Teenage childbearers, when they wed, marry quite young, and young marriages are at a high risk of dissolution (McCarthy and Menken, 1979; Morgan and Rindfuss, 1985). As with other indicators, why and how early childbearing affects the chances of marital stability are unanswered questions (Marini, 1981a, b; Moore and Waite, 1981; see references in Hofferth and Hayes, 1987, ch. 8). Some believe that early marriage, not early childbearing, is the source of disruption whereas others contend that the out-of-wedlock births diminish the prospects of a stable union (Hofferth and Hayes, 1987); some evidence suggests that *both* early marriage and out-of-wedlock births increase the risk of marital disruption (Morgan and Rindfuss, 1985).

Although teenage marriages are less likely to survive, those that do produce a greater number of children than later marriages. An increased number of children is a further disadvantage to teenage parents. Several studies have shown that adolescent parents experience great difficulty in restricting their family size (Bumpass et al., 1978; Millman and Hendershot, 1980; Trussell and Menken, 1978). The most recent investigations point to a decreasing disparity in the completed family size of early and later childbearers, but the differences are still significant (Teachman, 1985).

It is widely assumed that the disadvantages associated with premature parenthood for parents are transmitted in one form or another to their children. The effects of early childbearing on children are, however, not well documented (Baldwin and Cain, 1980; Brooks-Gunn and Furstenberg, 1985; Hamburg, 1981). Only a few studies find that teenage mothers have problems in assuming the responsibilities of care giving and are less skillful in relating to young children; other research has failed to demonstrate differences in parenting skills (Bierman and Streett, 1982). Almost all investigators agree, however, that children of early childbearers may be disadvantaged in comparison to the offspring of women who delay childbearing because they are more likely to grow up in a single-parent household and more likely to be poor (Hofferth, 1986).

Have the effects of early childbearing been exaggerated?

The evidence that early childbearing increases the risk of social and economic disadvantage is compelling. However, it is less clear whether this risk is sufficiently high to justify the social stereotype of the teenage mother that has emerged from social science research and its portrayal in the mass media. The popular picture of the teenage mother is that of an unemployed woman with many ill-cared-for children who is living on the dole. And it is commonly assumed that teenage parents often end up neglecting, if not abusing, their children and that the children themselves are extremely likely to repeat the pattern of early childbearing, thus perpetuating the cycle of poverty and disadvantage. In short, teenage mothers are viewed both as victims and creators of their own fate as is illustrated in the following passage from an editorial in the *New Republic:* "The demographics tell a terrible story, presage a worse one: young women, girls really, still children themselves having children, passing on depression and helplessness from generation to generation" (1983:10).

This flamboyant rhetoric has shaped the political discourse about teenage childbearing, heightening the sense of urgency for remedial action. However, such interpretations seem to go well beyond the available evidence. To be sure, teenage mothers do not do as well as women who delay childbearing. But it is less clear whether social and economic differences due to the timing of parenthood are large enough to support the widespread beliefs that early childbearing almost completely determines a women's destiny in later life, the belief first articulated by Cambell and then elaborated and refined by the community of researchers and policymakers. Nor is it obvious that the fortunes of the offspring of early childbearers are so dismal as the preceding quotation, and others like it, imply.

The accuracy of the social stereotype of the teenage childbearer can be questioned on several grounds. First, virtually all existing studies show tremendous variation in outcomes of early parenthood, even though most do not highlight their individual differences. A substantial proportion of adolescent parents manage to recover from the handicaps imposed by early parenthood. Studies of teenage parents in later life show that many women have not followed the predictable course of lifelong disadvantage, even if they are not doing as well as their peers who postponed parenthood. Moreover, some portion of the adverse consequences presumed to be the result of early childbearing is, in fact, attributable to prior differences in the family backgrounds of early and later childbearers. When these differences are taken into account, the relative size of the disadvantage resulting from the timing of the first birth will diminish. The failure to take account of preexisting differences may have led to an overestimation of the impact of premature parenthood on the life course of women.

A second limitation of most studies of the consequences of early childbearing is their focus on the years immediately following the birth of the first child. The transition to parenthood is clearly quite difficult for teenagers, in part because adolescence is a troubled time for some (Adelson, 1980; Peterson and Craighead, 1985). Early and unplanned parenthood obviously complicates the normal course of adolescent development. Determining a young parent's adjustment at or shortly after the inception of motherhood may provide an especially negative impression of her eventual capacity to cope with parental responsibilities. A full and fair assessment requires a further examination of adolescent mothers in later life. Unfortunately, very few studies have followed up teenage mothers long enough to observe changes in the adaptation to early childbearing over the life course.

This failure to take account of individual variations in outcome has helped to perpetuate the negative stereotype of the teenage mother. By ignoring diversity, investigators have also missed an opportunity to understand why some young mothers manage to overcome the disadvantage associated with early childbearing while others are overwhelmed by it. Additionally, by not following teenage mothers over a significant proportion of their adult lives, and focusing on the teenage years, it is impossible to understand how early life decisions are translated into later disadvantage or success. This question addresses a broader theoretical issue: how events in early life shape adult adjustment and how much flexibility adults have to recast the misfortunes of childhood (Brim and Kagan, 1980; Elder, 1984b).

Turning to the children, the current research has limitations as well. When studying disadvantaged children, overdeterministic models are often applied.

Typically, young children living in poverty are thought to enter childhood and adolescence with their cognitive abilities in place, limiting change, even when their social circumstances improve. It is also assumed that all children respond similarly to environmental conditions, especially negative ones. Thus, being born in poverty is regarded by many researchers as tantamount to a life sentence to adult disadvantage. This portrait is identical to the one just drawn for these children's mothers. As with adults, research on the children has not adequately attended to individual differences nor to long-term change.

More recent views of child development characterize it as the interaction between environment and individual characteristics (Bronfenbrenner, 1985; Scarr, 1985), leading to the possibility that not all children growing up in poverty will have problems and that environmental variation will have an impact on growth. Oversimplified views about the impact of poverty do not do justice to the complexity and variability of development or to the possibility of change over the life span.

This oversimplified conception of human development neglects the biological and psychological differences among children as well as the coping strategies of families in facing similar hardships. In recent studies, investigators have begun to pay attention to "invulnerable" or "resilient" children who seem to respond well to adversity (Garmezy and Rutter, 1983). Although the idea that some disadvantaged children manage more successfully is hardly revelatory, investigators have only begun to explore the sources of variation among individuals facing common life circumstances.

An assessment of the coping strategies of adolescent parents and their children also is useful to policymakers and practitioners who seek to ameliorate the adverse effects of premature parenthood and prevent the transmission of social disadvantage from one generation to the next. Despite a considerable body of research on both the antecedents and consequences of early childbearing, the application of this knowledge to program interventions has been fairly meager, and the success of programs that have been attempted has been generally modest (Furstenberg and Brooks-Gunn, 1985; Hofferth and Hayes, 1987; Moore, Simms, and Betsey, 1986). A closer look at the recovery process among teenage parents who do well in later life may reveal what part of their prosperity is explained by individual determination, social support, or provision of service programs.

The Baltimore study

This study describes long-term variations in the careers of teenage mothers and looks at the situation of their children as they encounter adolescence a short generation later. Our data come from a longitudinal study of a sample of some three hundred women and their children from Baltimore who were first interviewed in the mid-1960s shortly after they became pregnant. The initial phase of the research, carried out over a 5-year period, primarily documented the consequences of early childbearing on the transition to adulthood, showing how the timing of the first birth altered the life course in early adulthood. The results left no doubt that premature parenthood profoundly influenced the educational, occupational, and marital decisions of the early childbearers, which resulted in considerable detriment to their economic position at the time of the 5-year follow-up. Nevertheless, the evidence clearly demonstrated that early childbearing affected some women much more negatively than others (Furstenberg, 1976). Indeed, a substantial minority of the young mothers seemed to have managed the transition to parenthood quite successfully, leading the author to conclude:

One of the most impressive findings was the diversity of responses to a common event. Despite the fact that virtually all the participants in the study were low-income black females in their midteens who were premaritally pregnant for the first time, the outcome at the five-year follow-up was enormously varied. In fact, by the time of the last interview, the sample hardly could have been more diverse in every important area we explored. Whether it was the decision to wed, marital stability, subsequent childbearing, work and welfare experiences, or methods of childrearing, the young mothers were extremely dissimilar. (pp. 218–219)

This observation of diversity was the end point of the 5-year follow-up. It is also the beginning point for the current study, which explores and attempts to explain differences in the life course of the young mothers in later life and their children in adolescence. The remainder of this chapter provides a brief history of the study, situating it in time and place. Any longitudinal study is also a historical study for it represents the experience of a single cohort. It is essential to say what is both common and unique about the participants in this study, compared to other cohorts of teenage mothers. The following section then serves as a description of the study design, an introduction to the participants, and an assessment of the quality of the Baltimore data.

The origins of the Baltimore project

The Baltimore study was initiated in 1966 as an evaluation of a comprehensive care program for adolescent mothers located at Sinai Hospital, a large community-based institution located in the northwestern part of the city. In the early 1960s, Sinai, like many other urban medical centers throughout the country, experienced a noticeable shift in the composition of its obstetrical population. A growing proportion of women delivering babies were young, unmarried blacks. This trend resulted in large part from the rapid decline in fertility among older women, especially within the Jewish population that had been the hospital's main clientele. At the same time, because of a rapid migration of blacks from the central city to northwestern Baltimore, the hospital was suddenly delivering the babies

Table 1.2. *Design of the Baltimore study, 1966–1984*

Interview schedule	Interview dates	Participants	Attempted interviews	Completed interviews[a] N	%
Time 1: during pregnancy	1966–1968	Adolescent mothers,	404	404	100
		their mothers	379	350	92
Time 2: 1 year after delivery	1968–1970	Adolescent mothers	404	382	95
Time 3: 3 years after delivery	1970	Adolescent mothers,[b]	404	363	90
		classmates	361	268	74
Time 4: 5 years after delivery	1972	Adolescent mothers,	404	331	82
		children of adolescent mothers,	331	306	92
		classmates	307	221	72
Time 5: 16–17 years after delivery	1983–1984	Adolescent mothers or surrogates	404	289	80
				35	
		Children of adolescent mothers	392	296	76
		National Survey of Children (blacks, 14–16 years old)		450	

[a] This category includes a small number of interviews that were excluded from the analysis because of a large amount of missing information. At time 5, 288 adolescent mothers and 33 surrogates were used in the final analysis.
[b] Interviews were also obtained with about one-third of the fathers at this time.

of between two and three hundred pregnant adolescents each year, the majority of whom were poor and black.

Alarmed by this trend, several public-minded physicians at Sinai designed a special program for pregnant adolescents to offer comprehensive medical and social services aimed at improving the quality of prenatal and neonatal care provided to the mothers and their offspring. This program, along with several others sponsored by the Children's Bureau at the same time, represented a bold experiment in social and health intervention to reduce the high levels of repeat pregnancy and infant mortality and morbidity sometimes associated with adolescent fertility (Howard, 1968; Klerman and Jekel, 1973).

In 1965, the Great Society was still in ascendancy, and a strong commitment existed to breaking the cycle of poverty by offering assistance to the socially and economically disadvantaged. Teenage childbearing was identified as a strategic link in the perpetuation of poverty. Some visionary program planners believed that reducing the medical complications associated with early childbearing, discouraging school dropout, providing vocational assistance, delaying additional pregnancies, and offering parent education would decrease economic dependency of the young mothers in later life and create more favorable opportunities for their offspring. (For a more detailed discussion of the political origins of the issue, see Furstenberg [1976] and Vinovskis [1981].)

As a precondition for funding ameliorative services, the Children's Bureau required that comprehensive programs be systematically evaluated. In the case of the Sinai Hospital program, the evaluation eventually led to a 5-year follow-up of a cohort of 404 adolescent mothers and their firstborn children. The study contrasted their transition to adulthood to the experiences of their classmates who delayed childbearing. The follow-up also measured the impact of early child-bearing on the life chances of the teenage childbearers and their offspring. Individual differences in the adaptation to early parenthood were explained as a function of the Sinai Hospital prenatal program, characteristics of the young parents, assistance provided by their families and friends, and services offered by welfare agencies in Baltimore (Furstenberg, 1976, 1981; Furstenberg and Crawford, 1978).

The participants in the Baltimore study were visited again in 1972, about 5 years after their first child was born. At that time, more than 80% of the original sample were reinterviewed, 331 of the young mothers and 306 of their children (see Table 1.2). The modest attrition, discussed more extensively later in this chapter, occurred disproportionately among the small group of whites who were originally interviewed, the mothers who married early in the study, and the women who moved away from Baltimore. Most of the loss of the children resulted from death or severe disability. The rate of refusal was negligible.

Designing the 17–year follow-up

The 5-year follow-up concluded the first phase of the Baltimore study. The idea of revisiting the families was not seriously entertained until a decade later, when the children of the teenage mothers themselves were approaching adolescence. By this time, the participants had not been contacted for over 10 years and the residential information last collected in 1972 was clearly out of date.

In the summer of 1982, the Commonwealth Fund provided a planning grant to determine whether the families could be found and whether another follow-up was feasible. Selecting 50 cases at random, two survey research firms traced the former respondents using all available information from earlier interviews. The Institute for Survey Research (ISR) of Temple University achieved the best results, locating about 90% of the subsample. On the basis of this encouraging outcome, the Commonwealth Fund provided a grant in 1983 to carry out the study, and ISR was selected to conduct the fieldwork.

Much of the following year was spent in preparing and pretesting the two interviews for the parents and children. For purposes of comparison, some items were retained from questionnaires used in earlier phases of the study. A large number of new questions also were taken from the National Survey of Children (NSC), a nationally representative survey designed to tap the development and well-being of adolescents, and the parenting patterns of their parents (Furstenberg et al., 1983). Since funding was not available to reinterview the classmates of the Baltimore study mothers, the NSC sample provided a baseline of later childbearers and their children against which to compare the school and fertility experiences of the Baltimore youth as well as their psychological adjustment and misbehavior. The final version of the parent's interview included an extensive life-history calendar, described in Chapter 2, recording significant residential, marital, childbearing, occupational, and economic events taking place since the birth of the child (see Appendix A). The life-history calendar deliberately covered portions of the parents' lives described in earlier interviews, permitting a reliability check of reported events at the time of the birth of the first child and the years immediately following delivery.

The fieldwork

The fieldwork spanned from November 1983 to June 1984, during which time 89% of the respondents were eventually located.[1] The tracing process was difficult and time-consuming. Only a few of the respondents still lived where they had resided when last contacted in 1972. Half had moved at least four times since the child's birth, and a third had spent some time living outside Baltimore. The respondents located and reinterviewed were undoubtedly the more sedentary segment of the original sample. Even so, a third reported that residential mobility had forced their children to change schools at least three times in the past 10 years or so. Only by eliciting the cooperation of school and welfare agencies was it possible to find those families who had moved frequently.

For the most part, when the mother was located, so was her firstborn child and vice versa. But in 30 cases, the child was deceased or had been given up for adoption in the early years of the study. In such cases, the parent was contacted; our interview completion rate was somewhat lower for these parents than for mothers who were residing with their children (79% v. 90%). In 33 additional cases, mothers were living apart from their children and saw them less than once

1 The ISR trained 17 interviewers in November of 1983 to trace the respondents and conduct the interviews. Careful monitoring of the initial contacts resulted in the dismissal of five interviewers because of poor work or lack of perseverance in tracing the more elusive subjects. During the fieldwork, which lasted 7 months, several interviewers left the study for new employment or because of pressing family obligations; others became weary of the rigors of interviewing. As a result, 10 fieldworkers conducted nearly 90% of the interviews, each averaging roughly 25 parent–child pairs.

a week. A few of these parents were no longer alive, some were in jail or had been hospitalized, and others had turned over childrearing responsibilities to some other family member or to the child's father. As might be expected, we had little success contacting mothers living apart from their children. If a child was living apart from his or her mother, a surrogate parent was interviewed (33 cases).

In the 358 families where either a mother or child was located, interviews were completed in 90% of the cases. Among those located, 42 potential respondents (mothers or children) initially refused to be interviewed. These persons were contacted again by Vivian Washington, a well-known black community leader in Baltimore and the former principal of the Edgar Allan Poe School, a program for pregnant students that many of our study respondents attended. Mrs. Washington was able to persuade a number of these individuals to participate, reducing the overall refusal rate to 8% of the total sample and 9% of those located. Of the 322 adult interviews, 263 consisted of mother–child pairs, 15 of mothers without study children, 10 of mothers with no child interview, 33 surrogate respondents, all but 2 with corresponding child interviews, and 1 mother who was interviewed a second time about the second of a twin pair. Additionally, 2 children were interviewed with no corresponding adult interview.

The quality of the data

Reports from both the field staff and the participants indicated that the interview generally proceeded smoothly. According to the interviewers, most respondents had no difficulty understanding the questions; about 14% of the adults and adolescents had a comprehension problem. All but a tiny fraction (3% of the adults and less than 1% of their offspring) were rated by the interviewers to be completely or usually truthful. However, in a few areas, primarily concerning teen delinquency and substance abuse, interviewers questioned the veracity of some respondents' reports. As might be expected, both parents and children may have underreported deviant actions. This pattern of underreporting was also evident in the National Survey of Children, especially among urban blacks. Consequently, the information on misbehavior is probably an understatement of the actual prevalence in our sample. The reliability of the data is examined in Appendix B. Overall, the results are quite satisfactory. When information assembled from the life-history calendar was compared to data collected in earlier interviews, the alpha coefficient averaged .75, and even higher levels of reliability were obtained on items reported in a validation form sent to the respondents just after the interview was completed.

The interviews were long. Among the adults, the average duration was 82 minutes; a third took more than 90 minutes, and 7% lasted 2 hours or longer. The adolescent interview was shorter, but still it averaged 49 minutes, and 14%

lasted at least an hour. Nevertheless, according to the interviewers, only 10% of the adults and 2% of the adolescents were "fairly" or "very" tired by the end of the session. This is an indication of the general level of involvement in the interview. The vast majority of the adults (92%) and adolescents (90%) were judged to be attentive and responsive during the interview, and all but a few (7% and 5%, respectively) were evaluated as very or somewhat interested in the questions. Another indicator of respondent interest is their willingness to participate in a subsequent interview. Only 2% of the adults and 1% of the adolescents refused permission to be contacted again.

Sample attrition

Although the overall completion rate of 80% of families (and 72% of mothers) is quite acceptable in a longitudinal study spanning nearly two decades, it is still important to assess whether the attrition in the sample created any bias. At the 5-year follow-up, dropout from the original sample was higher among whites than blacks and young mothers who were married at the time of the initial interview compared to those who were still single. Every effort was made in the 17-year follow-up to contact individuals who had previously been considered ineligible because they had moved from Baltimore as well as those who had refused participation in the 5-year follow-up. Therefore, the biases detected in 1972 may have been reduced in the current interview. On the other hand, since sample attrition increased somewhat over the past 12 years, the biases may have become even more pronounced in the 1984 follow-up. Appendix C examines this question.

In most respects the sample in the 17-year follow-up looks very much like the original sample of pregnant teenagers. The results do not seem to be influenced by selective dropout with the exception of the racial bias mentioned earlier. Most of the losses result from residential mobility, which, other than race, is the only strong predictor of sample attrition. A priori, it is difficult to tell whether women who moved out of Baltimore were any more or less likely to succeed economically. Our guess is that, if anything, they may be a little better off than those who remained in the sample. However, so few differences exist in the socioeconomic and academic background of participants and dropouts at the outset of the study that any biases due to residential mobility must be very small.

The representativeness of the Baltimore sample

When first studied, the participants in the Baltimore study were all under 18, presumably pregnant for the first time, seeking prenatal services at Sinai Hospital.[2] Clearly, the subjects were not selected in a way to ensure the representa-

---

2 In subsequent interviews, several women acknowledged that they had been pregnant prior to 1966, when the study began. Apparently, they had neglected to report a previous miscarriage.

tiveness of pregnant youth in Baltimore city. To what extent can we generalize from this hospital-based sample? This question cannot be completely resolved; however, at the time of the initial study, the characteristics of the teenage women were compared to available census information and vital statistics data assembled by the Baltimore City Health Department. These comparisons revealed that the adolescent parents served by Sinai were reasonably representative of the population of women under the age of 18 who delivered a child in the mid-1960s in one of the Baltimore hospitals. Although at that time Sinai served a predominantly white population, about three-fourths of the adolescent parents were black, which was generally true elsewhere in the city. And most of the teens under 18 delivering at Sinai were unmarried at the time of the birth. This also was characteristic of the population of teenage childbearers in other hospitals throughout the city.

The black, unmarried teens who sought prenatal care at Sinai Hospital came from families who were similar to the larger population of blacks in Baltimore. The vast majority had moved to northwestern Baltimore from the central areas of the city, where overcrowding and urban renewal were forcing a mass migration from a large inner-city ghetto. In certain respects, the recent migrants may have been slightly better off than their former neighbors who remained in the most deteriorated parts of the city. However, the migrants were relatively poor even in their new neighborhoods.

Only half of the sample lived in a two-parent household, a figure that seems unremarkable today but was shockingly low by the standards of the time. A quarter of the families were on welfare, again a figure that was considered quite high in the mid-1960s. Only a fifth of the household heads were high school graduates, and about the same proportion held jobs that could be classified as skilled employment. Three-fourths of the adolescents' mothers had been teenagers when their first child was born, and half had been under 18. A fifth were unmarried when their first child was born, and many others had been premaritally pregnant. At the time of the first interview, when many of the parents were still of childbearing age, half already had borne five or more children.

Examination of census data suggests that the participants in the Sinai Hospital study resembled the general demographic profile of the black population in Baltimore. (There are too few whites in the sample to draw comparisons with the white population.) Yet the hospital probably did not serve the most destitute neighborhoods in the city. As the special prenatal program became known to welfare agencies, pregnant teens seeking antenatal services were sometimes referred from neighborhoods beyond the hospital's catchment area. This had the effect of broadening the composition of the teenage clinic population, but it may have also enlisted more motivated teens to the program. Still, the clinic largely catered to the local population, which, as shown by the figures cited earlier, consisted primarily of the poor and the near poor. Most teens did not come to the hospital for special services, but were instead merely seeking the closest place to deliver their baby. In sum, we are reasonably confident that the findings of our follow-up can be extended beyond the population studied, at least to the general population of urban blacks, who comprise about a third of all teenage parents under 18 in the United States. Further evidence of the representativeness of the Baltimore women will be presented in the next chapter, when we contrast participants in this study to women in several national surveys.

Even though this sample may be reasonably typical of black school-age mothers, it includes only teenagers who had their first birth between 1965 and 1967. The situation for teenage mothers today may be very different from what it was two decades ago when the study began. In the first place, most women in this study did not have an adequate opportunity to terminate their pregnancy by abortion. Although illegal abortions certainly occurred, access to abortion among the very young and the very poor was quite limited. Some young mothers in the study no doubt would have sought an abortion if their pregnancy had occurred in 1985 instead of 1965. Today, close to half of black teenagers under 18 who become pregnant obtain an abortion, more than triple the proportion in 1972.[3]

Two decades ago, early childbearing was generally not regarded as a social problem so long as it was accompanied by marriage. Most teenagers who became pregnant hastily married to avoid social stigma. Today, relatively few are prepared to wed merely because of a pregnancy. Thus, the Baltimore mothers gave birth at a time when out-of-wedlock childbearing was less common and special services for unmarried teens were less readily available. Although it is not possible to assess precisely how changes in the availability of services have altered the career of teenage parents, we must recognize that the life course of adolescent mothers today may differ from those in this study because of differences in the community response to teenage parenthood. When this study began, teenagers were often discouraged from continuing in school, and infant day care was virtually nonexistent. At the same time, employment opportunities for both young men and women were somewhat better than today. In the future, as we begin to describe the family-formation patterns of the *third* generation, the offspring of the children of the women studied here, it will be possible to see how the changing structure of opportunities has altered the life chances of young parents. However, our results may be somewhat cohort specific, influenced by the fact that the study began in the years of the Great Society.

Organization of the results

What follows is an account of what we learned from the 17-year follow-up. This volume reports on how well the young mothers were doing as they entered their

---

3 Figures on abortions are not available prior to 1972; it is safe to assume that the number increased dramatically after abortion became legal in Maryland in 1968.

thirties and on the situation of their children as they entered their middle teens. Chapter 2 provides a profile of adolescent mothers, viewed from two separate perspectives. The first calculates the extent to which the social and economic circumstances of the early childbearers have changed in the intervening 12 years, contrasting two cross-sectional snapshots taken more than a decade apart. The situations of the early childbearers in Baltimore are compared to those of mothers of similar age in several nationally representative samples. This contrast allows us to assess the generalizability of our results and, because the national surveys contain older childbearers as well, informs us about the fortunes of the early childbearers relative to women who postponed parenthood.

Chapter 3 addresses the primary issue in this study: What conditions affect the adaptation of the early childbearers in adulthood? We test the effect of several kinds of potential determinants on the divergent careers of the teenage mothers. One broad category consists of *individual differences* in social background, life plans, motivation, and ability. These personal attributes provide an indication of how social resources and individual characteristics exerted an influence on later life outcomes. A second set of potentially important influences, also related to the availability of social resources, is the woman's access to *informal networks of support,* in particular her own family. A third, and possibly the least explored of the possible determinants of successful adaptation to early parenthood, is the impact of *formal programs of social intervention.* Finally, we shall assess the significance of yet another set of determinants of the impact of early parenthood on adjustment in adulthood, *career contingencies,* how the patterning of life events around the time of the first birth structured the course of adult experience.

Chapter 4 turns from the situation of the mothers to the circumstances of their children. Although it is still too early to tell whether the children, or which children, are following in the footsteps of their parents, we will be able to form a preliminary impression. In 1984, the children were the same age as their mothers had been at the time of the first interview. Chapter 4 examines how the mother's life decisions translate into child life events. As a way of gauging the relative well-being of the children, we shall also compare the offspring of the young mothers to children of later childbearers who participated in the National Survey of Children.

Chapter 5 explores the intersection between the mothers' and children's lives. We shall see how the trajectory of the mother's life course affects the development and well-being of the children in the adolescent years.

In the final chapter, the findings are reviewed in light of a series of ongoing policy debates about appropriate strategies for dealing with the problem of adolescent fertility. As implied earlier, the political discourse about teenage parenthood tends toward the inflammatory. Careful and objective analysis of the policy and program initiatives is sadly lacking. Based on the empirical results, some suggestions are offered about the kinds of programs and policies that might be most effective in ameliorating the consequences of early childbearing. But we shall also try to provide a more realistic picture of the dimensions of the problem, sorting out potentially fruitful and fruitless approaches to intervention. This picture is derived to a considerable degree from our findings regarding the flexibility of human development over the life course.

2   Experience in adulthood

Looking back on the transition to parenthood

Nearly all participants in the Baltimore study were in their middle teens when they first became pregnant and in their early twenties at the 5-year follow-up. This chapter reviews their life histories in the subsequent period from 1972 to 1984. We have omitted a full description of the teenage years, when most of the young mothers were struggling to remain in school, enter the job market, and establish a marital relationship while raising a child. These experiences are recorded in an earlier account of the study (Furstenberg, 1976). Because the next chapter will show how the early adjustment to parenthood significantly shapes the course of later life, however, it is useful to begin with a few observations about the transition to parenthood, even at the risk of covering familiar ground.

As we have said, it was not an easy time for the women in the study. Looking back on that period, many, recalling the problems that beset them after their first child was born, said they did not understand how they were able to get through those difficult years.

There is no "typical" transition to motherhood. The modal pattern, as will become more apparent later in this chapter, was unpredictable and disorderly, to borrow terms sometimes used to characterize the occupational careers of lower-status workers (Wilensky, 1961). Many women resumed their education only to drop out when marriage, child-care arrangements, or another pregnancy interfered with their school routines. Similarly, they moved in and out of the labor force with the availability of jobs and the competing claims of child care. Marital disruption accounted for a good deal of the erratic quality of early adulthood. Dissolution of a relationship often prompted the young mother to seek refuge with her family until she was able to marshal resources necessary to establish an independent household (Furstenberg and Crawford, 1978; Furstenberg, 1981).

Even in 1972, 5 years after the birth of their first child, most women's lives were still quite unsettled. While substantial educational and occupational gains were made in the early years of the study, the majority of the women were still living in precarious economic circumstances at the 5-year follow-up. When compared to their classmates who had postponed parenthood, most of the young mothers appeared destined to live a life of social and economic disadvantage.

Methods of updating the life course

How accurate was this preliminary assessment of the young mother's chances of recovery in later life? We rely on two different strategies to investigate patterns of success and failure over the longer term. The first simply provides a cross-sectional comparison of the women's lives over the time period of the 17-year follow-up. Using a variety of indicators of economic and social well-being, we trace the trajectory of the women's fortunes during the period from 1972 to 1984. In effect, we are using the young mother's status in early adulthood as a baseline against which to compare her status in later life. Was she better or worse off or was her situation about the same?

A second strategy is to compare the young mothers to a group of women from similar backgrounds who postponed childbearing. In the first stage of the study, former classmates of the young mothers served as a comparison group. Unfortunately, funding was not available to reinterview the classmates in 1984. However, a lower-cost version of the same technique was employed, namely, assembling comparable information from several large national surveys of women conducted close to the time we completed our 17-year follow-up. Throughout this chapter, the Baltimore women are compared to their counterparts in the national studies who waited until their twenties or early thirties to have their first child.

The life-history calendar

Following other researchers who have studied the life course, we devised a calendar for simplifying the task of collecting detailed biographical information. Previous studies suggest that retrospective data are easier to gather and more readily recalled when diverse life events are reported together in a single format (Freedman et al., 1986). So, for example, women in our study found it less difficult to remember when they had moved in or out of their parents' household if they were asked about concurrent marriage, schooling, and employment experiences. An additional benefit of this technique for interviewers was the possibility of cross-checking responses that seemed logically inconsistent or implausible as respondents filled out the calendars.

The procedure for collecting the data was simple. Each respondent was given a calendar with blank grids to fill out. The columns listed the years from the birth of the first child to the time of the interview and the rows listed a set of specific life events. On this matrix, information was recorded on: (1) years living in the parental household (i.e., with mother), (2) years of attendance in school, (3) marital and cohabitational history, (4) pregnancies and childbearing, (5) separations from the study child, (6) job history, and (7) the years in which public assistance was received.

Respondents experienced few difficulties filling out the calendar, and the information supplied appeared to be quite reliable when cross-checked against the data collected from earlier interviews. Although some inconsistencies inevitably occurred, no evidence of systematic bias occurred in the reports of early life events that suggested respondents were editing negative events from their lives or reconstructing them to appear more successful than they were in fact. (See the discussion in Appendix B.)

The completed calendars provide a general overview of the life course of the Baltimore mothers over the entire span of the study. Even a cursory glance at the life histories revealed the diversity of the lives of the participants in our project. Three completed calendars have been reproduced in Figure 2.1 for purposes of illustration. Although based on information supplied by actual respondents, some personal details and life events have been deliberately altered to protect their anonymity.

The first woman, whom we shall call Doris, was 34 at the time of the interview. In many respects she resembles the popular stereotype of a teenage mother. Doris was unmarried and a school dropout when she became pregnant in 1966 at the age of 16. She went on welfare immediately and continued to receive public assistance for the next 17 years, even during the period of her brief marriage, which lasted for only 3 years. Doris had three children by three different men, none of whom was her husband. She has been employed periodically but never for more than a few years at a time and never yielding enough income to lift her off the welfare rolls. During her late twenties, she had a lengthy relationship with Harris, who fathered her third child. But in 1980, Harris left the household, and Doris has been living alone with her three children, and her grandchild, the 2-year-old son of Dalia, Doris's second oldest child. By the end of this chapter, we will know how many women in our sample resemble Doris.

Other Baltimore mothers may be more like Iris, whose life history also is depicted in Figure 2.1. Iris became pregnant at 16 and waited to marry the baby's father until finishing high school, the year after her child was born. Her marriage lasted about ten years, during which time she had a second child. Except for the periods right after her children were born, Iris has always worked. After her marriage broke up, she received public assistance for 2 years; she began a new relationship with a man named Lester, which was brief. When it dissolved, Iris moved in with her mother for a year as an alternative to going back on welfare. As soon as she could afford it, she moved out and is now living with her two

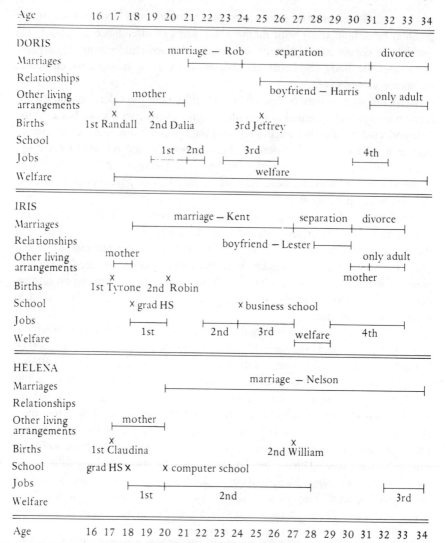

Figure 2.1. Outline of three calendar histories

children as a single parent. For the past 5 years, Iris has been steadily employed as a business administrator for the Baltimore School District.

Iris has managed reasonably well with the occasional assistance of her family and supportive services from the government. Her best financial years were when she was married and working at the same time. But most of her adult life, she has been economically hard pressed, relying primarily on her own income to support her children.

Helena's life history, as shown in Figure 2.1, is different still. At her parents' insistence, Helena delayed her marriage to Nelson, the father of her child, until she had completed her schooling and had a secure job. She and Nelson were married in 1971 around her 20th birthday. They have been married continuously for nearly 14 years. During most of this period, both Helena and Nelson have been steadily employed. They now live in a comfortable garden apartment on the outskirts of Baltimore with their two children.

These three case histories, though unique in some sense, were selected to represent prototypes of varying adaptations to early childbearing. Despite efforts to find employment and settle into a stable relationship, Doris has not managed to achieve domestic or economic security. Iris has done somewhat better though she, too, has struggled to maintain economic independence and has barely scraped by as a single mother for the past 5 years. Both would envy Helena's marital and economic career, which since her early twenties has been progressively secure and stable.

This chapter explores the distribution of life histories. First, each career component – schooling, patterns of residence, marriage, fertility, and employment experience – is examined in turn. Then, in the conclusion, we see how the separate components cluster together. Chapter 3 will explore the reasons why careers sharply diverge over time.

Schooling

No consequence of teenage childbearing has received as much attention as the effect of early parenthood on school achievement (Hofferth and Hayes, 1987). Most existing studies examine patterns of dropout at pregnancy or soon after delivery on the assumption that initial exit from school is tantamount to the termination of education. In general, the results of the first phase of the Baltimore study appeared to be consistent with this assumption. Most teens who dropped out of school before or soon after their child was born did not return.

By the 5-year follow-up, just under half of the mothers had completed high school. A majority of the dropouts continued to report that they would like to complete high school, but in 1972 only 8% of the women who had not graduated were currently enrolled (along with 9% of the high school graduates). The prospects of further education for the large number of dropouts seemed poor, judging from their performance to date.

In fact, a surprising amount of educational activity took place in the second phase of the study. Over half of the sample (56%) reported that they had attended school for at least part of one year. Most of these women had a limited amount of additional schooling, which may have consisted of only a school term or perhaps some course in adult education. But a quarter of the sample were in

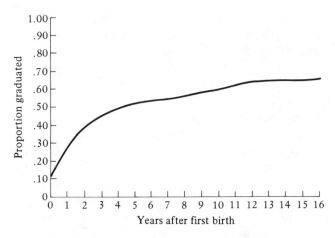

Figure 2.2. Proportion graduating from high school by years after first birth ($N = 288$)

school for at least part of 2 or more years and 15% attended classes for 3 or more years during their twenties and early thirties.

Years of schooling listed on the calendar did not necessarily translate into actual educational attainment. About one grade was attained for every 2 years of schooling attended. *Of all the educational attainment that occurred following the birth of the first child, more than half took place in the second segment of the study.* High school graduates, pursuing higher education, accounted for a significant proportion of the further schooling. But one woman in six completed high school in the second segment of the study or a third of the young mothers who had not graduated by 1972.

The pattern of high school graduation is depicted in Figure 2.2, which shows the year of completion relative to the timing of the first birth. Most women completed high school within 5 years of the birth of their first child. However, a steady trickle of women graduated during the second segment of the study (see also Fig. 2.3). Clearly, many women returned to school to obtain a diploma, or more often, a GED, when they were well into their twenties. This often occurred when their youngest child entered school.

Viviana James is an example of such a women. She returned to school as soon as her second child entered the first grade. She felt bored in the poorly paid clerical job she had held for several years and was told that she could qualify for a more responsible and better-paying position if she only had a high school diploma. She persuaded a cousin to stay with her child while she took a GED preparation class. She had no difficulty passing the examination and received a promotion the following year. When we spoke to Viviana following the 17-year follow-up, she commented about the importance of completing high school:

Table 2.1. *Educational level of Baltimore women in 1972 and 1984 (in %)*

	1972	1984
Less than high school graduate	49.2	32.6
High school graduate, only	41.2	37.5
Some post high school	8.8	24.7
College graduate	0.8	5.2
Total	100	100
	(250)	(288)

I wanted a [better] job to help out because things were starting to get tough. And the only jobs available were waitresses and jobs that you work so hard in and didn't make any kind of money. Then I realized I needed to go back to school.

Many women in the Baltimore study went beyond high school, and much of this education occurred in the second segment of the study. Table 2.1 compares the educational level of the sample in 1972 and 1984. About a tenth of the women in 1972 had some schooling after high school, 6% had attended college, and less than 1% had completed college by the 5-year follow-up. Twelve years later, their educational profile significantly improved. Nearly a third of the sample had some postsecondary education, about a quarter had some college, and 5% had graduated from college. Moreover, 9% of the sample attended school in the previous year, indicating that the educational level of the sample will rise a bit more in the future.

Did schooling experience during or just after the first pregnancy set the pattern of educational achievement in later life? We anticipated that early dropouts would typically not go much further in school once they left and that most would never graduate from high school. The actual results were not as we expected. Although early dropouts were certainly less likely to complete high school than those who remained in school throughout their pregnancy, slightly more than half of the women who dropped out before or soon after conception eventually completed high school (compared to about four-fifths of the women who remained in school throughout their pregnancy).

Close to half of the dropouts reported some schooling in the second segment of the study, compared to two-thirds of the women who never left school during their pregnancy. Evidently, early dropout reduces, but does not foreclose, a young mother's chances of further schooling. Like Viviana James, many teenage mothers resumed their education only after their youngest child entered school. And more than a few of the teenage mother's parents returned to school in later life. A college graduate boasted that her mother completed a 2-year college program the same year that she received her baccalaureate. Many women were able to make good on their strong commitment to education only much later in life.

The results in Table 2.1 do not imply that the adolescent mothers would have caught up to their classmates, whose educational achievement was significantly greater at the 5-year follow-up. In 1972, only 9% of the classmates who deferred childbearing had dropped out of school before graduating as compared to 51% of the young mothers. More than a fourth of the high school graduates were still in school, and 3% had already completed college. The delayed childbearers had reached a higher level of educational attainment in 1972 than the early child-bearers achieved a decade later. While we can only guess how much higher the classmates' academic achievement would have been had they been reinterviewed in 1984, it would have unquestionably exceeded the level attained by the early childbearers. Whether the gap between the young mothers and their classmates widened or narrowed over time cannot be known. In any case, the findings are consistent with other cross-sectional studies showing that status-attainment differences resulting from early parenthood do not disappear later in life (Card and Wise, 1978).

This is apparent when the educational level of the Baltimore sample in 1984 is contrasted with women who postponed childbearing. Three separate national data sets are tapped for the comparisons: (1) the National Survey of Family Growth (NSFG), commissioned by the National Center for Health Statistics in 1982 to survey the fertility of American women; (2) the Current Population Survey (CPS), a monthly survey of employment behavior carried out by the Census Bureau that in June 1983 included questions on fertility and birth expectations; and (3) the 1982 National Longitudinal Survey (NLS), a longitudinal study of women's labor-market experiences sponsored by the Department of Labor. The research design, sample, and content of each of these studies are described more fully in Appendix D. Using somewhat different sampling criteria, each study collected data from a representative sample of women, similar in age to the Baltimore mothers.

Our analysis is confined to black women between the ages of 29 and 36 who had at least one child and were living in metropolitan areas. (There are too few whites in the Baltimore study to make reliable comparisons.) Table 2.2 contrasts the educational achievement of the Baltimore women with their counterparts in the national surveys subdivided into early and later childbearers. This breakdown reveals two distinct comparisons. First, the Baltimore mothers are contrasted to their counterparts in the national survey who were teenage mothers. Second, differences can be observed between the educational attainment of *early* and *later* childbearers.

The result of the first comparison is extremely reassuring. The Baltimore mothers have about the same educational level as the early childbearers in the national

Table 2.2. *Socioeconomic variables among black women ages 29–36 with at least one biological child*

	Baltimore[a] (1984)	CPS[b] (1983)		NLS[b] (1982)		NSFG[b] (1982)	
Age at first birth	14–19	14–19	20+	14–19	20+	14–19	20+
Age (mean)	32.7	32.3	32.7	32.1	32.2	32.3	32.4
Education							
High school graduates (%)	70.5	73.4	86.3	59.0	86.2	69.9	87.9
Years completed (mean)	12.0	12.3	13.1	11.4	12.8	12.0	13.3
Marital status (%)							
Currently married	30.2	35.1	47.9	37.5	57.2	32.2	56.9
First marriage	80.8	—	—	82.0	91.0	73.7	88.3
Remarriage	19.2	—	—	18.0	9.0	26.3	11.7
Previously married	45.7	41.5	32.9	45.4	23.3	43.3	26.1
Never married	24.0	23.5	19.3	17.1	19.5	24.5	17.0
Biological children (mean)	2.3	2.7	2.0	2.9	1.9	2.9	2.0
Currently employed (%)	67.8	56.1	65.6	61.5	71.8	63.7	70.3
Welfare received in past year (%)	29.1	—	—	29.7	14.3	27.5	20.0
Family income							
Less than $15,000	52.8	61.7	51.2	61.9	41.1	54.6	35.0
$15,000–$24,999	23.6	19.4	20.4	18.6	19.3	20.9	22.6
$25,000 or more	23.6	18.9	28.4	19.4	39.6	24.5	42.4
N (unweighted)	(258)	(242)	(233)	(252)	(231)	(289)	(310)

Note: Dash indicates that data are not available.
[a] A few white respondents (30) were excluded from analysis.
[b] Respondents residing in metropolitan area only. Figures were weighted to represent national population.

surveys. The percentage of high school graduates varies from a low of 59 in the NLS to a high of 73.4 in the CPS, no doubt reflecting some differences in the data-collection procedures and sampling variation.[1] The Baltimore women with a graduation rate of 70.5 are within this range, supporting the impression that the Baltimore women are similar to the larger population of black teenage mothers who had a first child in the mid-1960s.

Table 2.2 also corroborates the results of many previous studies, namely, that teenage mothers are significantly less likely to complete high school than women who delay childbearing until their twenties (Mott and Maxwell, 1981). Later childbearers are considerably more likely to complete high school than are teen-

1 The NLS follow-up interviews were not well designed to elicit full responses on schooling after the initial interview. It seems likely that educational attaiment is somewhat understated.

age mothers (13–27% more graduate) and attain about a year more of education on the average. These differences, though sizable, are perhaps not as large as some observers might expect. And it would be inaccurate to attribute all of the difference in Table 2.2 to the effect of early childbearing because women who become mothers early in life are generally less able and motivated students than those who avoid premature parenthood. Given this initial dissimilarity, the disparity in educational attainment might have been even greater. This result could be taken as evidence that young mothers probably narrow the gap in educational attainment in later life.

On the other hand, it is important to remember that these comparisons are confined to black teenage mothers. Existing studies, including our own, show that black adolescents who become parents are both less likely to marry and to leave school than whites. Accordingly, blacks may be somewhat less handicapped educationally because of early parenthood than whites (Mott and Maxwell, 1981). But even black teenage mothers, as Table 2.2 shows, are significantly less likely to complete high school and, as we indicated earlier, much less likely to complete college than their counterparts who avoided early childbearing. Even if the size of the educational deficit is not as large as some have claimed, doubtless the Baltimore mothers, and women like them, would have attained more schooling had they postponed parenthood.

Marital history

In the late 1960s, when the Baltimore study was initiated, most women who became premaritally pregnant elected to marry before or soon after the child was born. The majority of the young mothers were married by age 20, a pattern that varies sharply from the one seen today. At the 5-year follow-up, close to two-thirds had entered marriage as compared to only one-fifth of the never-pregnant classmates.

By 1972, more than half of the early marriages had dissolved. Among those still married, a substantial proportion reported severe problems in their relationship. Moreover, many of the single women, both never and previously married, despaired of their chances of finding a mate and expressed deep misgivings about the institution of matrimony. One-third (34%) stated that they sometimes thought that women were better off if they never married, and two-thirds (66%) estimated that less than half of all marriages worked out. The results suggested that a substantial number would be permanently disinclined to enter or reenter marriage.

This prediction was only partially borne out. By their early thirties, only 22% of the entire sample had never married (Table 2.3); about two-fifths of those still single in 1972 had married by 1984. Many of the never-married women were

Table 2.3. *Current marital status among Baltimore*
women in 1972 and 1984 (in %)

	1972	1984
Never married	37.8	21.5
Currently married, 1st marriage	34.4	26.0
Currently married, 2+ marriages	2.1	8.3
Previously married, 1 marriage	25.7	35.4
Previously married, 2+ marriages	0	8.7
Total	100	100
	(288)	(288)

living with someone (11%) or had lived with someone in the past (31%). By the 1984 interview, only 14% of the sample had never entered a marital or cohabitational relationship that lasted at least 6 months.

However, most relationships with men were impermanent. Helena, the third woman whose life history is portrayed in Figure 2.1, managed to enter a stable marriage but is an exception. A third of the women were currently married, but 24% of these were in a second or third marriage. Only 26% of the sample were in a first marriage; just 16 percent had remained married to the father of the study child.

Because of the impermanence of marriage, the distribution of marital status at the 5-year and 17-year follow-ups is almost identical (Table 2.3). This comes about because about half of the women married for the first time or remarried in the second phase of the study while nearly half separated or divorced. The net result is almost no change in the proportion of currently married: 36.5% were married in 1972 and 34% in 1984. The only real difference over the 12-year span was that the number of never-married women declined, especially if we take into account "quasi"-marriages, cohabitational relationships that never result in a formal marriage.

Women who delayed marriage or whose first relationship dissolved complained in 1984 that it was impossible to find eligible males. Though only in their late twenties and early thirties, these women, in fact, face a dismal marriage pool (see Darity and Meyers, 1984; Wilson and Neckerman, 1985). Many unmarried black males of an appropriate age are either unemployed or have serious social and psychological liabilities.

I learned through bitter experience. When I first had the baby, I thought that her father was going to do everything for her, you know, take care like he's supposed to and everything. But things turned out different. Like they say you learn through experience, and that's what I'm doing. . . .When I first got married, I went the wrong way. Well, it wasn't the wrong way at the time. I thought it was right. My husband didn't want me to work. [I was] sitting home, cleaning up, cooking and everything. When he decided to leave, I was left with nothing – just me and my daughter. If it wasn't for the welfare, we could have starved to death. She would have had no clothes, and we would have been sitting outside. So that's why I figured, you know, get your own job. Try to keep it. That the way you're going to take care of yourself if anything happens.

Interviewer: So what about marrying again?

Respondent: Oh my goodness. It would be nice. I do think about it every now and then. But, the men out here now these days are for the birds. Really. They are all, I guess just about everybody's doing the same thing. Everybody is trying to get over something or someone. And I have had a lot of relationships if that's what you want to call them. I've always been the one to get hurt.

Are early childbearers especially disadvantaged in their prospects of entering and maintaining a stable union? Are they any worse off than black women who postpone parenthood? As observed in the previous chapter, marriage rates have drastically fallen off for blacks, divorce is endemic, and remarriage is relatively rare. It is just possible that the teenage mothers' inability to maintain a stable marriage is not very different from that of women who delay childbearing.

The national surveys were again consulted, serving as a baseline for comparison. Table 2.2 contrasts the marital distribution of the Baltimore women with their counterparts in the three national surveys, broken down by their age at first birth. The results further confirm that the Baltimore women look very similar to the early childbearers in the national surveys. Roughly the same proportion had ever been married. The Baltimore women are slightly less likely to be currently married and slightly more likely to be previously married than early childbearers in the three national surveys, but the differences are trivial. Since women who married early were less likely to remain in the study, sample attrition may well explain this difference.

Noticeable differences, however, are evident in the marital patterns of early and later childbearers. Even though they had a headstart on family formation, early childbearers are actually less likely to enter marriage than women who delay parenthood. And later childbearers are far less likely to dissolve their marriages than early childbearers. About half of the women who had their first child at 20 or older were currently married (usually in their first marriage), compared to about a third of the teenage parents of whom fewer were in first marriages. Some of this difference is artifactual. Early childbearers married on the average about 2 to 3 years before later childbearers and therefore have had a longer exposure to the risk of divorce. Even if we correct for the difference in the timing of marriage, the rate of divorce among women who postpone childbearing is distinctly lower.

These results corroborate previous findings demonstrating a link between early childbearing and marital instability (Coombs, Freedman, and Friedman, 1970; McCarthy and Menken, 1979; Morgan and Rindfuss, 1985). The nature of the causal links between these events is, however, in dispute. Some researchers have argued that it is early marriage, not childbearing, that leads to a higher risk of divorce; others believe that premature parenthood independently increases the risk of disruption. We find this debate uninformative since most early marriages would not occur were it not for an impending pregnancy. However, it is still unclear whether early childbearing/early marriage diminishes the prospects of stability or whether the individuals who become teenage parents are at greater risk of divorce because of personal attributes, e.g., low education, personality problems, and the like. This issue will be taken up in the next chapter when the association between early adjustment to parenthood and success in later life is examined.

Residential experience

Marital status and residential patterns are inevitably linked. Looking back at the life histories depicted in Figure 2.1, all three of the women resided with their mothers until they married, and Iris returned to her family home when she and Lester broke up. Indeed, almost all of the women remained with their parents until they married or, in some instances, had a second child. Marital disruption, loss of a job, or housing problems often brought them back to their parents' residence for a brief stay.

Though a complete residential history was not taken at the 17-year follow-up, information was collected on the frequency of moves and the pattern of coresidence with parents. As might be expected, most of the families had moved about quite a bit – half had changed residence four or more times since their first child was born, a fifth moved six or more times.

The life-history calendar recorded all the years during which the women resided with their mothers for at least part of the time. Figure 2.3 graphs the proportion of early childbearers who were living with their mother during the entire course of the study. From a high of 72% at the time of the child's birth, the rate of coresidence drops off sharply during the first phase of the study. By 1972, about a quarter of the sample still resided with their parents, though some of these women had been out on their own for a time and, like Iris, were temporary refugees from broken marriages. By the end of the 1970s, when most women were in their late twenties, the proportion levels off to about one in ten, where it remained. In the 5-year period preceding the 1984 interview, 86% of the sample had not lived with their parents whereas only 8% had lived with them at least 4 out of the 5 years.

Although comparable information from the national surveys does not exist on the proportion of three-generation households, the low incidence of coresidence in the Baltimore sample tells us that the differences cannot be very large. The

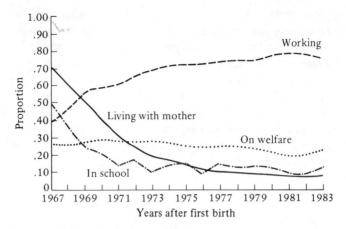

Figure 2.3. Proportions working, on welfare, in school, and living with mother by cal-endar year following first birth ($N = 288$)

picture emerging from this study challenges the view held by many researchers that most teenage mothers remain dependent on their parents and become en-trapped in three-generation households. Instead, it appears that the three-generation constellation is an exception. Even among women currently receiving public assistance, the incidence of three-generation households was only 10% – almost the same rate as for the entire sample.

The patterns of household residence were regulated in part by changes in the marital situations of the Baltimore women. Only 5% of the currently married women lived with their mother at any time during the past 5 years as compared to 13% of the previously married and 27% of the never-married women. The higher prevalence of coresidence among single mothers seems to result less from preference than from necessity. Living with parents following the birth of a child or after an economic crisis can be a temporary boost to social mobility, but as will be seen in the next chapter, persistent coresidence is a predictor, and may be a source, of long-term economic dependency.

Fertility

Almost all of the young mothers grew up in very large families; half had four or more siblings. Their family size preferences, expressed at the outset of the study, were far more modest, but even so, close to half wanted to have three or more children. By the 5-year follow-up, it appeared that many women were going to have even more children than they either wanted or expected. The tempo of childbearing in the years immediately following the first birth exceeded the young mothers' plans. Close to a third of the young mothers had been pregnant two or more additional times and a sixth had already had a third child. Over half had already reached their desired number of children.

Doris's situation was not unusual. She became pregnant only a year after the birth of her first child. Like her first pregnancy, the second was unplanned. Doris had emphatically stated at the postpartum interview that she did not intend to have another child until she was married, but at age 17 she was unmarried with two children. When asked how the second pregnancy happened, she replied that she had stopped using the pill because she was afraid of getting cancer and had thought her boyfriend was going to "use protection."

Throughout the first part of the study, young mothers reported great difficulty using birth control effectively. All but a few wanted to practice contraception, almost all attempted to use birth control, and most used it at least occasionally. But only a small minority – about a fifth of the sample – were reliable contraceptive users. Birth control was practiced more faithfully among the women who had participated in the comprehensive prenatal program, but even many of these women were not able to avoid rapid repeat pregnancies. Perhaps the most discouraging finding was that more than half of the single women, who were working or in school and who explicitly stated a desire to defer further childbearing, failed to use birth control regularly.

Predictably, the young mothers were well ahead of their classmates in family building at the 5-year follow-up. Even when compared to the classmates who had already had a child, the adolescent mothers were much more likely to have had an unplanned and unwanted repeat pregnancy soon after their first birth (Furstenberg, 1976). Their fertility at the 5-year follow-up led us to anticipate that fertility a decade later would not closely conform to the young mother's original intentions.

We were wrong. Data collected in 1984 revealed that the vast majority were able to control their fertility in the second phase of the study. Indeed, most had fewer children than they originally intended and not even as many as they had expected in 1972. Table 2.4 shows the number of additional children born to the women who participated in the 17-year follow-up, broken down by whether the births occurred in the first or second segment of the study. Overall, about a fifth of the women never had a second birth, two-fifths had only one more child, 26% had two additional births, and the remainder (12%) had three or more children. *Of all additional births, 61% occurred in the first segment of the study.* On the average, the young mothers had .81 births in the 5 years after their first birth and .52 children in the 12 or so years of the second segment. The average per year fertility in the initial phase of the study was three times greater than it was in the second period (.16 compared to .05 births per woman in an average year). By

Table 2.4. *Number of additional children born to women by 1984, by phase*

Number of additional children beyond study child	Total		Phase 1		Phase 2	
	N	%	N	%	N	%
0	60	20.8	116	40.3	170	59.0
1	119	41.3	121	42.0	93	32.3
2	75	26.0	41	14.2	19	6.6
3	24	8.3	8	2.8	5	1.7
4+	10	3.3	2	0.6	1	0.3
Total	288	100.0	288	99.9	288	99.9

the time the young mothers reached their late twenties and early thirties, child-bearing for most had concluded. *Only 13% of the women had given birth in the 5 years immediately preceding the 1984 interview.*

The next chapter examines the determinants of subsequent childbearing and identifies characteristics of women who successfully limited their family size. Our attention here is confined to *how* most women managed to curtail their fertility in the second segment of the study. Did they become more adept at practicing birth control, resort to abortion more frequently, or employ some other strategy of family limitation? Each of these explanations has some bearing on the dramatic reduction of fertility, but two were especially important.

First, the greater availability of abortion in the second segment of the study is obviously one reason why our prediction of high lifetime fertility was not borne out. Even in 1972, just after abortion had been legalized in Maryland, a substantial number of the young mothers reported that they had terminated or would terminate a pregnancy once they reached their desired family size. About a fifth of the mothers who had become pregnant for a third time before 1972 reported they had obtained an abortion.

By 1984 the use of abortion had become more widespread. No doubt, self-reported data underestimate the true incidence because many who disapprove of abortion are reluctant to admit that they obtained one. Nevertheless, Figure 2.4 shows a predictable rise in the abortion rate from .20 for women with one child to .52 for women with three children. Abortion rates at every parity were more than twice as high in the second segment of the study than in the first. Of course, women, irrespective of parity, may have been more capable of managing the outcome of an unwanted conception when they were older. Nevertheless, the legalization of abortion, the ensuing changes in public opinion, and the greater accessibility to low-cost abortion all made it a more acceptable means of resolving an unwanted pregnancy (Sklar and Berkov, 1974). One mother, reflecting back on her early life, observed how different it might be had she become preg-

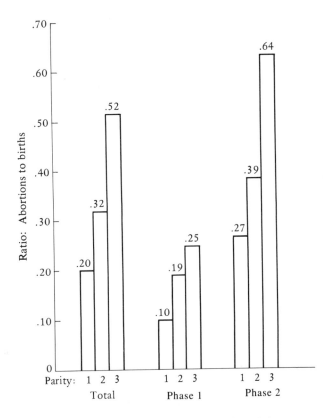

Figure 2.4. Ratio of abortions to live births by parity and phase

nant in her teens today: "It's 1985, and I would have to honestly admit that with abortions being legal, which they were not in 1967, I'd have to think about it."

The other principal source of the decline in fertility is sterilization. Several national studies have shown that many women experience the same problems in using birth control that plagued the participants in the Baltimore study (Tanfer and Horn, 1985; Zelnik, Kantner, and Ford, 1981). As a result, a growing proportion of females in their late twenties and early thirties have shifted from pill use and barrier methods to contraceptive sterilization. Among all currently married women in the NSFG, the proportion who were sterilized more than doubled from 1973 to 1982, rising from 12 to 26%. Blacks, probably because they reach their intended family size earlier, are even more likely than whites to elect sterilization (Bachrach, 1984).

No national trends on sterilization among formerly married and never-married blacks are available. However, it is reasonable to assume that the incidence of

Table 2.5. *Percent sterilized among Baltimore women by total number of children born and current marital status, 1984*

	Number of children born			
	0–1	2	3+	Total
Blacks				
Currently married	50.0%	55.2%	73.3%	61.0%
	(18)	(29)	(30)	(77)
Previously married	36.4	62.0	71.7	61.0
	(22)	(50)	(46)	(118)
Never married	29.6	31.6	68.8	40.3
	(27)	(19)	(16)	(62)
Total	37.3	54.1	71.7	56.0
	(67)	(98)	(92)	(257)
Whites, total	—	—	—	67.9
				(28)

Note: Dashes indicate fewer than 15 cases.

sterilization has been increasing here as well. The Baltimore data show a startlingly high level of sterilization. Over half of the women (56%) have been sterilized. Table 2.5 shows the patterns of sterilization by marital status and parity for blacks. (Because they are too few in number, comparable breakdowns for whites cannot be provided though the data suggest that racial differences are not large.)

As might be expected, sterilization among blacks rises with parity. This pattern is almost identical regardless of whether the woman is currently married or previously married. Never-married women are somewhat less likely to have become sterilized if they have had only one or two children, but they are no less likely to have been sterilized if their family size is three or more. A high proportion – nearly a third – of the never-married women elected to become sterilized even when they had only one or two children. Sterilization resolved the fertility dilemma that existed in 1972: Most women did not want additional children, but they also had great difficulty using contraception and were reluctant to resort to abortion when unwanted conceptions inevitably occurred. As women reached or exceeded their desired family size, sterilization became an increasingly attractive option, at least compared to the alternatives.

Again it is instructive to look at the three case histories we have been following. After having a third unintended pregnancy in 1974 when she was 23, Doris's childbearing ended. In 1984, Doris reported that she was sterilized. Since the date of the sterilization was not ascertained in the interview, we do not know how long she waited after her third child was born to have the operation. It probably coincided with the delivery, however, even though Doris was only 23 at the time.

One woman in Doris's situation described the lengths she went to obtain a sterilization in her early twenties.

I used to take the pill . . . and when I knew I couldn't take it anymore, I said "Forget it, do something." I had two kids. I was supposed to get it down at Brady Hospital, but they said, "If both of your kids get killed in a car accident, there is only a one percent chance that we can undo this, and blah, blah, blah." So I went to another hospital.

Despite encountering considerable resistance from the medical community for what many physicians regarded as a premature closure of life options, most young mothers expressed few reservations about ending childbearing. Having started 5 to 10 years earlier than many of their peers, they elected to conclude childbearing 5 to 10 years earlier. By their mid-twenties, most were ready to forgo the possibility of having more children.

As a result, the women in the Baltimore study managed to limit their fertility to levels comparable to delayed childbearers. Table 2.2 compares the mean number of children born to the Baltimore women, with the mean number of children produced by early and later childbearers in the national samples. Unlike the figures on schooling and marital status, the Baltimore women stand out from their counterparts nationwide. They average about .5 births fewer than the early childbearers in the national surveys. Several reasons could explain this difference, including regional differences in fertility, fewer number of years married (the Baltimore women have spent less time in matrimony), and, most important, better opportunities to obtain sterilization at an early age because of ample medical facilities in the community.

The participants in the study have nonetheless produced more children than the delayed childbearers in the national sample, consistent with a general pattern of higher fertility among teenage mothers. In time, however, later childbearers may match the number of children born to the Baltimore women since more delayed childbearers are currently married and probably fewer are sterilized. Were we able to compare the two groups again in another 10 years, the small disparity might have disappeared.

These results, showing modest or no differences in the number of children ever born to early and later childbearers, are in line with several recent studies on the impact of early childbearing on fertility. Apparently, as sterilization and abortion become more available, the effect of age of childbearing may become less pronounced (St. John, 1982). The rapid tempo of family building among early childbearers is curbed by marital dissolution and the availability of birth control and abortion. In all likelihood, the Baltimore women will bear only about half the number of children that their mothers produced and about the same number as all black women in their same birth cohort who have at least one child.

Economic status: welfare, work, and family income

Teenage childbearing arouses public concern largely because it is believed to be a nearly certain path to poverty and economic dependency. Though the young mothers and their classmates come from roughly equivalent socioeconomic backgrounds, their economic situations in 1972 had sharply diverged. Close to a third of the young mothers were receiving public assistance at that time as compared to only 15% of all the classmates and fewer than 5% of the classmates who had not become pregnant in their teens. Disparities in employment levels between the young mothers and their classmates were similar. Slightly under half of the young mothers held jobs and were partially or wholly self-supporting as compared to 70% of the classmates who had delayed childbearing. Low education, child-care responsibilities, and limited employment experience were severely restricting the economic status of the young mothers in 1972 and seemed to point to a bleak economic future.

As we discovered in examining the educational careers of the adolescent parents, the prognosis at the 5-year follow-up was somewhat worse than the actual outcome a dozen years later. Unlike the popular stereotype, most teenage mothers did not become chronic welfare recipients. In 1984, slightly under a quarter of the women (and exactly a quarter of the blacks) had received public assistance in the past year, a small decline from the proportion who had been on welfare in 1972.

Of the 70% who ever received welfare during the course of the study, close to two-thirds went off the welfare rolls by 1984. These results are quite consistent with the findings of other investigators who have studied patterns of welfare use among AFDC families. Studies by Duncan and his colleagues at the University of Michigan clearly demonstrate that the welfare population is quite transient. Only a minority of women have lengthy stays on public assistance. Bane and Ellwood (1984) also show that welfare stays are typically short: Half of all women exit from welfare within 3 years, though some later reapply for public assistance. Still, only about a fourth of women who receive public assistance become welfare dependent, that is, remain on welfare for a significant proportion of their childbearing years. Chronic recipients nevertheless receive the lion's share of resources simply because their duration on welfare is so long. They may be compared to the chronically ill hospital patients who consume a large fraction of health-care dollars even though they are a small fraction of those hospitalized.

Most women in our study used welfare like Iris, who spent 2 years on public assistance after her marriage broke up and she switched jobs. Iris and others like

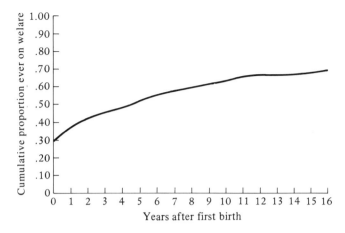

Figure 2.5. Cumulative proportion ever on welfare by years after first birth ($N = 288$)

her despised the welfare system and felt humiliated by going on welfare. One informant, whose situation was similar to Iris's, commented in an interview:

Welfare helped at the time, but I really didn't like it . . . I didn't want to get used to depending on getting a check and food stamps every month. It was enough just to take care of the rent, the gas, and the telephone. . . . But my daughter needed other things like clothes, and it didn't take care of that. That's why I decided I had to get off and find me a job quick.

Even those like Doris, who were on welfare for most or all of the study, had little good to say about the welfare system. One woman who had been on welfare for a decade recalled in 1984:

I hated it . . . I would always make it a habit of not going to market when welfare recipients were there. The only thing that keep me going was "It's not going to go on forever."

Most of those who went on welfare did not have stays as lengthy as Doris or the woman quoted above. Two life tables were constructed showing the probability of ever going on welfare and, for those women who ever received public assistance, the probability of remaining on welfare. As Figure 2.5 shows, the probability of becoming a welfare recipient rose rapidly during the early years of the study and then leveled off. Most women who ever went on welfare did so by the end of the initial phase because stints on welfare were more common when young children were in the home.

The probability of exiting from welfare was even steeper in the early years of the study (Fig. 2.6). Within three years, more than half of the women on welfare ceased receiving payments. Some of these women ultimately returned to the welfare rolls during the course of the study, but most who went back on welfare

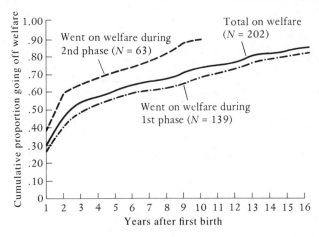

Figure 2.6. Cumulative proportion going off welfare among women who ever went on welfare

went off again when circumstances permitted. Only one woman out of eight who went on welfare in the first phase of the study was still receiving public assistance in 1984.

By examining the patterns of welfare use in the most recent 5-year period, we obtain the clearest picture of how the women in Baltimore are faring at the present time. *Two-thirds of the participants did not receive welfare during any of the past 5 years*. Among the third who did, most (22% of the entire sample) were on public assistance at least 3 out of the 5 years. Clearly, chronic or near-chronic welfare dependency is the exception rather than the rule among the early childbearers in our sample, though a significant minority of the Baltimore women are reliant on welfare.

Is this proportion of welfare dependents high or low? We return to our national data to provide a baseline for comparison (see Table 2.2). Once again, the experience of the Baltimore women is quite similar to that of their counterparts. In each case slightly more than a quarter of the women had been on welfare in the past year. The CPS did not collect information on welfare experiences, so a comparison must be confined to the other two surveys. In contrast, about a fifth of the later childbearers had received welfare in the past year. Although the difference is consistent across surveys and sizable enough to be statistically significant, it is not large.

The rather modest differential may be explained partly by the fact that welfare use is more prevalent among women with young children. Many teenage mothers no longer have young children. Eligibility requirements may force them off welfare, but they are probably also willing and able to enter the labor market. The early schedule of childbearing experienced by the Baltimore mothers and their counterparts in the NSFG and NLS, therefore, confounds the contrast among early and later childbearers. Nonetheless, the finding that the great majority of adolescent mothers in the Baltimore and national samples are not reliant on public assistance is unexpected, as is the rather small difference between early and later childbearers.

Employment experience

The occupational careers of the participants in the Baltimore study paralleled their welfare experience. The rate of employment rose steadily during the course of the study. About a third were employed the same year their first child was born, another third began working within 2 years of their first birth, and all but a sixth had held a job by the end of the first segment. Nevertheless, in 1972, significantly fewer mothers were employed than classmates (45% v. 59%), despite the fact that more classmates were full-time students. Moreover, the jobs held by classmates required greater skill and were better paid. Many of the young mothers who had found employment appeared to be stuck in low-paying jobs.

Their situation improved a little during the second segment of the study, but many of the early childbearers remain at the bottom of the economic ladder. By 1984, all but 2% had accumulated some work experience, and the majority had worked more or less continuously in the decade following the 5-year follow-up. Figure 2.3 shows the proportion of women employed during each year of the study. The percentage working rose from 40 in 1967 to 72 in 1983, the last year for which we have complete information. This does not mean that all women working in a given year were continuously employed, but it denotes that they were employed for at least 3 months of a given year. Sixty percent of the sample worked in each of the 5 years preceding the 1984 interview, 11% held jobs in 4 of the 5, and the remaining 29% worked 3 years or less. Slightly less than a tenth of the sample had no employment during the most recent 5-year period.

The job histories of the three women depicted in Figure 2.1 are illustrative of the varied occupational experiences. Doris worked intermittently at five different jobs during the course of the study. All of her jobs were unskilled employment and her last position paid no more in 1982 than she had earned a decade earlier, correcting for inflation. Iris was somewhat better off, having worked a greater number of years and having acquired some skills. She took a civil service test several years ago and qualified for a position as business administrator in the school district. Her income is not high, but she has security and job benefits that are likely to hold her in the position.

Helena's situation is similar to Iris's. Except for 2 years when she decided to stay home with her second child, she has worked every year since graduating from high school. On the basis of a good recommendation from her second employer, 2 years ago she became executive secretary to the head of a small cosmetics business. Helena is hoping some day, when her children complete school, to start her own business.

Like Iris and Helena, most of the women in the study switched jobs infrequently. During the entire study, 18% of the women had only one job, 20% two jobs, 18% three jobs, 19% four jobs, and fewer than a fourth of the women had five or more jobs. Of those currently employed, more than half had held the job for 5 or more years, and a quarter had been at the same place of employment for 10 or more years. Whereas some of the women attributed their job stability to contentment with their place of employment, many did not feel they had the option of leaving. About three out of five of the working women thought it would be extremely or fairly difficult to find a different job.

Just as welfare use among later childbearers was somewhat lower than among teenage parents, participation in the labor force was higher among the women who postponed parenthood. Although employment levels differ somewhat among the three national studies (presumably reflecting economic conditions and sample differences), in all cases later childbearers were more likely to be working. These results are consistent with previous research showing that early childbearers are at an economic disadvantage, albeit a small one. The Baltimore data are in line with the national figures, though a somewhat higher proportion of women in our study were currently employed owing to lower rates of marriage and fertility.

Income

In 1984, 67% of the women were currently employed and another 9% were actively seeking work. Almost all of those who were working (94%) were employed for at least 30 hours a week . Most held unskilled or semiskilled jobs, were working in the service sector of the economy, and were paid modest wages. Before deductions, the average hourly wage was $6.40. Assuming no periods of unemployment, this yields an average annual income of $13,304 per working woman, barely a sufficient income to support a family. Of course, many women were in fact underemployed, working less than full time. Their actual earnings often fell short of what was needed to support their family.

In 1983, 40% of the women were the exclusive breadwinner in their family; in another 24% of the cases, they provided the principal source of income. Only 12% contributed nothing to the total family income. Of course, some women had other sources of income such as child support, supplementary assistance, or aid from family members. Table 2.6 lists the different sources of income received during 1983 by current marital status. Personal earnings were a major source of income even among married women.

Because women had difficulty determining exact income from each source

Table 2.6. *Sources of income for Baltimore mothers by marital status,*
1984 (in %)

Income source	Currently married (99)	Previously married (127)	Never married (63)
Employment	78	76	84
Welfare	10	38	32
Husband/partner[a]	94	26	17
Father of child	6	26	17
Family	10	15	19
Other income	26	23	22

[a] Twenty-one (17%) of the previously married and 10 (16%) of the never-married mothers currently have a partner.

and because some were reluctant to volunteer this information in the pretest, they were only asked to report their total family income within broad categories. Although the figures they supplied are less precise, they provide a reasonable estimate of the economic status of our respondents.

Many of the early childbearers are poor. A third have annual incomes below $10,000, about the poverty level for a family of four in the United States in 1983. While many of the early childbearers are not doing well economically, a surprising number are relatively well off. A quarter of the sample had an income exceeding $25,000 a year, which placed them above the median for the country. Combining the income and welfare data into a single measure, the sample divides into four categories. About a quarter of the respondents are on welfare, a quarter are working poor with incomes below $15,000, about a quarter have modest incomes between $15,000 and $24,999, and the remaining quarter are economically secure with a family income exceeding $25,000. The economic circumstances of the three women whose lives we have been following throughout this chapter illustrate the diversity within the Baltimore sample. Doris relies primarily on the meager income she obtains from public assistance, supplemented with occasional employment, sporadic child support, and emergency assistance from her mother and an older brother. Iris is totally dependent on the income she receives from her job, which amounts to just under $15,000 a year, including additional earnings she receives for overtime work. She is occasionally called upon to assist her mother and younger sister, who are living on welfare. Helena's situation is quite different. With her husband's earnings and her income, she recorded a family income of $37,000. Helena was among the top 10% of the sample in the amount of family income. Helena sometimes feels economically pinched, but she realizes that she is doing well in comparison with many of the women she knows.

Women like Helena are likely to recognize that they are relatively well off economically just as women like Doris often feel on the edge of utter destitution. When asked how often they worry that ''your total family income will not be enough to meet your family's expenses and bills,'' 8% of the economically secure replied most or all of the time as compared to 39% of those with modest incomes, 44% of the working poor, and 69% of the women on public assistance. Evidently, many of the early childbearers are living a precarious economic existence.

Whether they are any worse off than they would be if they had postponed parenthood is a question that can be answered by turning again to the national surveys. Returning once more to Table 2.2, we find data on family income levels of early and later childbearers in the national surveys. Variations from survey to survey are to be expected as the questions seeking income information differed. Nonetheless, we find again a similar pattern of results. Like the Baltimore women, early childbearers generally have incomes near or below $15,000. At the other end of the continuum, between a fifth and a quarter had incomes above $25,000. Again, it appears that the Baltimore women resemble their counterparts in the national surveys.

The comparison of these women with older childbearers reveals a substantial difference in the level of family income. Later childbearers are much more likely than teenage mothers to have incomes of $25,000 or more. Conversely, many fewer are poor. Compared to other indicators of well-being, family income is quite sensitive to the timing of childbearing. The following chapter provides more information on why teenage mothers are so much less likely to attain a secure family income than women who postpone parenthood.

Summary

The 15-year follow-up provides some good and some bad news about the situation of early childbearers in later life. The popular belief that early childbearing is an almost certain route to dropping out of school, subsequent unwanted births, and economic dependency is greatly oversimplified, if not seriously distorted.

A substantial majority of the young mothers in our study completed high school, found regular employment, and even when they had been on welfare, eventually managed to escape from public assistance. Relatively few ended up with large families. Like other women in the United States, they seem to have revised their fertility expectations downward during the 1970s. Most had even fewer births than they wanted or expected at the time they first became pregnant. In the past 5 years, when the young mothers in the Baltimore sample were in their late twenties and early thirties, just under a third had spent *any* time on welfare, 60% were working in *each* of the 5 years, and less than 10% of the women, with two or more children, had an additional child. Half of the sample in 1984 were living on incomes that provided at least a modest level of security, and a quarter were making $25,000 a year or more.

The young mothers appear in the most favorable light when we compare their current situations to their circumstances 12 years earlier, when the 5-year follow-up was concluded. In almost all respects, they are far better off today than a decade ago. Many more have advanced their schooling, found employment, gone off welfare, established their own household, and regulated their fertility. Only in their marital status was no substantial change observed. Although many of the young mothers entered marriage during the second segment of the study, just as many were separated or divorced in the period from 1972 to 1984. More of the women had partners in the recent follow-up, but cohabitational relationships appear to be even less stable than marriages. Thus, most of the mothers were largely dependent on their own incomes for support.

While the popular image of the adolescent childbearer in later life is not completely accurate, the assumption that premature parenthood creates lasting social and economic disadvantages is strongly corroborated by the results of our long-term follow-up. When the black women in the sample, who comprise the great majority of the participants in the study, were compared to black mothers of similar age in several national studies, we discovered that the Baltimore mothers were doing less well on all of the outcomes examined.

Even if the stereotype of the adolescent mother in later life is much exaggerated, it is not wholly wrong. Many teenage mothers manage to break out of the seemingly inevitable cycle of poverty, but the majority did not make out as well as they probably would have had they been able to postpone parenthood. These findings lend some credibility to the belief that the life course remains to some degree fluid and flexible, but they also suggest that there are definite limits as to how much room early childbearers have in which to manipulate their circumstances in later life. In the next chapter, we shall examine the conditions that constrained or promoted subsequent adaptation to early childbearing in adulthood.

3   Pathways to success in adulthood

To understand how social contexts affect the life choices of individuals, social scientists often focus on cohorts that share a common experience or set of experiences. As Elder (1974) has demonstrated in his study of children of the Great Depression, the experience of certain events at a particular age can have important implications for subsequent behavior. Additionally, a particular cohort may have vastly different options available when confronting life events. Changing abortion laws provide a relevant example. Abortion was illegal during the 1960s, when the women we studied first became pregnant. Teenagers who became pregnant a decade later faced quite a different set of options. In short, a cohort's unique history can affect attitudes, opportunities, and behavior (Ryder, 1965).

The mothers in the Baltimore study are from roughly the same birth cohort. They also constitute, in demographers' terms, an age-parity cohort; that is, they had their first birth as teenagers. Not only do they share age-graded and historical experiences, which may be considered normative events (Baltes and Nesselroade, 1973), but they share a nonnormative event – teenage parenthood. They also made the crucial transition to parenthood at the same ages and in the same historical period. In addition, these teenage mothers grew up in the same city, almost all are black, and most came from relatively disadvantaged families. Despite these commonalities, enormous variation in outcomes occurred, as we learned in the previous chapter. For instance, a fourth of the mothers were on welfare in 1984 while another fourth were relatively comfortable economically, with a family income of more than $25,000 per year. By the 17-year follow-up, slightly under two-fifths of the sample had three or more children, and about one-fifth had never had even a second child.

This diversity highlights the fact that life courses are determined by complex interactions between individual characteristics and social contexts (Bronfenbrenner, 1979, 1985). Chance life events and other factors beyond individual control also influence the life course. Over time, the cohort identity – the experience a cohort shares – becomes less salient as subsequent experience blurs the differences between cohorts (Ryder, 1965). Stated differently, cohort members

48

become more dissimilar over time as the implications of their different choices and opportunities alter the subsequent life course.

This chapter focuses on this intracohort diversity. Given similar origins, how can one explain the broad array of outcomes observed among these adolescent mothers? We will examine some of the events, individual characteristics, and environment factors that determine the circumstances of the Baltimore study women 17 years after their first birth.

Strategy for data analysis

The abundance of the data, interviews, and records assembled over a 17-year period allows us to examine the unfolding life course of the Baltimore mothers. Our organization and analysis of the data retain the longitudinal, sequential character of the life course. Norman Ryder (1965:859) has written: "The raison d'être of the longitudinal approach is the organization of personal data in temporal sequence, to determine the causal potentiality of otherwise isolated acts." In effect, a woman's past affects her present, and her present affects her future.

Even with the organizing concepts of the cohort and the life course, we risk drowning in the available data. To provide further focus, our findings are organized around two key indicators of well-being in 1984: (1) *economic status* (based on the classification developed in Chapter 2 that divided the sample into four groups – welfare recipients, the working poor, those with modest incomes of $15,000 to 24,999, and the economically secure who have incomes of $25,000 or more) and (2) *fertility* (i.e., the number of living children). Selection of these two outcomes was somewhat arbitrary. We could have considered educational achievement, stable marriage, or childbearing skills as alternative indicators of well-being. However, the measures selected are widely regarded both by concerned professionals and by the women in the study themselves as appropriate yardsticks for gauging the success of teen mothers. Additionally, these measures provide some indication of the economic costs of early parenthood on social services, especially public assistance. Both indicators are also strongly related to expressions of well-being voiced by the participants in the study such as personal happiness, emotional health, and psychological security. Finally, the measures have the virtue of being simple, straightforward, and easily interpretable. The task of this chapter, then, is to explain the variability in economic status and fertility in the Baltimore women 17 years after the birth of their first child.

Chapter 1 identified several possible explanations for the intracohort variability observed: (1) *individual differences* in motivation and competence; (2) *availability of resources,* including informal networks; (3) *involvement in formal programs;* and (4) *career contingencies,* the decisions during or following the first pregnancy that may have facilitated or constrained events in later life. This chapter examines information collected over the past 17 years that is directly or indirectly linked to one or another of these explanations. We begin by examining a broad range of factors that could affect the economic or fertility outcomes. Those factors that prove most important will then be examined together, taking account of their temporal sequence, in order to identify their relative role in the prediction of economic success and fertility. For example, remaining in school throughout the pregnancy and following the birth was related to economic security in the first phase of the study. Does this early decision continue to influence economic status later in life, and how much variability does it explain?[1]

Variability in economic status at the 17-year follow-up

Previous research has considered income attainment as a measure of life outcome. Most of these studies have looked at the situation of males; very few have looked at women, much less those who became parents at an early age (for exceptions, see Bane and Ellwood, 1983; Card and Wise, 1978). However, some of these studies have illuminated the pathways through which antecedent events affect economic status. This prior work influenced our choice of variables and the form of our conceptual model.

The Blau and Duncan (1967) study has been the starting point for much of the stratification research of the past two decades. The explanatory model posits that parent's background status affects occupational and economic status largely through the son's educational attainment. Specifically, the father's education and occupation, and to a lesser extent family size, influenced aspirations and resources for the son's education. Thus, fathers passed on status to their sons primarily by providing them with schooling, which can then be translated into high-status occupations with generally high incomes.

Subsequent research examined the status-attainment process in greater detail and for different subgroups, such as women and blacks. For instance, Jencks et al. (1979) argue that academic success is a crucial mediating variable for economic outcome and, like Blau and Duncan, traces some of the variability in academic success to family background variables. But controlling for background variables, individual academic ability still had strong effects. Thus, academic ability is one source of subsequent variability in the life course. Academic ability, however, not only is a measure of cognitive skills, but also is influenced

---

1 No single analysis, nor any single data set, will allow us to substantiate fully or rule out completely any of the possible explanations. Instead we present evidence gathered from applying a quantitative social science methodology. The data we analyze are consistent with the explanations we offer. But this information does not prove them. Greater certainty can come only with additional studies that replicate our results. But for those who wish to develop policy now, the best available information and evidence are crucial.

by motivation and general competence, which are themselves influenced by environmental conditions and individual characteristics. The predictive power of academic ability appears to derive in large part from its relation to these stable underlying attributes (Jencks et al., 1979).

The Blau and Duncan model of intergenerational mobility has been elaborated in recent years. Featherman and Hauser (1976a) argue that the process underlying status attainment is different for blacks than for whites. Blacks are less able to pass on status to the next generation such that the relation between the father's education and occupation and the son's education would be weaker for blacks than for whites. Also, within a level of education or an occupation, blacks may be less able to obtain a high income, given discrimination in hiring and promotion. Indeed, lower income returns for a given level of education or a given status job were observed for blacks. Featherman and Hauser (1976a) also show that the status-attainment model for blacks became more similar to the white male model across the 1960 decade. They attribute such changes to less discrimination, both at individual and institutional levels.

Women, like blacks, were found to have more difficulty translating their schooling and occupational status into income (Featherman and Hauser, 1976b). For women, economic status is linked to her own marital and fertility experience, more so than for men. Women can achieve status and income via their own human capital in the workplace or they can, through marriage, create a partnership with a man who has high income potential. Thus, women can compete in a wage market or a marriage market, or both. Recently, the number of women in poverty has risen substantially because fewer marriages occur and those that do are less stable; because women usually retain custody of children in the case of marital disruption; because men often do not provide support for their children; and because women suffer discrimination and structural barriers in the job market (Bane, 1986; Bane and Ellwood, 1984; Fuchs, 1986; Garfinkel and McLanahan, 1985).

Based on these and other findings, we anticipate the following results in our study. First, background variables should predict economic attainment as they do in all of the classic studies on status and income attainment. But since our sample is primarily black, the links between background variables and economic status may be weaker than in samples of whites. Further, black women may have an especially difficult time translating parents' status into income because of discrimination based on race and sex. Second, educational attainment should be a crucial factor in the unfolding life course, with general competence and motivation important variables underlying academic success. Third, marital and fertility experience will be crucial in predicting economic security. Marriage may provide an avenue to economic security, but if the marriage fails the woman may be left in a nearly hopeless situation, with several dependents and few marketable

Teenager's background variables
+*race
  welfare status as a child
* mother's education
+*mother's age at first birth
  mother's number of children
  mother's employment status
  mother's marital history

Time 2 variables
* education level
+*school attendance during pregnancy
+*Poe School attendance
  meetings with clinic group
+*birth control use
+*household composition
  welfare status
  discuss birth control with mother

Time 1 variables
  mother's marital status
+*welfare status at time of birth
+*marital status
+*marriage relative to birth
* education level
  reaction to pregnancy
  negative school attitude
+*educational aspirations
* marital expectations
  age began intercourse
  friends' premarital fertility
  birth control use
  age

1st Segment variables
+ welfare status
+*years lived with mother
+*additional children born
+*interval to 2nd birth
+ school in 1st segment
* reliance on mother
+ return to school following birth

Time 3 variables
+*welfare status
+*educational level
+*marital status

Time 4 variables
+*welfare status
+*educational level
+*marital status

Outcome variables
+economic status
*fertility

*Significant bivariate association with outcome measure of economic status at .05 level.
+Significant bivariate association with number of children ever born at .05 level.

Figure 3.1. Selected variables examined as potential determinants of economic status and family size

52

skills. Finally, subsequent fertility may overwhelm a woman, making it difficult to provide for her family without resorting to public assistance.

Figure 3.1 shows some of the available indicators that we considered as potential predictors of the adolescent mothers' 1984 economic status. Consistent with the preceding discussion, family background and educational, marital, and fertility experiences are highlighted. Also as mentioned before, the heart of the longitudinal approach is the temporal alignment of data collected at various time points. We will consider events and experience early in the life course as potential determinants of later events and attitudes. Consistent with this life-course perspective, we have arrayed the variables from left to right by their time of occurrence. Variables that have significant bivariate associations with 1984 economic status are indicated by an asterisk; those related to family size are marked with a plus sign.

Background variables

Familial background variables, in part, reflect childhood experiences, which might produce differences in motivation and skills, as well as access to strategic resources. Surprisingly, background variables prove to be only modest predictors of economic status. Welfare experience as a child, number of siblings, and parental education do have important effects and will be discussed at length later. But a number of other potentially important familial variables were inconsequential. For instance, whether the parent of the adolescent mother was herself an early childbearer was not significantly related to the eventual success of the women in our study. If the parent had a child out of wedlock, her daughter was only slightly more likely to be economically disadvantaged in adulthood. While virtually all of the respondents' mothers had eventually married, close to half were separated or divorced at the outset of the study, so that variation in family composition was evident. But adolescent mothers living in two-parent households at the time of their pregnancy were not significantly more likely than those living in single-parent households to achieve economic security as adults.

Of the family background variables, only two emerged as significant predictors of economic status. The first of these is race. Whites were more likely to attain a higher economic level than blacks, which could reflect the discrimination that blacks still face. Discrimination may be overt, as in the case of favoring whites for jobs and promotion, or more subtle, as in the case of knowing the right people. However, the race differences in part might be due to other factors. As mentioned in Chapter 1, almost all of the whites in our follow-up sample are married, partly owing to the high attrition of unmarried whites over the course of the study. And as we have shown, being married at the 5-year follow-up is a strong predictor of economic status. Thus, differential rates of marriage, marital stability, or attrition could be influencing the greater economic success of whites. Because of this race difference and because of the small sample of whites, subsequent analyses only include blacks.

Only one other family background variable proved significant in the preliminary analyses, namely, the educational level of the respondents' parents. Two other variables, number of siblings and welfare experience as a child, were only weakly associated with economic status in 1984. They had strong and interpretable effects on some of the mediating variables and were included in subsequent analyses, in order to understand better the process by which family background influences economic and fertility status.

Characteristics of the pregnant adolescent

Moving from characteristics of the family to characteristics of the adolescent mother, we detected some unexpected results. Contrary to common expectations, but consistent with the results of the first phase of the Baltimore study, respondent's age at time of pregnancy was not related to economic status later in life. After controlling for other variables, the life chances of the mothers 15 years of age and younger are no worse than those of women who have their first child at age 16 or 17.

None of the attitudinal measures of responses to becoming pregnant tapped in the initial interview (with one exception, which will be discussed later) predicted economic status or fertility level in 1984. Specifically, we examined the pregnant adolescent's views about sex and marriage, her reaction to her pregnancy, her attitudes about birth control, and her feelings about doctors and medical care. None was related to adult economic status, either directly or indirectly. This finding is again consistent with the results of the initial phase of the study, which discovered no link between the young mothers' attitudes during pregnancy and their subsequent adjustment to parenthood. In addition, frequency of church attendance, age at first intercourse, birth-control experience prior to first pregnancy, and the timing of first prenatal visit also were either unrelated or only weakly associated with subsequent economic status. That attitudes about marriage, pregnancy, and health care are unrelated to economic success suggests that they do not figure importantly in the management of early childbearing.

The pregnant teen's educational ambitions and goals are the one set of attitudes that predict later economic success. In particular, a strong association exists between the pregnant adolescent's educational aspirations and her later economic well-being. Her self-evaluation of school performance and enjoyment of school were also modestly related to her economic status in adulthood. The strongest predictor of eventual economic success was being at grade level, suggesting that adolescents who were performing below grade level were especially susceptible to economic disadvantage in later life.

These findings seem to confirm the earlier observation that competence and motivation, as inferred by early educational commitment, are important sources of variation in later life. This interpretation is further bolstered by the fact that those reporting higher aspirations were more likely to remain in school throughout the pregnancy and to finish high school eventually. And, of course, school completion is an important path to subsequent economic well-being (see also Bane and Ellwood, 1983).

Characteristics and experience of the adolescent mother 1 year postpartum

The picture derived from the initial interview does not change much when we look at the life course 1 year postpartum (time 2). The young mothers' school experiences during pregnancy and immediately following childbirth were important predictors of economic status in adulthood. In particular, women who remained in school throughout their pregnancy and after their child was born were significantly less likely than early dropouts to be on welfare and more likely to be economically secure in 1984.

Another finding helps to explain the strong association between school continuity and economic success. Women who attended the Edgar Allan Poe School, a special school for pregnant teens, were much more likely to be economically well-off in adulthood than women who either dropped out or remained in their regular school program. The Poe School emphasized academic achievement, delaying marriage, and postponing further childbearing as indicated by its informal motto, "Never More." Adolescent mothers who continued their education had fewer children in 1984, and those who attended the Poe School had an especially low number of additional births. It is, of course, entirely possible that the school program attracted students who were more educationally ambitious and competent, which may explain why its graduates were more successful. We will address this issue in the multivariate analysis later in this chapter.

The Sinai Hospital provided a special program for teenage mothers emphasizing health care, family-planning services, and counseling. The pregnant teens were randomly assigned to this program or the regular prenatal care program, so that selection factors are not relevant, as they are for Poe School participants. But in contrast to the apparent success of the school program for pregnant teens, participation in the comprehensive health-care program sponsored by Sinai Hospital was not strongly associated with economic well-being. Because of its policy relevance, however, we retain this variable in the subsequent multivariate analysis.

Both the Poe School and the Sinai Hospital program increased the likelihood that teenage mothers used birth control at the 1-year follow-up. Contraceptive use is crucial for preventing rapid, additional births, as subsequent analyses will show. Preventing or delaying such births, in turn, is crucial because the burdens of additional children can virtually guarantee economic dependency. Consistent with this line of reasoning, birth control use has a clearly significant bivariate association with 1984 economic status.

Finally, the postpartum interview included several measures of the strength of family bonds in the period following childbirth. A good deal of information about the quality of the relations between the adolescents and their parents was collected to assess how family functioning affected adjustment to early child-bearing. Adolescent mothers who were living in two-parent families were no more successful in later life than those living with a single parent. Most families got along well at the time of pregnancy and even better once the child was born; however, young mothers who reported more harmonious relations did no better economically than mothers who had more tumultuous relations. Adolescents who relied more on their parents for advice were slightly less likely to experience later economic success. This could be due, in part, to the fact that women who married early were less reliant on their parents, and these women, as shown before, tended to fare better economically. Additionally, long-term reliance on the parents may indicate a lack of self-reliance or autonomy, psychological di-mensions not measured in this study.

The postpartum interview yielded four variables to be included in the multi-variate analyses: remaining in school continuously, use of birth control at the 1-year follow-up, attendance at the Edgar Allan Poe School, and participation in the Sinai Hospital comprehensive health-care program.

Characteristics and experience of the adolescent mother 5 years after her first birth

The young mothers' circumstances five years after delivery, based on the 1972 interview and the 1984 life history calendar, constitute the final set of potential explanatory factors. We expected to find, and generally did find, that what hap-pened to them in the early years of the study strongly shaped their adaptation in later life.

First, additional fertility in the first segment of the study forecast economic problems in later life. Both the length of the interval between births and the occurrence of a subsequent birth were significantly related to economic disad-vantage in later life. This result is consistent with the evidence collected in the first phase, showing that repeat pregnancy led teenagers to discontinue their ed-ucation, drop out of the labor force, and rely on public assistance. However, the long-term picture is a little more complicated. Educational achievement at the 5-year follow-up is clearly associated with economic success in adulthood, but we did not find that early work experience or receipt of public assistance stongly predicted economic status at the 17-year follow-up. If this result holds up in the multivariate analysis, it would indicate that early entrance to the labor force is not always a wise choice and that welfare may enable some teens to complete their schooling and thereby improve their long-term economic prospects.

One other unexpected result emerged from our examination of the relationship of early career patterns to the young mothers' success in later life. In the initial phase of the study, women who remained with their parents were more likely to remain in school and avoid repeat pregnancies. As one mother said, "I never would have been able to make it [finish school] had I not lived with my mother." This favorable effect of coresidence did not hold up over the long-term. In fact, the more years women lived with their parents in the first phase of the study, the more likely they were to have economic problems at the 17-year follow-up. Possibly, coresidence offers temporary relief but, if extended, may foster long-term dependency. Alternatively, women who lived apart from their parents may have entered stable marital unions, whereas those who were divorced or separated returned home to live with parents. In effect, those who remain or return to the parental household may be the less successful members of our study.

Consistent with these preliminary analyses, the following life situations from the 5-year follow-up are included in subsequent analyses: additional childbearing in the first 5 years (had two or more additional children), current marital status (married or not married), welfare experience in the first 5 years of the study (2 or more of the first 5 years on public assistance versus less than 2 years on welfare), and completion of high school by the 5-year follow-up.

Paths of influence

The influence of these various competing sets of factors, entered sequentially into the multivariate analyses, is the primary analytic task of this chapter. Both direct and indirect paths of influence will be traced in order to understand how a particular event or life choice actually operates on eventual outcome.

Background status

The background variables entered into the analyses were the educational level of the respondent's parents,[2] the respondent's number of siblings (those with 4 or more siblings v. those with three or fewer siblings), and whether or not the respondent was on welfare as a child. Figure 3.2 shows the direct and indirect effects of the background variables on economic status in 1984. Indirect effects are represented by dashed lines, direct effects by solid lines. Indirect effects are

---

2 When more than one parent was in the household, we measured parental education by the educational level of the parent with the most education.

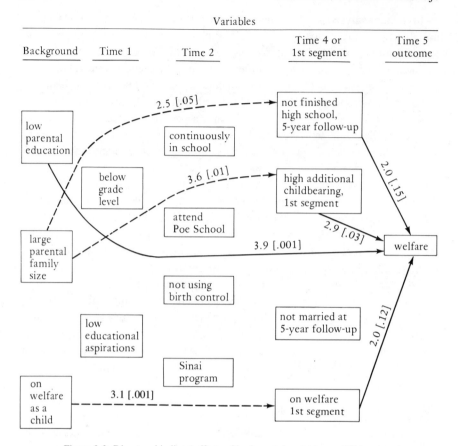

Figure 3.2. Direct and indirect effects of background variables on 1984 economic status

those that operate by causing a change in a more proximate variable; that is, their influence is mediated through an indirect path. Large parental family size, for instance, affects 1984 economic status by increasing the likelihood that the respondent will have high fertility in the interval following the first birth. This high fertility, in turn, reduces the likelihood that the young mother could or would escape economic dependency.

The unidirectional arrows suggest causal relationships. The magnitude of the coefficient indicates the strength of this relationship; using the same examples as earlier, the value of 3.6 indicates that coming from a large sibship increases by 3.6 times the likelihood of having high additional childbearing (i.e., two additional children) in the first 5 years. High fertility at the 5-year follow-up, in turn, increases by 2.9 times the likelihood of being on welfare at the 17-year follow-up. Likewise, large parental family size more than doubles the likelihood of not finishing high school, which similarly doubles (i.e., increases by a factor of 2.0) the likelihood of being on welfare at the time of the most recent survey. Coming from a large family seems to result in a significant long-term disadvantage, operating through the lower education and higher fertility of the next generation.

The number in brackets is the *p*-value, which indicates how often a coefficient of this magnitude would result from sampling variability alone. We use this statistic as a rough guide to which effects are large enough to be interpreted substantively. Finally, any given path shown in Figure 3.2 is estimated net of unique others in Figures 3.3– 3.6. Thus, the complete model could be pictured as an overlay of these five figures. (See Appendix E for details of model selection and estimation.)

Background variables may be reflecting differential familial experience and/or differential access to resources. Therefore, we would expect such factors to influence later economic success, perhaps through schooling or aspirations. Somewhat surprisingly, then, parent's education is not strongly associated with the pregnant adolescent's grade level or educational aspirations. Although the estimated paths were in the expected direction (i.e., low parental education is associated with being below grade level and having low educational aspirations), they were quite weak (see Appendix E). We had expected that those with more educated parents would have more stimulating experiences, more encouragement, or higher cognitive abilities, all of which would improve school performance and increase educational aspirations. For instance, models of status attainment for the general population show that parental education is a major factor affecting the educational attainment of children and, indirectly, their eventual socioeconomic status (see Blau and Duncan, 1967; Featherman and Hauser, 1978; Jencks et al., 1979).

Why do we find no significant path here? Some may suggest that we have a truncated sample with respect to parents' education. Although variability in parental education in the general U.S. population is greater than in this sample of black adolescent mothers, substantial variability in educational level within this sample does exist, weakening this explanation. Another possibility is that parents' education has its effects earlier – in reducing the likelihood of early sexual intercourse, by increasing the likelihood of using contraception, or of having an abortion, for instance. In other words, parental education is an important variable affecting the likelihood of getting into our sample, but given a teen birth it has little additional influence. This explanation is almost certainly part of the story.

Finally, weak effects of parental education on the adolescent mother's educational performance or aspirations could also result from discrimination. As we saw earlier, during the 1960s blacks were less able than whites to transmit their status to their children, via education, and were less able to translate educational and occupational attainment into income. These results, indicating discrimination, make the weak effects of parental background on children's educational aspirations and performance less surprising.

In contrast to the weak effects operating through educational performance and aspirations, we discovered that parental education has a powerful direct effect on economic success. After controlling for the other variables, those with less-educated parents are almost four times more likely to be on welfare in 1984. Because attitudes and values of the pregnant and postpartum teenagers were generally unrelated to subsequent economic status and because indirect effects of parental education were weak at best, we interpret this direct effect as indicating that less-educated parents had fewer economic or social resources to dispense. These resources may include economic wealth as well as informal networks that provide crucial opportunities, such as stable jobs, child care, and emotional support. Also, drive, cognitive ability, and social skills of the parent may be reflected in parental education. In short, parents with less than a tenth-grade education may have pushed their children less, been less able to support them in their return to school, less effective in getting them jobs, and less discouraging about resorting to welfare. Finally, educational level may be tapping a general cognitive component that is moderately heritable. Were this the appropriate explanation, however, stronger effects on educational attainment would have been expected. In sum, the observed pattern of associations leads us to conclude that educational level of the parent taps a greater determination and ability to help the child make the best of a bad situation.

This interpretation is consistent with statements of respondents themselves. Consider the statements of a teenage mother who was stably married and in the middle class at the 17-year follow-up.

I depended on my mother a lot. . . . And she helped quite a bit. I guess that was probably the only thing that kept me going. His family wasn't able to help us . . . [my mother] had a little bit of money saved, and said anytime we needed anything, just give a call and she would [help].

[My] whole family, they encouraged me . . . they saw if I was more or less standing still or I was losing interest in improving myself. . . . I guess I'd have to say my family was the greatest pushing force in my life.

Two other background conditions influence economic status indirectly. Large parental family size increases the likelihood of high fertility in the first 5 years of the study by a factor of 3.6. It is often stated that women coming from large families view additional children more favorably. In fact, evidence collected in the first phase shows that some of these subsequent births were wanted (Furstenberg, 1976), suggesting this premise might be true. However, attitudes about family size did not predict subsequent outcome. Therefore, we suspect that the size of family of origin influenced economic success because it affected the parent's capacity to provide assistance to the young mother. Lacking assistance, the young mothers' prospects of overcoming the burden of early childbearing were realistically perceived as dim, providing a lower incentive to avoid additional births.

To turn to the second leg of this pathway, high fertility during the first part of the study increased the likelihood of economic dependence at the last interview in 1984. Additional childbearing further constrained the young mother's educational and occupational choices.

Parental family size also was associated with not finishing high school by the 5-year follow-up, which itself is associated with later economic dependency. One could argue that the fewer available economic and social resources for larger sibships reduced the likelihood that these teen mothers could stay in school. Reduced schooling, in turn, lowered their ability to support themselves in the long run.

Finally, being on welfare as a child increased sharply (by a factor of 3.1) the likelihood of receiving welfare over a substantial portion of the first 5 years. Being on welfare in the first 5 years, in turn, roughly doubled the likelihood of being on welfare in 1984, although this effect is one of the weaker ones shown. Nevertheless, this causal pathway of welfare experience to current dependence is consistent with the popular intergenerational welfare-dependency notion. That is, children raised in a household receiving public assistance continue this economic dependency as adults in providing for their own families. It is believed that those with welfare experience as children are more willing to accept public assistance as adults because they were raised in an environment where accepting such payments was condoned. In contrast, this path also could reflect the reduced resources of these families, who resort to welfare because they cannot rely on assistance from their families. Given that attitudes about welfare did not differentiate those who accept welfare from those who do not, the second explanation must be regarded as the more likely one.

Somewhat surprisingly, no direct path from welfare as a child to welfare at the 17-year follow-up was found. Evidently, if a woman escapes this welfare trajectory early, she is no more likely than other women to go on welfare. This may reflect, in part, the marginal economic existence of this sample, but it also challenges the notion that once on the rolls, even as a child, one develops a predilection to dependency that is not shaken by periods of economic independence.

Measures of competence and motivation

Figures 3.3 and 3.4 show the direct and indirect effects, respectively, of educational competence and motivation during the teen years on eventual economic success. As noted before, these measures, probably because of sample selectiv-

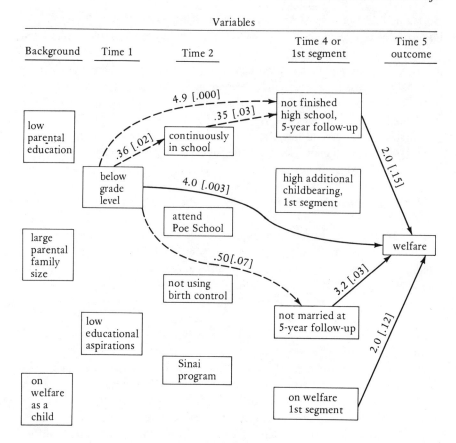

Figure 3.3. Effects of educational competence at time 1 on 1984 economic status

ity, are largely independent of parental background information. Consequently, the adolescents' levels of motivation and competence provide strong independent forces producing variability in the life course. This finding is not unique to our study. Remember the study of men's occupational outcomes discussed earlier (Jencks et al., 1979:121): Academic ability has strong effects even controlling for background variables and a host of attitudinal variables that might be influenced by background variables.

Earlier research from the initial phase of this study indicated that young mothers who remained in school during the pregnancy and afterward were doing better at the 5-year follow-up than those who did not. Now we are able to examine this career contingency more closely. Specifically, being below grade level (see Fig. 3.3) and having low educational aspirations (Fig. 3.4) both decrease sharply the likelihood of remaining in school throughout the pregnancy. Better and more motivated students probably find school more enjoyable and are likely to receive

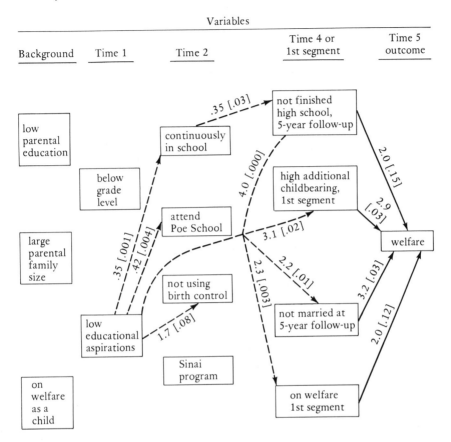

Figure 3.4. Effects of educational aspirations at time 1 on 1984 economic status

more support from teachers and others to remain in school. Of course, not all of the better and more motivated students remain in school. But remaining in school during and following pregnancy are important paths for explaining 1984 economic status, since educational continuity significantly affects the likelihood of finishing high school. Specifically, remaining in school more than doubles the likelihood of high school graduation at the 5-year follow-up.

Being at grade level, our measure of academic competence, has a direct effect on the likelihood of economic dependence in 1984 (see Fig. 3.3). Those below grade level at the beginning of the study are four times more likely to be experiencing economic hardship in 1984. Evidently, those girls who are bright enough and well-behaved enough to do well in school are better able to become economic successes later in life. Jencks et al.'s classic study (1972) of status attainment reached similar conclusions in the population at large.

Note that those below grade level when first pregnant are more likely to be married at time 4. Perhaps these students chose marriage because they foresaw few other opportunities, given their school failure and/or dislike of school. Since marriage is strongly predictive of economic status, a marriage, if it remains intact, can greatly improve a family's economic prospects. As noted earlier, women have two routes to economic security, one via the job market and one via the marriage market.

Although we do not show the associations among the contemporaneously measured variables in these figures, being at grade level is clearly associated with higher initial educational aspirations. In fact, those at grade level are almost three times more likely to plan on attaining post–high school training. In all likelihood, those who do better in school receive more encouragement from parents, teachers, and peers. They also find school more pleasurable and rewarding, which undoubtedly fosters higher educational aspirations. Even net of grade level, educational aspirations have an effect on the subsequent life course. High aspirations increase the likelihood of attending the Poe School. And the decision to attend this school apparently had important consequences, which will be discussed further in the following section.

Those teenagers with low educational aspirations are (1) more than twice as likely to be on welfare for much of the study's first segment, (2) over twice as likely to be unmarried, (3) more than three times as likely to have high additional childbearing in the first segment, and (4) four times as likely not to have finished high school by the 5-year follow-up (see Fig. 3.4). In the open-ended questions, respondents themselves often credited their educational drive for their successes. In fact, in response to the question "What would you say enabled you to do as well as you have?" almost all women mentioned their drive, determination, motivation, or initiative. One woman doing well at the 17-year follow-up says: "I wanted that degree . . . and I wanted to come out [of school] with all of my friends. I was just determined. I wanted to come out in that Sixty-Seven class. . . . I'm just ambitious." Another woman explained it this way: "Just that I wanted to be better than the people I was around. I had a lot of gumption, will power, I went forward. I wanted to do things, and I guess I had dreams that I just wanted to fulfill."

By themselves such claims would be highly suspect, possibly due to the women reinterpreting their determinants of success, especially given the dominant American ideology that reifies individual motivation and initiative. For instance, most individuals, particularly men, attribute their own success to drive and determination (Crandall, 1969). But a quantitative analysis of the longitudinal data supports these women's claims. Based on their reports as teenagers, the more educationally motivated did have greater chances of economic self-sufficiency in later life.

In sum, educational competence and motivation provide largely independent

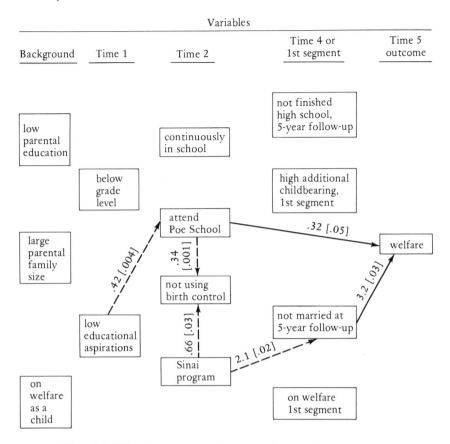

Figure 3.5. Effects of program variables measured at time 2 on 1984 economic status

sources of variation that account for substantial subsequent variability in the life course. Respondents rightly credit their success to these characteristics.

The effects of formal programs

Figures 3.5 and 3.6 illustrate the effects of early postpartum experience upon economic status. As mentioned earlier, women who chose to attend the Poe School tended to have higher educational aspirations, so we cannot attribute all differences between Poe School students and others to the effects of the school. Apparently, however, the Poe School staff also reinforced and extended their students' educational aspirations. Poe School students were over two times more likely to be using birth control a year after the study child was born. Birth control use was critical in curtailing a rapid repeat pregnancy. Women reporting no

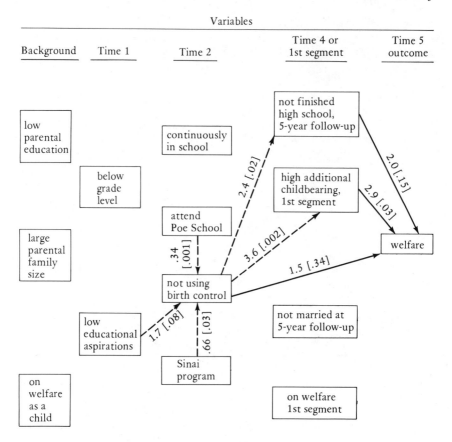

Figure 3.6. Effects of birth control use at time 2 on 1984 economic status

contraceptive use a year after birth are almost four (3.6) times more likely to have additional births by the 5-year follow-up (see Fig. 3.6).

Attending the Poe School has direct as well as indirect effects. Girls who attended Poe were much less likely (.32 as likely) to be on welfare at the 17-year follow-up than girls who did not, controlling for educational goals and performance (Figs. 3.5, 3.6). Whether attendance at the Poe School was more influential than staying in regular high school is still an open question.[3] Students who attended regular school were less successful than the Poe matriculants in avoiding welfare, though they clearly did better than the women who dropped out of school in the first year after delivery. In sum, results of the multivariate analysis

3 Since close to four-fifths of the young mothers who were in school a year after delivery had attended the Poe School, caution must be taken in interpreting our results.

indicate that the special school for pregnant girls had a decidedly positive effect on preventing disadvantage in later life over and above the regular school program, and that this effect cannot be merely explained by selective recruitment into the school.

Both the possible selectivity and the positive effect of the Poe School are mentioned by several of the more successful women in the open-ended interviews. Consider this statement from a teen mother who went on to finish high school, attend nursing school, and become a registered nurse. When asked about people who might have been a positive influence in her life, she responded:

The school for unwed mothers was instrumental in motivating me. They were, they were really good to us. . . . But you couldn't just go there and relax and that's it. . . . They were always talking about getting ahead. And the type of students that were accepted at the school were self-motivated.

Selectivity is less an issue with respect to the Sinai Hospital program. The young women were assigned to this program randomly, creating a classic experimental design. Selective attrition might still have resulted in the least motivated being more likely to drop out. However, we found no evidence that the special program served more educationally able and motivated teens. Women in the special clinic were more likely to be using birth control a year after the birth of the child than women attending the regular clinic. This intervention was not a major determinant of 1984 economic status, given its narrow and short-term focus. Nonetheless, interventions of this type are worthwhile because they provide a headstart on spacing additional children and avoiding unwanted pregnancies.

Another effect of the program may have been to reduce the likelihood of early marriage. Those participating in the special clinic were over twice as likely not to be married at the 5-year follow-up. Apparently, these young mothers heeded the counseling staff's general opinion that it was wiser to defer marriage until the completion of school.

But as Figure 3.5 shows, women who were not married at the 5-year follow-up were over three times more likely to be on welfare in 1984. We also must report that marriage per se contributes little to a woman's economic chances. Women married at the first or second interviews were not more likely to avoid welfare dependency in adulthood. Only those who married early and remained married escaped economic disadvantage, and as we saw earlier, many of the early marriages quickly dissolved. These women are extremely vulnerable to economic dependency if they have dropped out of school and have had additional children. However, those who enter a stable marriage or marry after completing schooling are far less likely to end up on the welfare rolls. Many of the women who are doing well credit their husband's hard work and contribution to the family, usually as breadwinner. As one women who has achieved a comfortable middle-class life-style with her husband of 16 years said, "My husband just really took on the responsibilities, you know father and husband at a very young age. He was brought up to be very family conscious. That has a lot to do with it (our success)."

In short, early marriage, though a high-risk strategy, is successful for those women who remain married. Some respondents clearly recognized its risks. As a result, not getting married was a conscious decision for some women. As one successfully employed mother said:

I didn't want to get married, then. All I wanted to do was finish school. People would get married for money, and the next thing you know they would be divorced. And the girls didn't have an education so they really couldn't get a job. They didn't have that extra umph to pursue their careers or anything.

Postpartum birth control use plays a role in determining adult economic self-sufficiency (Fig. 3.6). Attendance at both the Poe School and the Sinai Hospital Special Clinic increases contraceptive use. As noted earlier, birth control use has a strong indirect effect on economic status by reducing rapid family building. In addition, not using birth control has a modest direct effect on economic dependency in adulthood. Specifically, women who were not using birth control 1 year postpartum were roughly one and a half times as likely to be on welfare net of their fertility in the initial phase of the study. Early patterns of birth control use probably forecast more regular use in later life.

It is also possible that birth control practice measures the determination of the young mother not only to avoid pregnancy but also to exercise more control over her future. That birth control use taps a general dimension of motivation is signaled by its association with educational aspirations and achievement. The more educationally ambitious women are more likely to use contraception at the 1-year follow-up and were also more likely to finish high school by the 5-year follow-up. Use of birth control is probably associated with general competence and feelings of mastery as well. These traits, which are unmeasured in our study, no doubt contribute to a woman's prospects of becoming economically self-sufficient in later life. As one of our women put it, "You can make one mistake, but there is no excuse for another." Other mothers discussed the financial implications of having more children. A mother with only one child said: "My son started growing up and, of course, the living for him was expensive. I knew I couldn't afford it [to have more children]. As that was number one and as he got older, I just decided, I don't want any more children."

Table 3.1 summarizes the relationships shown in Figures 3.2–3.6. Using the same general model we also examined the determinants of economic security (i.e., having a family income greater than $25,000) at the 17-year follow-up. Results mirrored those already presented. In addition, analysis of additional variables indicates that we have captured the important sources of life-course varia-

Table 3.1. *Determinants of welfare*

Independent variable	Ratio	*p*-value	Odds of being on welfare
Direct effects			
Low parental education	3.9	[.001]	Almost 4 times more likely if parents' education 9th grade or less
Below grade level	4.0	[.003]	Almost 4 times more likely if below grade level
Attend Poe School	0.32	[.16]	Less than half as likely if attended Poe School
Not using birth control	1.5	[.34]	1.5 times more likely if not using birth control
High additional childbearing, 1st segment	2.9	[.03]	Almost 3 times more likely if had 2 or more additional children
Not married at 5-year follow-up	3.2	[.03]	Over 3 times more likely if not married at 5-year follow-up
On welfare in 1st segment	2.0	[.12]	2 times higher if on welfare during 1st segment
Not high school graduate, time 4	2.0	[.15]	Twice as likely if not finished high school by 5-year follow-up

Indirect effects

If large parental family, then:
 • almost 4 times more likely to have 2 or more children in the 1st segment
 • over twice as likely not to have finished high school by the 5-year follow-up

If on welfare as child, then:
 • over 3 times more likely to be on welfare for 2 or more years during the 1st segment

If below grade level, then:
 • roughly half as likely to attend Poe School
 • about 5 times more likely *not* to have graduated by the 5-year follow-up
 • roughly 60% less likely to have stayed in school during pregnancy and after

If low educational aspirations, then:
 • less than half as likely to attend Poe School
 • roughly 70% more likely to *not* be using contraception at the 1-year follow-up
 • roughly 60% less likely to have stayed in school during pregnancy and after
 • 4 times as likely to have *not* finished high school by the 5-year follow-up
 • 3 times more likely to have 2 or more children in the 1st segment
 • over 2 times as likely to be unmarried at the 5-year follow-up
 • over 2 times more likely to be on welfare during the 1st segment

If attend Poe School, then:
 • almost 60% less likely to report *not* using contraception at the 1-year follow-up

If participated in the Sinai program, then:
 • roughly 35% less likely to report *not* using contraception at the 1-year follow-up
 • over twice as likely to be unmarried at the 5-year follow-up

If not using birth control, then:
 • roughly 3.6 times more likely to have 2 or more additional children in the 1st segment
 • over twice as likely to have not finished high school by the 5-year follow-up

69

bility in our model. Beyond those variables in the model, few others we measured have important effects. There are some minor exceptions that are of interest. One of these is coresidence with parents. Contrasting women who lived with parents for over 2 of the first 5 years with those who did not, we discovered that living with one's parents slightly lowered (i.e., by a factor of .55, $p = .15$) the likelihood of achieving economic security. Evidently, living with parents for a short time is not a disadvantage; in fact, those living with parents were more likely to stay in school while pregnant and in the period following the birth. Those who became dependent on parents, as defined by living with them for longer than 2 of the first 5 years, were less likely to achieve economic security later in life.[4]

Variability in fertility at the 17-year follow-up

High fertility handicaps both the mother and her children – the mother because it limits her nonfamilial opportunities and may make it difficult to care effectively for her children, and the children because family resources have to be spread over a larger sibship. For these reasons most observers, and the women themselves, view small families as a successful adaptation to early childbearing.

As in the case of income and status attainment, prior research has focused on the determinants of family size. Early decision models assumed that couples decided on a family size and then set out to realize that intention. Subsequent research efforts have been sensitive to the fluidity of the life course. Specifically because children come one at a time, fertility is best analyzed in a step-by-step, sequential fashion (Namboodiri, 1972). All of the Baltimore sample entered parenthood in their early teens. Early childbearing is associated with a rapid subsequent pace of childbearing and high completed fertility (see Bumpass, Rindfuss, and Janosik, 1978). But as with economic status, much variability in family size exists by the 17-year follow-up.

A crucial variable for explaining differences in family size is the length of the period between the first and second birth. Several possible mechanisms may account for this result. First, rapid and early childbearing leaves many years in which an accidental pregnancy can occur. Those who have the number of children they wish by age 20, for instance, have over two decades to guard against further pregnancies. A woman who reaches her desired family size at older ages has fewer years at risk, i.e., before menopause. This argument, while still relevant, was more important prior to the legalization of abortion and prior to the

---

4 When we repeat this analysis contrasting those who are doing the best versus all others, the results are very similar. In fact, the indirect paths must be the same. The direct effects are given in Appendix E. The factors discussed here not only alter the likelihood of economic dependence but discriminate between those who are most and least successful.

widespread use of contraceptive sterilization. Second, not all women are equally fecund. Those who have births early and close together are disproportionately fecund. This higher fecundity increases the likelihood of additional pregnancies, all else being equal. To describe the influence of fecundity, Rodriquez et al. (1984) make the analogy between the fertility process and an engine with its own inbuilt momentum. Fecundity provides the momentum in the fertility process. The more fecund move to successive parities more quickly.

Another important consideration is the restrictive impact of subsequent births on the other roles the woman might hold. An additional child makes returning to school or getting a job more difficult. Given these lost possibilities, the opportunity cost of additional childbearing is reduced. In contrast, those who delay fertility have experiences and opportunities that may compete with additional childbearing, which in turn may delay childbearing even more. Delay can even extend to the decision to have no more children. Childlessness comes about by a series of decisions to postpone childbearing (see Rindfuss, Morgan, and Swicegood, in press). Postponement allows for competing interests to develop, possibly leading to further delay. We see the pace of later childbearing as crucial decisions having immense consequences for the subsequent life course. While there may be economies of scale in childrearing (i.e., a second child may not bring as many costs as did the first), the additional costs can push the burdens beyond a threshold level where dealing with motherhood and another demanding role (work or school) becomes very difficult.

Another focus of recent fertility research is on "intermediate variables" or "proximate determinants" (see Bongaarts and Potter, 1983; Davis and Blake, 1956). Fertility is a biological process, and social or economic variables can only influence it via proximate determinants such as the frequency of intercourse, the likelihood of conception, or the likelihood of successful gestation. In the mid-1960s to early 1970s in the United States, marriage, contraceptive use, and abortion were the most important proximate determinants. Marriage reflects more regular and frequent intercourse and a normative approved context for reproduction; contraception affects the likelihood of conception or successful gestation; abortion terminates a pregnancy. Our crude measure of contraceptive use in the period following the first birth should be a crucial variable through which various socioeconomic variables have their impact. Likewise, the pace of fertility should be more rapid for those who marry before or soon after the child is born (Bumpass et al., 1978; Grady and Landale, 1985).

Before constructing a multivariate fertility model, we examined separately a series of parity-progression ratios,[5] which provided some insights into the deter-

---

5 Parity-progression ratios are the proportion of women with x births who go on to have $x+1$ births. Such measures are consistent with the sequential nature of the childbearing process.

minants of additional births at each parity. Since our primary concern is explaining why certain women have large families, we ultimately elected to focus our attention on the contrast between the approximately one-third of the sample (39%) who had three or more children by 1984 versus those who had fewer. Contrasting families of large and small size highlights the substantively important findings from the more complex analysis of parity-progression ratios. Moreover, this analytic strategy makes intuitive sense. Women with three or more children are much more likely to be dissatisfied with their family size, more likely to have an unplanned child, and generally experience more economic and psychological difficulties at the 17-year follow-up.

Basically, we reexamine the same set of variables included in the model predicting economic success. An exception is the substitution of having a child within 2 years of the first in place of high additional childbearing in the first 5 years. But our analytic strategy remains the same in that we allow background variables and past experience to influence subsequent experience. Since we know from the previous chapter that about two-thirds of the additional childbearing occurred in the first 5 years after delivery, and that relatively few women who did not have additional children early in the study ended up with large families at the 17-year follow-up, we can be fairly confident that many of the determinants of short-term fertility are important elements in explaining who had large families in 1984. Therefore, many of the determinants of large family size are already familiar to us, as they appeared in the indirect paths determining economic status.

Rapid family building was strongly linked to the size of the family of origin. Also, women who were more educationally ambitious and academically competent were more likely to stay in school, and women who remained in school were less at risk of having additional children in the first segment of the study. Finally, participation in the special school for pregnant teens and the comprehensive hospital clinic both were indirectly linked to the pace of family building. Women who attended these programs were more likely to practice contraception early in the study, and contraceptive compliance early in the study had a strong effect on lowering the odds of repeat pregnancies and additional childbearing. Figures 3.2 through 3.6 show these indirect paths.

Figure 3.7 shows only direct effects on the likelihood of having three or more children at the 17-year follow-up. Table 3.2 briefly describes all of the direct effects in this fertility model. As one would expect given the preceding arguments, the effect of a rapid, early childbearing pace is very strong – if a woman bears her second child within two years of the first she is almost nine times more likely to have at least three children by the 17-year follow-up. This huge direct effect dwarfs all others shown in Figure 3.7.

The measures of personal competence and educational motivation from the

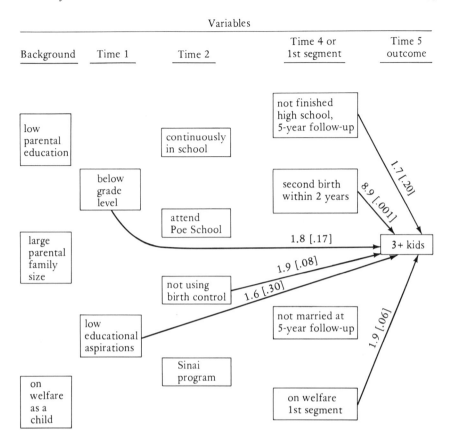

Figure 3.7. Direct effects on the likelihood of having three or more children in 1984

pregnancy interview have modest direct effects. Those below grade level at the time of pregnancy were close to twice as likely to have three or more children at the 17-year follow-up. Having high educational aspirations has a weaker direct effect. (But, as shown in Figure 3.4, it has a set of important indirect effects.) The direct effect of not using birth control also may measure personal competence and motivation: Those who are more competent and motivated may take active steps to control subsequent fertility.

Women who finished high school by 1972 were less likely to have three or more children. Disproportionately, these women had high competence and educational aspirations. This schooling probably provided them with the skills to obtain a job and the motivation to limit births. In contrast, those on welfare during the first 5 years, and disproportionately those who had received welfare as a child, were roughly twice as likely to have three or more children. Critics

Table 3.2. *Determinants of family size*

Independent variable	Ratio	*p*-value	Odds of having 3 or more children
Direct effects			
2nd child born within 2 years of 1st	8.9	[.00]	Almost 9 times more likely to have 3 or more if 2nd birth interval is less than 24 months
On welfare 1st segment	1.9	[.06]	Twice as likely if on welfare during the 1st segment
Not using birth control	1.9	[.08]	Almost twice as likely if not using birth control at the 1-year follow-up
Below grade level	1.8	[.17]	Almost twice as likely if below grade level at time of pregnancy
Low educational aspirations	1.6	[.30]	60% more likely if intends little additional schooling
Indirect effects			
Very similar or identical to those described in Table 3.1.			

of welfare have long argued that it promotes high fertility, although a strong argument can be made that high fertility also leaves many women with no option except welfare, given child-care constraints.

Clearly, our results show that early childbearing is less likely to establish a pattern of rapid family building when women remain in school, receive family-planning assistance, and avoid another birth in the next few years. Service programs, such as the Poe School and the Sinai Hospital special clinic, may aid teen mothers who have the ambition and ability to manage the demands of early parenthood. In contrast, adolescents who enter parenthood with severe educational deficits are at the greatest risk of dropping further behind, becoming reliant on welfare, and bearing additional children quickly. This pessimistic scenario, it must be said, applies only to a small number of women in our study. Nevertheless, this small minority consumes a large share of the social-welfare services. These data suggest that it is not difficult to recognize these high-risk teenage parents. In our final chapter on policy implications, we shall have more to say about this special population.

Summary

In this chapter we have attempted to explain the diversity of economic and fertility outcomes among a sample of teenage mothers. The number of pathways to success may come as a surprise, especially to those who subscribe to a highly deterministic view of the unfolding life course. Early childbearers clearly are disadvantaged when compared with peers who bear children later, but huge variability exists. Teen childbearing lowers the likelihood of economic success and increases the likelihood of having a large family. But the life course is sufficiently flexible to allow for a number of paths to recovery. And our mothers know it. Referring to the reasons she is successfully employed, Iris, one of the women introduced in Chapter 2, said, "I'm not a quitter, but once I did the best I can, then I have to look at the facts and either keep going or just take another route."

The four dimensions with which we began this chapter illustrate some of these different paths. First, differential resources, including informal networks and parental support and role models, are very important. We interpreted most of the variability associated with background factors as indicating such differential resources. Those with more economically secure and more educated parents have more direct aid and other family resources available.

Second, differences in competence and motivation are very important factors. Those who are doing well in school and who have high educational aspirations are much more likely to be successful.

Third, interventions in the form of the Poe School for pregnant girls and the Sinai Hospital Program had moderate effects. These interventions seem to be appropriately aimed at a crucial life-course contingency, the decision to postpone additional births and to complete high school.

Fourth, career contingencies are important as well. The major one mentioned here is the pace of subsequent fertility. Additional births at young ages severely constrain the mother's ability to attend school and accrue job experience, crucial human capital for economic self-sufficiency in later life. Also, women who have additional children seem to be less competent and motivated and to have fewer family resources on which to draw. Additional childbearing is thus selective of those on the more ominous life paths. Statistical controls on these prior variables suggest, however, that subsequent fertility still has an independent influence and does not just mediate the influence of earlier measured variables.

A second important career contingency involves marital decisions. Marriage is a high-risk strategy, but stable unions bring huge dividends in terms of higher economic status, as the case of Helena, discussed in Chapter 2, illustrates.

Decisions to remain in school and to accept welfare have weaker direct effects than do fertility and marriage. We suspect this is because of the nature of the mother and wife roles: Both are very time-consuming with long-term commitments. But student and welfare recipient are statuses more easily changed from year to year. Nevertheless, the weak effects of schooling may be a bit misleading. Schooling is associated with lower fertility. Likewise, the use of welfare allows some women to remain in school. Thus, both may help explain why some women postpone additional births and others do not.

Decisions regarding fertility, education, marriage, and welfare need not be independent but rather can be joint decisions. One may decide to marry, have additional children, and forgo additional schooling, for instance. Fertility may be the crucial element in such a strategy; in fact, our analysis suggests that it is. However, fertility is embedded in a larger strategy including decisions about marriage, work, and education.

Regardless of the strategies used to overcome the problems associated with early childbearing, most women were disadvantaged by teenage parenthood. The acceptance of doing less well than peers who postponed childbearing is embodied in the following statement made by a single mother of two. When asked if her early pregnancy set her back in life, she said:

No, I think had I been more serious about doing what I wanted to do that I could have probably been where I wanted to be now, financially and careerwise. I'm pleased with what I'm doing, with the salary and all. But I also feel that, had I given it my 100 percent instead of 75 percent that I would have reached the goal that I set out to reach. I have done a lot, but am not the best I could be.

4 The children's experience

The costs of teenage parenthood may not be limited to the mothers themselves but may extend to their children as well. Children might be affected in a variety of ways. Adolescent mothers may not have much time to spend with their children due to the competing demands of school or work; they may need to piece together complex childrearing arrangements; they may not be the most competent of parents because of social immaturity or inadequate knowledge about childrearing; and of course, they are likely to be economically disadvantaged. Such conditions are believed to place the children of teenage parents at risk of developmental delays, social and emotional problems, school dropout, and early childbearing, thus helping to perpetuate a cycle of disadvantage. On the basis of rather little evidence, the supposition that disadvantage is transmitted intergenerationally in families with teenage parents seems plausible if not compelling. Recall the quotation cited in Chapter 1, which referred to the rising rates of teenage childbearing as revealing "a terrible story . . . children having children, passing on depression and helplessness from generation to generation."

Popular accounts of teenage childbearing rarely fail to mention its devastating consequences for children, who are presumably likely to encounter parental neglect, child abuse, abandonment, family instability, and other forms of parental miscare. Additionally, the impoverished lives of teenage mothers and the conditions in which their children grow up are believed to contribute to high rates of school failure and juvenile delinquency. The children of teen mothers are seen as ill-fated. A recent *Time* cover story (December 9, 1985) on teenage pregnancy illustrates the pervasiveness of beliefs about the untoward effects of the cycle of having babies.

The offspring of teen mothers often experience educational and emotional problems. Many are victims of child abuse at the hands of parents too immature to understand why their baby is crying or how their doll-like plaything has suddenly developed a will of its own. Finally, these children of children are prone to dropping out and becoming teenage parents themselves.

In point of fact, very little is known about the life course of the children of adolescent parents, or whether and how early parenthood effects their life chances.

A recent survey of both the published and unpublished literature on this topic assembled what is known about the general level of well-being of the children of teenage mothers (Brooks-Gunn and Furstenberg, 1986). Across studies, young children of teenage mothers experienced small decrements in cognitive and social functioning compared to same-age children of older childbearers. So few studies were conducted with older children and adolescents that we do not know if these small, early negative outcomes become more conspicuous, merely persist, or just disappear over time. Whether early parenthood per se results in deleterious outcomes through some unspecified pathway, or whether the children of early childbearers are only worse off because their parents are more disadvantaged has not been determined. In short, the links between the mother's life experience and that of her child have not been elucidated (see also Hayes, 1987).

The 17-year follow-up of Baltimore study participants was designed to identify these links. This chapter describes the life course of the children against the backdrop of the mothers' changing life situations. Information is drawn from the early interviews as well as from mothers' retrospective accounts in 1984 to reconstruct the life course of the children from birth to adolescence. This chapter also provides a look at the possible negative outcomes of teenage motherhood at three different age points: the infancy, preschool, and high school years. At the child's first birthday, mothers supplied information on neonatal health. At the 5-year follow-up, cognitive and social tests were administered to the children, and the mothers answered questions pertaining to their children's well-being. At the 17-year follow-up, an extensive amount of information was collected on the adolescents' social and psychological adjustment by interviews with the adolescents themselves, their parents (or parent surrogates), and their teachers. Most of our attention will be focused on adolescent outcomes, partly because information about the children when they were infants and preschoolers is described in an earlier report (Furstenberg, 1976). Also, the adolescent's experience is most relevant to the central issue of this study, namely, whether and how social disadvantage is perpetuated or alleviated. Therefore, particular attention is given to several key arenas of behavior: school performance, antisocial acts, and, of course, sexual and fertility experience.

Before turning to the findings, it is useful to provide a capsule description of the sample. Of the 404 pregnant women initially studied, 15 had children who died and 15 had children who were adopted early, leaving 374 potential adolescent respondents. Two hundred and ninety-six, nearly 79% of the available children, or 74% of the original sample, actually participated in the 17-year follow-up. In 10 cases the mother but not the child was interviewed; in 6 cases the child refused to be interviewed; in 3 cases the child was retarded; and in 1 case the child was away for the duration of the study. Typically, the biological mother was interviewed as well (264 cases). In 2 cases no parent was interviewed; in the remainder (30) a surrogate parent was interviewed. One twin pair was included; both were interviewed and the mother was asked questions about each twin's behavior separately. On the average, the teenagers were seen 16.4 years after their birth. Thirty-two percent were 15 years of age, 42% were 16 years old, and 26% were 17. Approximately equal numbers of boys and girls were interviewed (154 and 142, respectively), and the vast majority of the teenagers were black (91%).

The life course of the child

The complexities of the mothers' lives, as they juggle child care, schooling, jobs, and relationships with men and family members, are mirrored in their children's life course. Although children were not asked to fill out a calendar in the 1984 follow-up, their life histories can be reconstructed from their mothers' calendars, supplemented by information from their interviews. Child life events of interest include separations from the mother, child care arrangements, living with an adult male figure (father or otherwise), and paternal support.

To illustrate both the complexities of the children's lives as well as the influence of the maternal life course upon them, we focus on the three families introduced in Chapter 2 (see Fig. 4.1). Doris's son Randall was 17 at the time of the last interview. He has lived with a varying combination of adults over his life. During his preschool years, he resided first with his mother and grandmother, then with his grandmother alone, before moving back with his mother after she married Randall's stepfather. Following the breakup of this marriage, Doris's boyfriend, Harris, moved in. By Randall's adolescence, however, Harris had left the household and Randall lived with his mother, two siblings, and Matthew, his infant nephew, the son of his younger sister.

Doris was the primary caregiver throughout Randall's early years, during which time she dropped out of school and worked only sporadically. Randall's grandmother assisted in child care but had primary responsibility for him only briefly when Doris first moved in with Randall's stepfather. Randall still sees his grandmother several times a month. Although Randall knows how to contact his biological father, he sees him very infrequently (not even once a year). Randall considers Harris to be like a father to him. He and Harris still keep in touch regularly, getting together every other month, even though Harris left the household 2 years ago. Randall does not see his stepfather.

Other Baltimore children had experiences more similar to those of Iris's son, Tyrone, who lived with his mother and grandmother as an infant, while Iris completed her schooling. For the next 9 years, Tyrone lived with his mother and father. After the dissolution of his parents' marriage, Tyrone lived with his mother

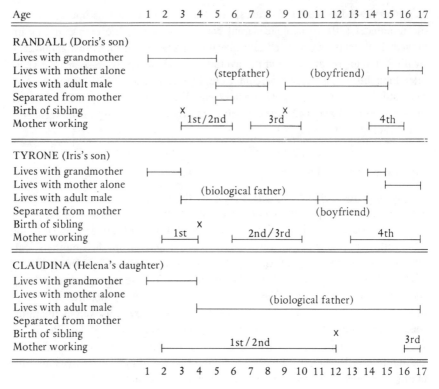

Figure 4.1. The life course of three children of adolescent mothers

and, for a brief time, with Lester, Iris's boyfriend. As an adolescent, he and his mother moved in with his grandmother for a brief time when Iris and Lester broke up. Now, he lives with his mother and his sister. Iris and her mother shared child-care responsibilities during Tyrone's early years when Iris was in school and when she began work. Tyrone still feels very close to his grandmother and often goes to stay with her for weekends. Tyrone also sees his father, although not as regularly as his grandmother. When he was younger, Tyrone spent several summer vacations with his father. He does not see his mother's boyfriend, Lester, whom he does not consider to be like a father.

In contrast is Helena's daughter Claudina, who, at 17, has lived most of her life with her mother and father. However, she lived in her grandparents' home until Helena completed her schooling and had a job. When Claudina was 4, her mother and father married, and Claudina has lived with them ever since. Helena's mother was the primary caregiver during Claudina's infancy, in order to help her daughter complete school. She also participated in child-care throughout Claudina's preschool years, as her daughter was working. Claudina still feels close to her grandmother and sees her weekly.

As we have stressed, these three families, like all of the others from the Baltimore study, are unique; no family had identical experiences (indeed, when attempting to find two families with daughters who had the same schooling, fertility, job, welfare, and marital history as Doris and Iris, who had sons, no perfect matches could be found in the entire sample). However, they not only illustrate the diversity of life experiences and residential patterns but may be considered prototypes of the ways families respond to early parenthood. This chapter documents the vagaries of the child's life history, including patterns of residence with the father and other men, separations from the mother, child-care configurations during early childhood, and paternal support. Then, we will examine child health and behavior over the 17-year period – infant status, schooling and academics, misbehavior and maladjustment, and sexuality. Chapter 5 then will explore how the maternal life course influences adolescent behavior.

Separations from the mother

The mother's life-history calendar reveals the instances in which she was separated from the child for at least two months.[1] The proportion of children separated from their mother at each age is presented in the last column of Table 4.1. In the first year, virtually all of the children lived with their mothers. This percentage is probably an underestimate since there was a lower likelihood of obtaining interviews with the mothers who gave up their children for adoption and foster care, or who eventually relinquished the care of the child to a relative or friend in the community. Nevertheless, we know that 97% of the children were living in the same households as their parents at the 1-year follow-up when 95% of the original sample were reinterviewed.

The proportion of children experiencing a separation from their mother increased gradually over the life course, from a low of 3% in the child's first year to 11% when the child was 15. It is surprising that twice as many children were separated from their mothers in the adolescent as in the preschool years. Teens sometimes live with their father or grandmother either because the mother and adolescent are having difficulties getting along or because the mother has moved

1 The analyses concerning separations from mother and living arrangements (Tables 4.1 and 4.2) were based on information in the mother's rather than the child's interview. The number of cases is 273. Surrogate respondents were eliminated, which would indicate that these findings probably underestimate the incidence of separations because maternal separations may have been more frequent in surrogate parent situations. Separations due to summer vacations or marriage (in the case of a few of the girls in their adolescent years) were not counted. In these analyses, the child was coded as being in only one state (separated from mother, living with biological mother and father, etc.) per year. This was done hierarchically, not by longest duration. This may render the per year and cumulative figures approximate, and underestimate the number of transitions within a year.

Table 4.1. *Children living with mother only, mother and biological father, mother and stepfather, mother and boyfriend, mother and any man, and separated from mother at each year of life* (*in %*)

Age	Mother only	Mother and biological father	Mother and stepfather	Mother and boyfriend	Mother and any man	Separated from mother
< 1	60.1	33.3	1.5	2.2	37.0	2.9
1	52.4	34.4	5.5	4.8	44.7	2.9
2	45.1	34.1	11.4	7.0	52.4	2.5
3	42.1	28.9	13.9	11.4	54.2	3.7
4	40.3	26.7	17.2	11.7	55.7	4.0
5	39.2	24.5	19.8	13.2	57.5	3.3
6	35.9	23.8	19.8	15.0	58.6	5.5
7	34.8	22.0	22.0	16.5	60.4	4.8
8	34.8	21.2	23.1	16.8	61.2	4.0
9	34.8	20.1	21.6	18.7	60.4	4.8
10	34.8	18.7	22.0	19.0	59.7	5.5
11	37.4	17.6	21.6	17.6	56.8	5.9
12	37.7	16.8	22.7	16.5	56.0	6.2
13	35.5	17.2	23.8	16.8	57.9	6.6
14	37.4	15.0	23.1	16.1	54.2	8.4
15	40.7	13.9	22.0	12.1	48.0	11.4

Note: Ages 16 and 17 are omitted because not all children had reached these ages by 1984. This table also excludes the 30 cases in which a surrogate parent was interviewed, and 2 cases in which no parent was interviewed. Therefore, our estimates of maternal separation are somewhat low.

out of the city to the suburbs and the child wishes to stay in Baltimore. Paradoxically, the mothers perceive the move out of the city as moving up; their teenagers often do not. One mother explained the lure of the city to her daughter.

Out here you don't see kids hanging out. During the summer you might periodically hear them out there but normally not after eleven o'clock. In the city, the kids stay out to four in the morning. And see, she likes that rough crowd, fighting. She just likes that rough crowd, and it's not out here. She's with who she wants to be, she can walk around.

The percentage of children who ever lived apart from their mothers during the course of the study was, however, quite a bit higher than percentages by any given year. Thirty-two percent of the children lived apart from their mothers for at least two months during the course of the study, with the percentage rising to 39% if children with surrogate adult respondents are included. Among those who were separated from their mothers, the majority (62%) experienced only one separation, 22% experienced two separations, and 16% experienced three or more.

Parents were asked to report why children were not living with them during these separations. The most common reasons were disciplinary problems, difficulties in arranging child care, and maternal absence. A few mother–child dyads had been separated because of the mother's marital problems, custodial problems, her schooling, employment, or the institutionalization of the child (jail, juvenile facility, home for the mentally retarded). Children typically moved back with their mother when the specific problem causing the separation was resolved (e.g., mother returned home, custody case was settled, mother's life circumstances improved). For example, Doris's son Randall lived with his grandmother for a brief time when Doris first moved in with her husband, but they were reunited after she and her husband found a suitable apartment.

Primary caregiver

Merely because mother and child resided together continuously is not necessarily an indication that the mother played an active or the primary role in childrearing. At the time of delivery, most mothers planned to assume primary child-care responsibility. In many cases, this ideal proved incompatible with maternal desires for additional schooling or entrance into the work force. At the 3-year follow-up, nearly two-fifths of the mothers reported that they were not the primary child-care figure during the day: Their parents, other adults in the home, or siblings provided much of the daily supervision of the child during the child's earliest years.

This pattern of shared responsibility often continued throughout the later years of childhood. Remember that almost a quarter of the Baltimore mothers were still living in their parents' households in 1972. Thus, these women had a "second" parent (in this case the child's grandmother) and in some cases a "third" parent (the child's grandfather, uncle, or aunt) available for child-care support. Even mothers not living in their parents' households often turned to them for help. Many women continued to rely on their families for child-care assistance at the 5-year follow-up. Close to half reported that someone else, usually a parent or relative, provided the primary child care or, at least, spent as much time as they did caring for the child. In nearly 30% of the families, another person was spending 50 or more hours a week supervising the child, and a tenth of the mothers were living with their children only part of the time or not at all. These collaborative child care arrangements were, for the most part, described in quite positive terms by the young mothers. Except for the few extreme situations when the Baltimore women were spending very little time with their children, most women, especially those receiving assistance from relatives in the home, expressed satisfaction with the quality of care provided by parents and relatives.[2]

2 In general, the Baltimore women turned to their relatives for child care rather than to community services. The qualitative maternal interview suggests that the mothers were reluctant to use day-care centers (even when they were available), not only for financial reasons but out of preference for care by kin. Even today, day care for children under 3 or 4 years of age is not considered the

Only 10% of the women reported discontent or unhappiness with the current arrangements.

Because the mother was often not the primary child-care agent during the preschool years, it should not be assumed that she was disengaged from her maternal role. Most parents said that they took an active part in child care, even when they were aided by relatives or friends. For example, 75% of the mothers reported that they typically had dinner with their children almost every day and only-a tenth ate with them once a week or less. (Presumably, most mothers not having dinner with their children were living outside the home.) About the same proportion of parents reported that they watched television with their children on a regular basis, close to half of the parents read to their children at least several times a week, and two-fifths of the mothers answered that they took their children to a playground on the average of once a week or more.

These reported patterns of activity suggest that despite the fact that many young mothers needed their parents' help in child care to realize their own ambitions, a majority were actively involved in caring for their children. These situations might accurately be termed shared caregiving arrangements. Over half, especially women who were neither working nor in school, stated that they spent about the right amount of time with their children. A sizable minority (36%), however, indicated that they had too little time with their children, suggesting that shared caregiving exacted an emotional toll on the mothers. Only 7% complained that they spent too much time in child care. Shared caregiving, then, seemed to be a compromise between the mother's desires to further herself (and ultimately to make a better life for her children) and to provide high-quality care for her offspring.

In summary, at the 5-year follow-up, about half of the mothers were primary caregivers, a large minority shared responsibility with family members, and a small proportion (about a tenth) assumed only a marginal role in the routine supervision of the child. Most mothers who did not take care of their preschoolers full-time were subject to competing career demands. Many of the young mothers had been urged by their parents to remain in school or enter the labor force. These women frequently expressed ambivalence about relinquishing so many responsibilities to their parents but saw few alternatives. From the children's perspective, shared child care often resulted in having a "second mother." Indeed, at the 17-year follow-up, one-third of the adolescents had someone other than their biological (or surrogate) mother whom they considered to be "like a mother." In the majority of the cases, the "second mother" was the maternal grandmother.

ideal arrangement by a sizable number of women (Clarke-Stewart, 1977; Congressional Budget Office, 1978; Zigler and Gordon, 1982).

Fathers and children

Chapter 2 noted the impermanence that generally characterized the Baltimore women's relationships with men. The high rate of marital dissolution, the relatively large number of women who never married, and the frequency of short-term cohabitation relationships translate into a fleeting and unpredictable presence of adult men for the Baltimore offspring. With the exception of 9% who have never lived with an adult man (father, stepfather, or mother's boyfriend), all of the children had spent some time in such a household, but in many respects, the three families we have been following typify the patterns of cohabitation with fathers and father figures.

Claudina lived with her biological father and mother from her fourth year onward, representing the so-called traditional but quite infrequent pattern in this sample. Doris's son has never lived with his biological father, although the fathers of his two siblings were present for a time; one, Harris, was like a father to Randall. Tyrone, Iris's son, lived with his father from his second year until he was 11. Since then, he has resided with his mother and sister and, for a brief time, with his mother's boyfriend.

We have calculated the proportions of children living with both biological parents, a mother and stepfather, a mother and her boyfriend, the mother only, or someone else at each age (the column headed "separated from mother" in Table 4.1). Examining the presence of the biological father first, almost all of the mothers intended to marry the father of the child as soon as it was financially feasible or after completing their schooling. In fact, some realized their plans. About a fifth actually married their child's father before the child was born, and another fifth married them sometime after the delivery. Marriages between the biological parents slowed down to a trickle by 2 years after delivery, when most of the mothers were in their late teens. However, by this time, some of the women had begun to marry other men, thus introducing a surrogate father into the family. In addition, divorce made it less likely that children were living with their biological father as time passed. One-third were doing so in their first year, 29% in their fourth year, and 20% at their tenth year. Fewer than one in seven lived with their fathers by age 15. As might be expected, marriages with men other than the fathers were not nearly so concentrated in the first years of the child's life, so that 2% of the children had acquired a stepfather in the first year of life, 14% by age 3, and 22% by year 10. The number of children living with stepfathers remained at about a fifth from age 5 onward. The number of children who resided with their mother and her boyfriend also increased over time. Only 2% of the children in year 1 were in such a residential situation, as opposed to 11% at age 3 and 19% at year 10.

The implications of the fragility of marriage within the Baltimore sample and within teenage marriages in general are all too plain. While most Baltimore children have some experience living in a two-parent household, only a tiny minority (9.5%) resided continuously with both biological parents over the first 16 years of life. Seventy percent of the marriages to the study child's father had ended by 1984 (the majority by divorce, and most of the rest by separation). Even those with stepfathers were not likely to live with them for the majority of their lives. In order to look at the cumulative time spent with any father, we calculated the proportion of time each child spent living with different father figures. As an illustration, let's take the example of a 16-year-old girl interviewed in 1984 who had lived with her biological father from birth until she was 4, then lived for 8 years in a single-parent family until her mother remarried. For the past 4 years, she has been living with a stepfather. She is recorded as living with her biological father for 25% of her life, her stepfather for 25% of her life, and without a father for 50% of her life. Some of the children in our study had more complex careers, as their mothers moved in and out of relationships; others spent their entire lives in a single-parent household. When we calculate the cumulative experience living with an adult man and mother, 23% of the children spent a quarter or less of their lives in a household with an adult male, and only 29% spent more than three-quarters of their lives in such a household.

Finally, Table 4.2 reveals how much time children spent living with any particular father figure, illustrating the tremendous diversity in living arrangements over the course of the study. Only a handful of children spent the majority of their first 16 years in the same situation. Thirteen percent spent the entire first 16 years with a male in the home. The majority of these children resided with their biological father. Stepfathers were present continuously for under 1% of the children, and only 11% had a stepfather present for at least 10 years.

Dramatic as these data are, we cannot tell if the experiences of the children of adolescent childbearers are substantially different from those of their peers whose mothers were older when they were born. To address this question, we examined the family histories of black 15- to 16-year-olds in the National Survey of Children in terms of the age of their mothers at first birth. At the 1981 survey date, 21% of the early childbearers' children and 33% of the later childbearers' children were living with their biological fathers. The comparable figure for the Baltimore teens was 14%, indicating a somewhat higher rate of family dissolution in our sample than in the national sample. Fifteen percent of the NSC children with adolescent mothers and 6% with older mothers were living with a stepfather. In contrast, 22% of the teens in the Baltimore study resided with a stepfather at age 15. As expected then, black adolescents of older childbearers are less likely to be living with stepfathers and more likely to be living with their biological fathers than children of teenage childbearers. The Baltimore children seemed to have suffered somewhat higher rates of family dissolution than their counterparts in the NSC for reasons already discussed in Chapter 2.

Table 4.2. *Number of years spent in each of six living situations*
(*% of children*)

Number of years	Mother only	Mother and biological father	Mother and stepfather	Mother and boyfriend	Mother and any man	Separated from mother
0	15.0	52.4	55.3	54.6	9.2	75.5
1	5.9	7.0	3.7	6.2	2.2	7.7
2	7.0	5.5	5.1	7.7	4.4	7.0
3	7.0	6.2	2.9	7.3	4.4	1.8
4	7.3	2.9	5.5	5.1	3.3	2.9
5	7.7	1.8	5.9	4.0	6.2	1.5
6	7.0	2.2	2.6	4.4	7.0	0.7
7	4.0	1.1	2.2	2.6	4.8	0.7
8	6.2	1.5	3.3	1.5	7.0	0.0
9	2.2	1.5	2.2	1.5	4.4	0.4
10	5.9	0.7	1.1	1.1	5.5	0.4
11	4.8	0.4	2.9	1.5	6.2	0.0
12	4.4	1.5	3.3	0.4	6.2	0.4
13	4.4	0.7	0.7	0.7	4.4	0.7
14	3.3	2.6	2.2	1.1	5.9	0.0
15	1.1	2.6	0.7	0.4	6.2	0.0
16	7.0	9.5	0.4	0.0	12.8	0.4

Note: Age 17 is omitted because not all children had reached this age by 1984. This table also excludes the 30 cases in which a surrogate parent was interviewed, and 2 cases in which no parent was interviewed. Therefore, our estimates of maternal separation are somewhat low.

Paternal contact for the Baltimore youth was not confined to those fathers who resided with their children. An analysis of the data collected at the 5-year follow-up revealed that a substantial minority of the biological fathers not living with their children had regular contact with and provided financial assistance to their preschoolers. Surprisingly, unmarried fathers were almost as likely as previously married fathers to lend assistance to their young children. To what extent do these patterns of paternal involvement survive throughout the child's life? Some early commentators on the black family have observed that biological fathers living outside the home actually play a far more active role in childrearing than is popularly believed (Rainwater, 1970; Schultz, 1969).

Our results provide some support for this view though the level of support from fathers outside the home can only be described as modest. At the 5-year follow-up, a fifth of the children were living with their biological father and another fifth maintained at least weekly contact with him. The corresponding numbers at the 17-year follow-up were quite similiar: 17% were living with their biological father and another 16% saw him weekly. Thus, approximately one-third of the children had sustained contact with their biological father, and this percentage did not change appreciably during the 12-year period. Financial help in the rearing of the child is another way the father can provide support, over and above actual contact. In 1972, one-third of the biological fathers living outside the home contributed to the support of the child; only 13% provided support in 1984.

Thus far, we have only considered the amount of contact with the biological father living outside the home. What about "quasi-fathers" such as former stepfathers, boyfriends, or male relatives: Do they pick up the slack when no father (biological or stepfather) is in the home? One-third of the children with no father in the household reported that they considered a male other than a biological father or stepfather, either a former or current partner of their mother, a relative, or a friend, to be "like a father" to them. Nineteen percent were currently living with this type of person, 55% had lived with him, and 26% had never lived with him. Over half (52%) of those residing apart from the quasi-father saw him on a weekly basis, and only 10% saw him less than yearly. Thus, 15% of the teenagers not living with a father or quasi-father in the home received substantial attention from a surrogate father outside the home.

It should come as no surprise to discover that children living with their biological fathers or surrogate fathers are far better off economically than those living in female-headed families. This fact, well known from national income data, also was documented in the comparisons of income levels by marital status reported in Chapter 2. The question of whether economic status varies by the relationship of the father figure to the child has been given less attention. Specifically, are children living with biological fathers more economically secure than children living with father surrogates? Those living with biological fathers were much more likely to have family incomes over $25,000 (66%) than those living with stepfathers (41%). The disparity in cases of cohabitation – mothers living with boyfriends – was even greater. Only 12% of these households had incomes exceeding $25,000 a year. In contrast, few (9%) of those families with the biological father present were classified as the working poor (under $15,000), while over a quarter of those families with a stepfather or a boyfriend as the father figure were classified as such.

In sum, then, very few children had an enduring, or at least continuous, relationship with their father. Only a tenth had lived with their father from birth to age 15. At the same time, very few (7%) of the youth also lived in a female-headed household over these 16 years. The vast majority had a father figure, or some combination of father figures, in the home at least for part of their childhood. However, they also experienced changes in the availability of a father figure owing to high rates of marital dissolution, remarriage, and live-in arrangements. This had a profound effect on their economic well-being.

The mother's pregnancy and neonatal outcome

The pregnancy experiences of the Baltimore women may be critical events in establishing the later life course of the children because adverse antenatal conditions increase the likelihood of neonatal morbidity and mortality. Low birth weight, a common condition among teenage childbearers, poses significant health risks for the child (McCormick, 1985; Stewart, 1981). Premature infants with low birth weights are 2 to 10 times more likely to have academic or behavioral problems in childhood (Escalona, 1982; Harvey et al., 1982). It follows, then, that the offspring of the Baltimore mothers may be at increased risk of neonatal morbidity and developmental difficulties.

All but a few of the pregnancies were unplanned, and most were said by the mothers to be unwanted at the time of conception. Except for a small number of women who married prior to or just after becoming pregnant, consisting mostly of older whites in the sample, virtually everyone else recalled that they had been fairly or extremely distressed to learn that they were pregnant. As one young mother put it: "I guess I was devastated . . . I couldn't believe it at first and I was very disappointed because I . . . trusted my partner, and he said he would take care of me [contraception]." Others reported being "disappointed." Yet, with few exceptions, the women elected to keep the child and most quickly reconciled to early parenthood. (Of course, it should be recalled that abortion was not yet legal in Maryland when the study began, and adoption was and remains an unpopular option among teenagers.)

By the time of the first interview, which usually occurred in the second trimester, the majority reported that they were looking forward to motherhood and were fairly happy about the prospect of having a child. The rapid reappraisal of the pregnancy was in part due to the strong support provided by the pregnant teenagers' families, who, though initially quite upset, quickly rallied to their daughters' aid.

The young mothers provided information about the course of their pregnancy and delivery at the first-year follow-up.[3] Returning to our three families, we find that Doris first came to the clinic for prenatal care late in the second trimester. Doris's mother had not encouraged her to come sooner as "Doris has always been a healthy girl." Randall weighed a little under five pounds at birth and stayed in the neonatal intensive care unit for a week. He was plagued with upper respiratory problems throughout his first year. Iris entered the clinic at the beginning of the second trimester, immediately after her mother discovered that her daughter was pregnant. Iris had hidden her pregnancy because of embarrass-

---

3 Although medical record review would have been preferable, it was not done for budgetary reasons.

ment. Tyrone was a healthy seven pounder whose first year of life was fairly uneventful, from a health standpoint. Helena entered the clinic even earlier, in the first trimester, in part because she was spotting. Her health was monitored carefully, and Claudina was a healthy neonate.

Our prospective mothers and their newborns highlight both the diversity in the entire sample and the fairly normal perinatal course of the young women. Forty-one percent of the mothers received care in the first trimester, 52% in the second, and 7% in their third trimester. All of our young mothers received some antenatal care, in part because of our recruitment procedure (i.e., mothers had to be registered in one of two antenatal clinics to join the study). Consequently, the perinatal course was quite uneventful: Few prospective mothers (6%) were hospitalized prenatally, three-quarters reported no medical complications, and only 5% had cesarean section deliveries. Neonatal morbidity was as expected for black, poor mothers: Of live births, 11% were low birth weight (2,500 grams or less) and 11% had poor Apgar scores (six points or less). Thus, these teenagers and their babies looked similar to other national samples of black mothers, in keeping with the finding that more adverse health outcomes are not found for teenage mothers when quantity and quality of obstetric care are adequate (Baldwin and Cain, 1981; McCormick, 1985).

As mentioned earlier, the Baltimore study originally began as an evaluation of a comprehensive perinatal program devoted to the special needs of teenagers. Pregnant teens were randomly assigned to the age-targeted special program or to the regular clinic for prenatal and postnatal obstetric services. The patients in the regular obstetric clinic had roughly the same high quality of care as the teenage clinic patients. The special and regular clinic patients were similar with respect to perinatal status, including the month prenatal care began, type of delivery, prenatal hospitalizations, perinatal complications, and number of prenatal visits. Given these similarities, it is not surprising that the health status of the infants was comparable, in terms of Apgar scores, days spent in the nursery, the incidence of low birth weight, congenital malformations, and medical complications during the nursery stay. Finally, health status at 1 year, as grossly measured by incidence of hospitalization and number of well-baby and emergency-room visits, showed the babies to be doing equally well in the two groups. Thus, the effects of the special obstetric-care program were in the realm of fertility control, as discussed in Chapter 3, rather than in infant health.

Schooling experiences of the children

Of all the potentially deleterious outcomes of early parenthood, children's academic performance may be the most significant. Chapter 3 showed that school failure is a potent predictor of economic dependency in later life. The children of the Baltimore mothers who are doing poorly in school may be especially likely to perpetuate a cycle of disadvantage. This section describes the school experience of the teenagers in some detail, beginning with an overview of their academic readiness in the early childhood years. We then examine their subsequent school performance as measured in 1984.

Our three families illustrate the complex school careers of the children. Randall seems to have been at risk for academic problems from the beginning. As a 4-year-old, he was a very active child who had difficulty concentrating on any task for more than a few minutes. His distractibility was evident in the testing session, where he did poorly on the Preschool Inventory. By the 1984 interview, he had been held back two times and was currently in a remedial class. He has been in trouble repeatedly (skipping class, fighting in school). Exhibiting very little interest in academics or school-related activities, he looks forward to leaving school as soon as possible.

Tyrone, on the other hand, was characterized as an active and charming 4-year-old who performed well on the Preschool Inventory. He showed little patience or persistence on the tasks he found difficult. He progressed through elementary and junior high school on time but was held back in ninth grade, primarily because he skipped 55 days of school. Spending more and more time with older youth who have left school, he seems fairly uninterested in academics, even though he is a C+ student.

Claudina, compared to the boys, has had a fairly uneventful school course. A quiet and seemingly determined child, she performed at the 65th percentile on the Preschool Inventory. During the testing, she was persistent when given difficult tasks and seemed to enjoy the session. When last seen in 1984, she had not repeated any grades, was a B− student, and planned to go to college.

Like Randall, some of the children had difficulties from the beginning. As in Tyrone's case, school failure seemed to stem from later experiences and behavioral proclivities, rather than any early observable deficit in ability. And Claudina is illustrative of the child who does well throughout. Let us turn to the entire sample to see how representative these youth are.

School readiness

When the children were 3½ to 5½ years of age, over 200 were tested using the Caldwell Preschool Inventory, a measure designed to tap Head Start participants' cognitive competence (Cooperative Tests and Services, 1970). Half of the Baltimore study preschoolers were functioning above the 50th percentile and half below, similar to other samples of black urban preschoolers. Higher scores were found for children who saw their father regularly, lived in two-parent families, had single mothers who worked, and attended preschool. Enhanced functioning, as others have found, was related to more favorable economic and social conditions and to having participated in a preschool program.

Lest we paint too rosy a picture, the Baltimore preschoolers, while scoring like other Head Start participants (Schnur and Brooks-Gunn, 1986), had lower scores than did black middle-class children attending preschool in Philadelphia. Additionally, the preschoolers of the Baltimore mothers' classmates who delayed childbearing were doing better on the Preschool Inventory than were the children of the Baltimore adolescent childbearers. The study children, then, are at a disadvantage compared to preschoolers who did not have teenage mothers and who were not in such marginal economic situations. Other studies support these findings, showing that young children of early childbearers lag behind children of older childbearers, although the disparities are small (Brooks-Gunn and Furstenberg, 1986).

High school achievement

The story is quite different when we turn to the children's high school experience. We discovered what may only be described as massive school failure. While 92% of the adolescents were enrolled in school during 1984, half of the sample had repeated at least one grade during their school career.[4] Males were more likely to have been held back than females (58% v. 38%). In 1984, 12% of the students were enrolled in advanced classes, 17% in remedial classes, and the remainder in regular classes. Twice as many boys as girls were in remedial classes, and 15% of girls as opposed to 10% of boys were taking advanced classes.

Consistent with these high rates of school failure, only a quarter of the adolescents were rated by their mothers as being above average with respect to school achievement within their grade level and only about one-third of the teens themselves said they were one of the best or above the middle in school. According to the students' self-reports of grades in four subjects (English, mathematics, social studies, and science), 3% were A students, 35% B students, 54% C students, and 7% D students.[5] Surprisingly, most students express little dis-

---

4 Of the 22 who were not in school, 3 students had been expelled, 3 had left school because of pregnancy or the birth of a child, 8 had left ''because school was boring,'' 5 were in institutions, and 3 listed other reasons.

5 The self-reports of school progress and class standing were quite consistent. In order to assess the accuracy of the self-reports about school progress and class standing, we sent a brief questionnaire to each student's school principal, who asked the teacher who knew the student best to report on his or her current academic situation. One hundred and fifty-nine teachers returned the questionnaire. When the teachers were asked to compare the student to others in the class, 9% were considered one of the best, 20% were rated above average, 35% average, 20% below average, and 16% failing. About two-thirds of the teachers, the mothers, and the students thought that the adolescent could be doing better in school.

satisfaction with school: Four-fifths say that they are satisfied with school and two-thirds are interested in their schoolwork.

Another perspective on the level of school functioning is provided by the record of adjustment in school reported by adolescents and their parents. According to the adolescents' themselves, 36% had to bring their parents to school in the past year because of a behavioral problem, 34% have skipped school, 28% have fought at school, and 4% have damaged school property. According to the parents, 52% had received a note from the school about a behavior problem and 44% of the children had been suspended or expelled in the past 5 years. Males were more likely to exhibit school problems, as evidenced by a higher number of suspensions (51% v. 37%) and disciplinary problems (61% v. 43%).

Are the problems seen in this sample of teenagers typical of those seen in other samples who do not have teenage mothers? Comparisons of 15- to 16-year-old black adolescents in the National Survey of Children provide a partial answer to this question.[6] As can be seen in Table 4.3, school-related problems seen in the adolescents of early childbearers in the Baltimore Study are similar in magnitude to those seen in the National Survey of Children teens of early childbearers, and the adolescents of early childbearers are exhibiting greater difficulty in school than are the adolescents of later childbearers. Twice as many National Survey of Children adolescents whose mothers were early childbearers had repeated a grade as the children of later childbearers (46% v. 17%).[7]

Other school problems were more prevalent among the offspring of teenage mothers as well. School maladjustment was one and one-half to three times more likely to occur among the offspring of early than later childbearers (see Table 4.3). For example, almost one-half of the Baltimore adolescents had been suspended from school in the past 5 years as opposed to 17% of the adolescents of older childbearers in the National Survey of Children. In sum, adolescents whose mothers were teenage childbearers are at very high risk for school problems. They have a high chance of being held back a grade sometime during their school career, of having been expelled or suspended in the last 5 years, and of having their parents contacted about a problem. It is little wonder that so few have an above-average standing in class, or rate themselves as particularly competent in school.

The costs of grade failure, in terms of achievement and expectations, are substantial. Repeaters are more likely to have dropped out of school (12% v.

---

6 Since almost no age differences were found for schooling and academics and misbehavior and maladjustment when the 15-, 16-, and 17-year-olds were compared, the findings presented in Tables 4.3, 4.4, 4.5, and 4.6 for the Baltimore 15- and 16-year-olds are similar to those for the entire sample.

7 The national incidence of grade repetition for black high school sophomores is 17%, as reported in High School and Beyond, a longitudinal national study of over 20,000 high school students who were sophomores in 1980 (Rock et al., 1985).

Table 4.3. *School-related behavior of black adolescents, ages 15–16, by mother's age at first birth: the Baltimore study, 1984, and the National Survey of Children, 1981 (in %)*

	Baltimore childbearers	NSC: early childbearers 14–17	NSC: late childbearers 20 & over
	(202)	(33)	(52)
I. *School achievement*			
Child repeated a grade, ever	53	46	17
Standing in class (% above average)	26	31	31
II. *School problems*			
Child reports			
Parents brought to school because of behavior in the past year	41	42	17
Skipped school in the past year	29	27	14
Fought at school in the past year	28	39	15
Damaged school property in the past year	3	15	2
Parent reports			
Parents received note from school about behavior problem in the past 5 years	56	55	15
Child suspended/expelled from school in the past 5 years	49	36	19

Notes:

1. Base *N*'s are in parentheses.
2. All numbers are percentage of total. Don't Know and No Answer responses were eliminated from sample score.
3. NSC percentages were weighted to correct for oversampling.
4. The 17-year-olds from the Baltimore study are not included in this table to make the data comparable to the NSC data. The percentages for the total Baltimore sample are mostly very close to those presented here, in part because few age differences were found and because few 17-year-olds were seen.

5%), more likely to be in remedial classes (25% v. 10%), and less likely to be in a college preparation class (10% v. 45%). Grade failure also is associated with maladjustment in school; adolescents who have repeated a grade are more likely to have school discipline problems (68% v. 37%), to have been suspended from school (64% v. 25%), to have been in trouble at school (37% v. 10%), and to have received counseling in the past 5 years (34% v. 13%).

Grade failure also is associated with early sexual experience. Girls who had repeated a grade were twice as likely to have been pregnant than those who had not repeated a grade (32% v. 18%). Having intercourse, birth control use, or having had a child were unrelated to a grade failure among girls. By contrast, boys who had repeated a grade were less likely to use birth control than those who had not repeated a grade (25% v. 2%), but their reported incidence of intercourse or impregnating a girl was not higher.

As we saw earlier, grade failure is more pronounced in the boys than in the girls. Grade repetition spells future economic problems for females, as our earlier analyses of adolescent mothers in later life demonstrate. Is the same true of males? Given that unemployment rates for black youth hover around 40%, grade repetition may be even more ominous for them. Indeed, boys who have experienced grade failure seem to have psychologically distanced themselves from school, and perhaps even from mainstream activities, given the bleak odds of their obtaining employment. This seems to be more true of males than females, possibly because the former are more likely to face difficulties obtaining jobs and do not have other legitimate avenues of opportunity open to them, such as motherhood, child care, or homemaking. A record of school failure may predispose boys to disengage actively from the school environment, via aggressive actions leading to fighting, skipping school, suspensions, and so on. Girls who are failing in school seem less likely to use such direct means of exhibiting their discontent with school; instead, they are likely to become pregnant. Thus, school failure may lead to different outcomes as a function of gender – school dropout and/or alienation for boys, for whom achievement is not a viable avenue to employment, and pregnancy for girls, for whom early parenthood becomes an "excuse" for leaving a situation in which they are not achieving.

Educational aspiration

Chapter 3 revealed that educational expectations forecast adolescent mothers' success in later life. Is this same pattern evident among their offspring? Thirty percent of the adolescents were in the college-preparation track;[8] twice as many girls as boys were in academic high school programs (41% v. 20%). Two-thirds of the adolescents report that they plan to go beyond high school, and again, more girls than boys expect to go to college (72% v. 66%). These expectations may be quite unrealistic in view of their high incidence of school failure and behavior problems. Grade repeaters were less likely to expect to attend college than those at grade level (58% v. 78%). Nevertheless, a significant proportion of those who are having academic difficulty have post–high school expectations. Their performance to date makes such lofty ambitions highly suspect. Judging

8 The Baltimore sample is quite similar to a large national sample. In the High School and Beyond black subsample, 28% of the sophomores and 31% of the seniors were in the college preparation track.

from their mothers' experiences, we might expect to see a large gap between expectations and achievement. Most of the Baltimore mothers who expected to graduate from high school did so (86% expected to and 67% did), but few who expected to complete college actually achieved their ambitions (15% who expected to complete college and 5% who actually did). We suspect the adolescents may repeat the same pattern.

Maladjustment and misbehavior

Teenage motherhood is believed to lead to juvenile delinquency, substance abuse, and poor emotional adjustment, although little evidence exists to substantiate or refute these assertions. The Baltimore study contained extensive information on the incidence of misbehavior among the offspring of adolescent childbearers. When the children were about 4 years old, they were tested for their trust in others, their self-esteem, and their ability to delay gratification. And when they were teenagers, information was obtained from both the adolescents and their mothers on their level of psychological distress, receipt of psychological services, destructive behavior, substance use, and juvenile offenses.

Again the three case studies illustrate the wide range of problem behaviors manifested by the teenagers. As a preschooler, Randall had difficulty concentrating, was frustrated when asked to delay gratification, and exhibited low self-esteem, possibly as a consequence of his poor performance on the Preschool Inventory and his low cognitive ability generally. By age 16, Randall had been stopped by the police but had not committed any crime. He reports drinking alcohol regularly with his friends but does not report smoking marijuana. Tyrone, whose Preschool Inventory score was near the 50th percentile, also was unable to delay gratification. He exhibited a high activity level but did not exhibit any emotional problems. By high school, the picture had changed, as he began exhibiting destructive behavior around the time his mother became a single parent. Tyrone says that he has been stopped by the police twice, has seriously hurt another youth, and has stolen something in the past year. He drinks and smokes marijuana on a weekly basis. In contrast is Claudina, who, as a 4-year-old, seemed reserved and compliant. Claudina, like many other of our teenage girls, has not engaged in any destructive behavior, although she has lied to her parents and stayed out late. She says she has tried cigarettes and alcohol but does not currently smoke or drink.

In the entire sample, the children fared quite well as preschoolers. Their emotional behavior was generally well within normal ranges (see Furstenberg, 1976). However, by 1984 the picture is quite different. The Baltimore youth are exhibiting relatively high rates of misbehavior using a wide variety of indicators. A significant proportion appear to be headed for a life ''on the streets'' and have already spent or will spend time in a juvenile home or in prison. Of course, misbehavior may be considered normal "acting out," and experimentation with adult behaviors (drinking, smoking, sexuality) may not indicate future antisocial or criminal behavior. But the persistence and depth of much of the problem behavior suggest more serious outcomes for many of the youth in the study. A significant proportion report having been in serious trouble: 23% have run away from home, 19% have hurt someone seriously in the past year, and 11% have stolen a major item in the past year. A third have been stopped by the police, and 32% of the parents feel their child has needed emotional, mental, or behavioral help in the past year. Again, boys seem to be more troubled than girls.

Are these findings typical of adolescents in general, or is the incidence of serious problems higher among children of teenage mothers? The data from the National Survey of Children show that early childbearing is related to many indicators of maladjustment. Specifically, running away from home, stealing, and being stopped by the police occur more frequently in adolescents of early than late childbearers (Table 4.4). More of the Baltimore mothers felt their children needed emotional, mental, or behavioral help than did the National Survey of Children mothers, regardless of age of childbearing. Whether the Baltimore mothers are more likely to disclose such concerns to the interviewers given the long-term nature of the Baltimore study or whether differences result from the mode of interviewing or some other factor is not known.

Substance use, another possible indication of misbehavior, also occurred frequently in the Baltimore adolescents. Sixty percent say they have drunk alcohol, 25% have been drunk in the last year, 46% have smoked marijuana, and 5% have tried other drugs. Marijuana use, having gotten drunk in the last year, and having tried other drugs were considerably more likely to be reported by adolescents of teenage mothers than those of older childbearers in the National Survey of Children (see Table 4.5).[9]

Several summary scores were computed to measure behavior problems more generally. Three indexes, based on parental reports, tapped the level of delinquency, antisocial behavior, and psychological distress; the three using child reports measured delinquency, dissatisfaction, and psychological distress (see Appendix F for further description of the six scales). Table 4.6 shows that adolescents of the Baltimore and National Survey of Children early childbearers do not differ on five of the six measures, suggesting that the Baltimore sample is similar to black adolescents born to teenage mothers nationwide. However, the adolescents of later childbearers are faring better than the Baltimore adolescents or the National Survey of Children adolescents of early childbearers. Adoles-

---

9 More of the Baltimore black adolescents reported marijuana use than did the National Survey of Children sample. We suspect the NSC adolescents are underreporting this behavior, although urban–rural differences also may play a role in the higher incidence in the Baltimore sample.

Table 4.4. *Maladjustment of black adolescents, ages 15–16, by mother's age at first birth: the Baltimore study, 1984, and the National Survey of Children, 1981 (in %)*

	Baltimore childbearers (202)	NSC: early childbearers 14–17 (33)	NSC: late childbearers 20 & over (52)
Child reports			
Stayed out too late in the past year	74	76	67
Lied to parents about something important in the past year	56	52	39
Hurt someone seriously in the past year	16	9	15
Ran away from home, ever	23	6	0
Stole something in the past year	10	18	6
Stopped by police, ever	33	27	9
Parent reports			
Ran away from home in the past 5 years	17	3	0
Stole something in the past 5 years	16	15	8
Stopped by police, ever	26	24	10
Felt child needed emotional, mental, or behavioral help in the past year	12	3	4

Notes:
1. Base *N*'s in parentheses.
2. All numbers are percentage of total. Don't Know and No Answer responses were eliminated from sample score.
3. NSC percentages were weighted to correct for oversampling.

cents of early childbearers are much more likely to exhibit delinquency and antisocial behavior than are those of later childbearers, which is consistent with the results reported in Tables 4.4 and 4.5.[10]

The adolescent's sexual behavior

Perhaps the greatest concern of the public and policymakers alike is the specter of teenage parents perpetuating the cycle of early childbearing. One of the Bal-

10 The early versus late childbearer differences are much more pronounced when reported by the mothers than by the adolescents. Whether or not late childbearing mothers are underestimating their adolescents' delinquency or the early childbearers are overestimating it (relative to their children) is not known. The measure of well-being – psychological distress – is similar for adolescents of early and late childbearers, as reported by the adolescents themselves. In addition, the maternal and child ratings are quite discrepant. This suggests that mothers may not be good reporters of their adolescents' internal states, as opposed to their behavior. In brief, teenage motherhood is related to delinquency and misbehavior but probably not to adolescents' emotional states or feelings of well-being.

Table 4.5. *Substance use and sexuality of black adolescents, ages 15–16, by mother's age at first birth: the Baltimore study, 1984, and the National Survey of Children, 1981 (in %)*

	Baltimore childbearers (202)	NSC: early childbearers 14–17 (33)	NSC: late childbearers 20 & over (52)
Smoked cigarettes, ever	50	39	44
Drank alcohol, ever	54	42	44
Got drunk in the past year	21	18	10
Smoked marijuana, ever	44	24	25
Tried other drugs, ever	4	3	0
Engaged in sexual intercourse, ever	78	58	35
Reported pregnancy, ever	11	15	2

Notes:
1. Base *N*'s are in parentheses.
2. All numbers are percentage of total. Don't Know and No Answer responses eliminated from sample score.
3. NSC percentages were weighted to correct for oversampling.

Table 4.6. *Mean behavior problem scores of black adolescents, ages 15–16, by mother's age at first birth: the Baltimore study, 1984, and the National Survey of Children, 1981 (in %)*

	Baltimore childbearers (202)	NSC: early childbearers 14–17 (33)	NSC: late childbearers 20 & over (52)
Parent reports[a]			
Delinquency	1.6	1.3	0.5
Bad behavior	1.6	1.5	0.7
Psychological distress	2.4	1.7	1.6
Child reports			
Delinquency	1.2	1.2	0.8
Dissatisfaction	1.3	1.1	0.9
Psychological distress	2.3	2.1	2.0
Overall Problem Score[b]	4.4	4.1	2.0

Note: Base *N*'s are in parentheses.
[a] Mean of 0–5 and 0–4 scales; see Appendix F, p. 182 for description.
[b] Overall = 0 to 13 scale.

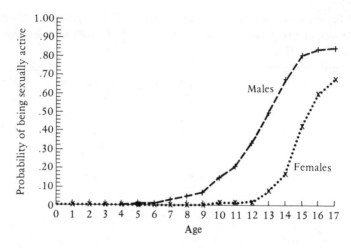

Figure 4.2. Cumulative probability of being sexually active by age (in years) and gender

timore mothers used the phrase, no doubt borrowed from the media, "the cycle of having babies." How does being raised in a family where teenage parenthood has occurred influence sexual behavior of the next generation of teenagers?

First, we examined whether having a teenage mother influences the timing of the sexual debut. The National Survey of Children provided data on the incidence of sexual intercourse among black 15- to 16-year-olds. Comparisons were drawn between the children of early and later childbearers. As seen in Table 4.5, having a teenage mother increases the likelihood of having had intercourse by age 16: Looking first at the NSC youth, 35% of those adolescents whose mothers were late childbearers have had intercourse versus 58% of those whose mothers were early childbearers. The Baltimore adolescents of the same age were even more likely to be sexually experienced. Seventy-eight percent reported sexual experience.[11] Within the Baltimore study, more boys than girls were sexually experienced (84% v. 70%). These rates are comparable to those reported by Clark, Zabin, and Hardy (1984), Ross (1979), and Zelnick and Kantner (1980) for urban black youth.

Not only are the rates of intercourse high, but typically intercourse first occurred at a fairly early age. The cumulative probability of being sexually active at each age, through age 17, illustrates this fact (see Fig. 4.2). One-third of the boys had had a sexual experience by age 12; two-thirds by age 14; 84% by age

11 Regional and rural–urban differences may account for the higher incidence of intercourse in Baltimore adolescents compared to the National Survey of Children adolescents of early child-bearers. Indeed, the percentage of adolescents having had intercourse is in line with the statistics reported in a recent survey of Baltimore city black adolescents (Zabin et al., 1984).

16. Girls reported a somewhat later age of intercourse overall. Only 2% were sexually experienced by age 12; the percentage was 17 at age 14; and by age 16, it was 60.

As has been reported by other investigators, most adolescents who report that they have had intercourse are not very sexually active. Within the Baltimore sample, only 40% of the teens had had intercourse in the past month (47% of the boys and 35% of the girls). Thus, much of the early intercourse is quite irregular, limiting the risk of conception but reducing the likelihood of contraceptive use.

Management of sexuality

Managing sexuality is one of the major tasks of the urban adolescent today, and this is certainly true for the teens in the Baltimore study. In order to understand how children and their mothers cope with almost universal teenage sexuality, teens were asked about their use of birth control and their mother's transmission of birth control information. Approximately 72% of the teens who have had intercourse reported using some form of contraception the last time they had intercourse. Boys and girls were equally likely to use birth control. Predictably, younger teens were less likely than older ones to have practiced contraception (43% v. 78%), supporting the findings of other researchers that young, sexually active girls are at the most risk for unprotected intercourse (Zelnick and Shah, 1983). Teens also were asked about the frequency of birth control use, with approximately 20% reporting rarely using birth control, 20% using it sometimes, 30% most of the time, and 30% always. Girls were more likely to report that they always use birth control than were the boys (41% v. 25%).

What role have the mothers played in their children's contraceptive practices? The Baltimore mothers are certainly not hesitant about discussing this topic with their teenagers; 93% reported they have done so, and a similarly high percentage believe that parents should discuss birth control with their teenage children. Most mothers remember that they initiated the first conversations, which is typical for most sexually oriented discussions (Brooks-Gunn and Ruble, 1982; Brooks-Gunn, 1984, in press).

However, the information transmitted may be quite vague. Typically, mothers talked euphemistically about the "need for protection." For example, one welfare mother told her son, "If you are messing around, use some sort of protection on yourself so you don't get those girls pregnant." Mothers are more likely to give more explicit information to their daughters. Many mothers mentioned that they were given little information as teenagers and have resolved that their daughters will not be at a similar disadvantage. As one mother said,

Well, my mother didn't talk to me about sex. She did talk to my sister so that helped. She would just say, well, "You know what not to do." My daughter and I talk about it with no problem. As a matter of fact, I took her to my gynecologist just last December and she had her first examination. It is totally different, totally different, the relationship my mother and I had.

Other mothers linked birth control information to their own early pregnancy. As one told her child, with reference to birth control, "I don't want to happen what happened to me. I don't want you to make no mistake. Protect yourself, then you don't have to worry about it."

In general, then, birth control is a topic of conversation in most households. The mothers seem to feel relatively comfortable or, perhaps more accurately, are not reluctant to discuss sexual issues with their teenagers. However, the information transmitted is often not particularly specific regarding birth control options, reliability of methods, and so on.

Fertility

As might be expected from the large differentials in the incidence of intercourse between teenagers born to early and later childbearers, the offspring of teenage mothers are also more likely to become pregnant. In the National Survey of Children, 15% of the adolescents whose mothers were early childbearers as opposed to 2% of the adolescents whose mothers were older childbearers reported a pregnancy (or getting a girl pregnant). In a comparable subsample of Baltimore 15- and 16-year-olds, the incidence was 11%. When the 17-year-olds are included, 16% reported a pregnancy – 26% of the girls and 7% of the boys.[12]

In order to chart the age at which these pregnancies occurred, the cumulative probability of being pregnant (or fathering a child) for each year of life is pre-

12 Perhaps it is not surprising that boys are much less likely to report having gotten a girl pregnant. This state of affairs is probably governed by ignorance, and girls may not tell their partners, especially if they choose to have an abortion. Information about actual live births also may be underreported. For example, virtually all of the fathers of the children born to our mothers in 1966–1968 acknowledge paternity. Historical changes in sexual patterns (in particular, less frequent intercourse with only one partner) make it less likely that all males will know they have fathered a child. However, surprisingly few national data exist on teenage paternity. For example, we know how many children each year are born to teenage mothers from information provided by the National Center for Health Statistics, but the proportion of these children who had teenage fathers is unclear. Paternal age is missing on one-third of all these birth certificates, in part because of the high rates of out-of-wedlock births (Sonenstein, 1986). The information we do have suggests that teenage paternity may be less prevalent than anticipated. In 1981, of births to teenagers, 47% were to fathers over 20, 19% to fathers under 20, and one-third to fathers of unspecified age (National Center for Health Statistics, 1983). Even if most of the "unspecified" cases were teenagers, one-half of the fathers were past their adolescent years. In the National Longitudinal Survey, four times as many 18-year-old females reported a birth as did 18-year-old males (9.5% v. 2%; Mott, 1983). For black males, the rate was 6.3%. Even with possible underreporting, then, adolescent fatherhood is probably much less common than adolescent motherhood.

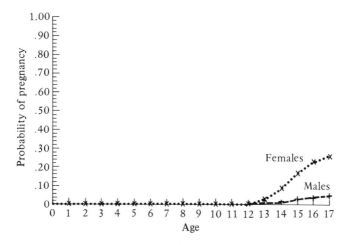

Figure 4.3. Cumulative probability of being pregnant (fathering a child) by age (in years) and gender

sented in Figure 4.3.[13] The first pregnancy occurred at age 12, and most births occurred when the girls were over 15 years of age. For the boys, the first report of fathering a child occurred at age 13, with the number increasing gradually thereafter.

As yet, most of the girls who have been pregnant have not had children. Just how many will end up as adolescent mothers is still unclear. Furthermore, many sexually active teenagers have managed to avoid pregnancy; of the sexually experienced girls, only 37% have been pregnant.

Nevertheless, it is clear that many of the teenagers are having intercourse without birth control and are therefore at risk of pregnancy and future parenthood. Have the mothers discussed this possibility with their teens, and if so, what have they said? According to the teens, almost all (over 90%) know that their mothers had them as teenagers, and 60% report that their mothers have talked to them about their experiences as young mothers. More girls than boys remember talking about this (77% v. 45%). Claudina, Helena's daughter, states quite matter-of-factly that "My mother does not expect me to have a baby so young." Tyrone reports: "She [my mother] told me that she wishes she had not had me so young [age 17] and she wishes that I don't make the same mistake." Two daughters whose families are on welfare remember their mothers as saying "It was very hard," and "I should wait until I finish school to have a child."

13 Since not all children had reached their 17th birthday, not all subjects are represented in this last data point in Figures 4.2 and 4.3.

When some mothers were asked how they would feel if their child became a teenage parent, their statements were remarkably similar to the children's. The predominant theme is "Don't repeat my mistake." Additionally, many mothers would be doubly disappointed if their advice were ignored since they feel that they, unlike their parents, explicitly gave their children information about managing sexuality. One mother said, "I did something with her that my mother did not have time to do with me; I talked to her even to the point of saying, 'Hey, I don't want you to have a baby. You and I know that I made mistakes; I don't want you to make the same ones.' " Another mother stated, "I could be a grandmother today, you know, and I'm so thankful that I am not. I taught him and I hope he goes through life with these little teachings because I look at some of his little buddies, they are fathers, and they are not ready."

Summary

The mothers' struggles to avoid poverty may have levied a cost on their children, costs in academic achievement, maladjustment, misbehavior, and, possibly, early parenthood. The amount of time the teenage mother had available for caregiving, the need for complex child-care arrangements, the absence of the father, lowered educational attainment, and, in some cases, reduced economic circumstances are all a familiar part of adolescent motherhood. Even with the help of family and friends, these obstacles were not (and probably could not be) totally overcome.

Yet we found little evidence that most mothers neglected their children. On the contrary, the energy put into providing adequate care while they were in school or at work, the pride they take in their teens' accomplishments, and the strong feelings of love are evident from the interviews. Most mothers feel they have done a good job, in less than ideal circumstances. In their own words, "I don't think I did bad in raising him"; "I know everyone thinks they have good children but I am not worried about him"; "I am proud of her."

At the same time, the mothers are very realistic about the consequences of early parenthood for themselves and, potentially, for their children. The mothers clearly know that avoiding pregnancy, completing school, and postponing marriage are most likely to ensure later success, and these three factors were, in fact, the best predictors of their own economic achievement, as we saw in the preceding chapter. As one mother said when asked what she wants her daughter to do, "I wouldn't want her to have a child early; I wouldn't want her to marry early, and I wouldn't want her to be a secretary."

Their goal, often explicitly stated, is for their children to avoid their mistakes, especially early parenthood. Over and over, mothers and adolescents alike voiced this theme. Perhaps the most eloquent statement was made by one parent who said, "I hope she does not completely walk in my footsteps because I could have left a lot of them out. If she is going to do it, I hope she takes a shortcut to better days.''

Some of the teenagers are on their way to a better life. Even with the mothers' best intentions, however, many seem destined to repeat the struggle, based on the startlingly high rates of high school failure, juvenile deliquency in males, and fertility in females. This bleak picture was somewhat unanticipated, based on the emotional and intellectual status of the children and preschoolers. The next chapter explores how the maternal life course determines the likelihood of children following in their mothers' footsteps.

5 The intersecting life courses
of adolescent mothers and their children

As we have repeatedly stressed, the variability in the life course of early childbearers was tremendous. Some mothers had a history of welfare dependence
while others managed to escape it; some married before the birth of the child,
some soon after, and some never; some mothers obtained additional schooling,
and others dropped out; some had many children, while others had few. By
examining the occurrence, timing, and sequencing of these early events in the
mother's life course, we were able to explain subsequent patterns of economic
achievement and fertility in Chapter 3. This chapter examines whether these
same life-course events also explain children's outcomes. Understanding the life
course of a single individual is complex, and the interrelation of multiple life
courses is even more so. The diversity of the mother's experience will result in
vastly different childrearing environments, which, in turn, influence children's
behavior. Four aspects of the maternal life course will be given special scrutiny
in this chapter: marital history, schooling, fertility, and changing economic resources.

Maternal life course and children's environment

Economic resources will determine much of the variability in children's environments. Material well-being may influence a variety of contextual conditions:
safety of the neighborhood, residence in a particular neighborhood, attendance
at a particular school, interaction with a particular peer group, access to cultural
opportunities, availability of informal networks of other adults, and importance
of the street culture in determining behavior. Specifically, children who are reared
in poverty are more likely to live in unsafe neighborhoods, to attend poor-quality
schools, and to associate with peer groups who do not value education or delayed
sexuality; they are less likely to be exposed to informal learning (camp, lessons,
cultural events) and to have achievement-oriented adult role models in their social network. The family's economic resources themselves, as we have seen in
Chapter 3, are largely determined by marital status, education, motivation, spac-

106

ing of children, and, to a lesser extent, the characteristics of the teenage mother's parents. All except the last are events about which mothers made decisions, even if constraints were placed on the decisions they could make.

Of the four aspects of the life course we will examine, economic, marital, educational, and fertility statuses, we expect that economic status will be the most powerful predictor of children's behavior. Past research has shown that equality of educational opportunities does not always promote greater equality, if students are differentially prepared to take advantage of these opportunities (Coleman et al., 1966; Jencks et al., 1972, 1979). The economic position of the family predicts school readiness in myriad studies. Indeed, the Head Start program originated in part because of these strong links (Zigler and Muenchow, 1984; Zigler and Valentine, 1979). In the Baltimore sample, economic status is expected to affect school readiness as well as subsequent academic performance. Additionally, economic status may affect school success in other ways, given that so many aspects of the environment are influenced by poverty. Of particular interest is whether poverty has differential influences on the child's behavior depending on the age of the child and the aspect of behavior under consideration.

The marital status of the mother also could be a potent force, accentuating or cushioning the disadvantages of early parenthood for children. Escaping poverty is more difficult for a family with only one wage earner, especially if that wage earner suffers from the lower wages and job discrimination women confront. Consistent with this argument, we found that marital status was strongly associated with economic security at the 17-year follow-up. Single-parent homes also might differ from two-parent homes in that child supervision is reduced, time spent with the parent is low, and emotional support is difficult in part because of competing demands on a single parent's time. Thus, a child in a single-parent home may have substantially different experiences than one in a two-parent home (see McLanahan, 1985).

Maternal educational goals and attainment also are likely to influence the child's development. Education is a crucial mechanism for occupational sorting and determining income in the United States. Many studies show clear links between maternal education and young children's cognitive, social, and emotional functioning. What are the mechanisms by which education may influence child development? Mothers who get further education probably value education more and may better communicate the importance of education to their children. They also may be more willing and able to invest in their child's education because they recognize its importance (Sewell and Shah, 1968). On a concrete level, they are more likely to read to their children, have books in the house, give verbal explanations for their behavior, take their children to the zoo and the park, and so on (Bradley and Caldwell, 1976; Wachs and Gruen, 1982). How and which of these possible mechanisms actually operate has not been well specified, but the link between maternal education and child outcomes is well documented in the sociological, developmental, and educational literature.

Finally, the mother's subsequent fertility may influence child development. Additional children, especially those who come in quick succession, make it increasingly hard for a woman or a couple to support their dependents. Independent of this economic link, more children and a rapid pace of childbearing result in parents' having less time to spend with any one child. Zajonc (1976) has argued that interaction with adults is critical for cognitive development and that such contact is lessened in large families. He attributes declining SAT scores during the 1960s and 1970s in part to the students' larger sibships. Whether Zajonc is right or not, supervision and emotional support are more difficult to provide in large families. Despite a popular belief that singletons are at a disadvantage, they actually have higher educational attainment and occupational prestige (Blake, 1981a). In economic terms, a trade-off exists between the quality and quantity of children. Fewer children mean that precious resources, time and money, will be in greater supply for children in one- and two-child families (see Blake, 1981b). In sum, we expect that low fertility will be positively related to enhanced child development.

Of course, none of these situations occurs in isolation. Economic stability is influenced by schooling, marital status, and employment. Educational attainment, in turn, is affected by family background, marital status, academic ability, educational aspirations, and, in our sample of mothers, attendance at a special school for teen mothers. Moreover, maternal life decisions in one arena often have an impact in other arenas as well. For example, we found that teens who delayed marriage were more likely to remain in school immediately after the birth of the child. Furthermore, early marriages were highly likely to dissolve, contributing to economic dependence. Thus, it is difficult to disentangle the separate effects of maternal life decisions since, in reality, they are intertwined. The following analyses consider the direct and indirect effects of life events on child outcomes, in an attempt to tease apart the relative contributions of separate life events.

Child development and the mother's life course

Typically, when studying mothers' influence on children's development, the mothers' characteristics at one point in time are the focus. This is true whether one is examining the effect of maternal education on young children's linguistic competence or young adult's educational attainment. The fact that maternal education can change over the life course is usually disregarded. And, as we have seen in Chapter 2, education, welfare, marital, and fertility situations changed dramatically over the course of 17 years. How such changes influence children is a sadly neglected topic.

This neglect can be traced to once popular views of development as relatively inflexible, primarily controlled by maturation, and malleable only at very young ages. The methodologies used, the topics chosen, and the conceptual models offered were constrained by the following three beliefs about development (Lerner, 1984). First, early experience molds an individual so pervasively that later change, though possible, is difficult to initiate and unlikely to endure. The seminal work of Bloom (1961), Hunt (1961), and others not only reinforced this notion but in part led to proportionately more research on early childhood than on any other life phase. Second, development was seen as essentially a ''within-the-person phenomenon,'' with contextual or environmental features having a relatively small impact. Research concentrated on cognition, language, and neuromotor growth, especially as age-graded and physiologically linked, rather than on environmental effects. Third, development was thought to proceed in a fairly standard sequence for all persons; individual differences in life courses and the existence of various developmental paths were not a focus of study. One of the most important contributions to developmental research has been a critical examination of these three beliefs, as well as the methodologies and models underlying them. Research has demonstrated that change occurs across the life span, that developmental life courses are not entirely determined by early childhood experiences, and that contextual features both enhance and constrain the potential for change, the end result being an alteration in all three beliefs (Baltes and Brim, 1979, 1980, 1981; Baltes and Nesselroade, 1973; Brim and Kagan, 1980; Gollin, 1981).

Even though development is now likely to be characterized as an interaction between personal and environmental characteristics (Bronfenbrenner, 1985), little research examines change in environmental or individual characteristics or how different environments may affect development at different ages. This chapter focuses on these concerns, rather than assuming that environmental conditions in early childhood are the only important source of contextual variation or that environment–individual links are present only in early childhood.

Analytic strategy

Several maternal life decisions and child outcomes will be employed in the following analyses. The key maternal events are marital status, economic situation, educational attainment, and fertility (both number and spacing of children). Child indicators of well-being include academic success (school readiness and grade failure), sexual experience, misbehavior or juvenile delinquency, and psychological functioning. Gender differences were found in all four domains, as we saw

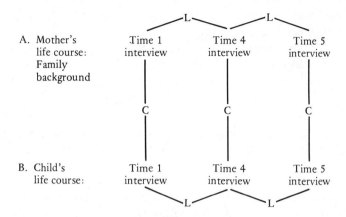

Figure 5.1. Analytic strategies for examining the life courses of mother and child

in Chapter 4. In the following discussions, boys and girls are combined since our analyses indicate that the influence of maternal decisions and environmental situations on child well-being was essentially the same for both. For example, more boys than girls have had sexual intercourse by age 15. But having a mother with recent welfare experience raises the likelihood of reporting intercourse by similar magnitudes for both boys and girls.

Whites are excluded in the analyses that follow. As mentioned in earlier chapters, few in our sample were white. In addition, a larger proportion of the whites were lost in subsequent follow-ups. Finally, findings may be different for whites and blacks. Also, only children whose biological mothers remain in the sample are included here because of our focus on the mother's influence on the child's well-being.

Our analytic strategy is presented in Figure 5.1 and is cross-sectional and longitudinal in nature. The horizontal lines represent the longitudinal comparisons, and the vertical lines the cross-sectional comparisons. First, a cross-sectional strategy allows us to compare associations between the mother's status and a particular child outcome at three points in time: at birth, when the child was roughly 5 years old, and when the child was 16 years old (times 1, 4, and 5 interviews, respectively). These cross-sectional comparisons are labeled C in Figure 5.1 and address whether maternal statuses are associated with child outcomes at three different developmental points and whether specific maternal statuses are associated with particular child outcomes. Second, life-course consistency will be addressed. These longitudinal comparisons, labeled L in the figure, tell us whether those mothers who start out disadvantaged remain so, and if children with early academic, behavior, or personality problems are more likely to have problems later in adolescence. Third, the interconnections between life courses are modeled using both the longitudinal and cross-sectional results. Thus, the chapter begins with a simple description of associations among variables and ends with the causal modeling of the interdependence of the mother's life course and the child's development.

Cross-sectional comparisons

Mothers and their newborns

The social transmission of disadvantage can occur very early, even prior to birth. If those mothers who are most disadvantaged are the least healthy and receive the least prenatal care, their infants are likely to exhibit higher incidences of mental retardation and higher morbidity rates (Bergner and Susser, 1970; Committee to Study the Prevention of Low Birthweight, 1985). Neonatal health can affect subsequent performance in many areas including academic, behavioral, and psychological domains (Beckwith and Cohen, 1984; Escalona, 1982; Newberger, Newberger Moore, and Richmond, 1976). Early childhood performance, in turn, can set life trajectories that are difficult to alter unless specific interventions are offered or environmental conditions are altered dramatically.

Two of the most extensively used measures of newborn health are birth weight and the one-minute Apgar score. The Apgar score measures an infant's functional status with regard to heart rate, breathing, color, and muscle tone just following the birth (Apgar, 1953; Apgar and James, 1962). Eighty percent of the Baltimore sample received very high (9 or 10) Apgar scores at 1 minute after birth. Birth weight is a commonly used measure of a newborn's health and is a powerful predictor of infant mortality and morbidity. Low birth weight is usually defined as below 2,500 grams, roughly 5½ pounds. Low birth weight is more common among blacks than whites, among very young mothers, and among disadvantaged socioeconomic groups (Hecht and Cutright, 1979; Taffel, 1980; Weiner and Milton, 1972). Clearly, the women in this sample are at high risk of having a low-birth-weight infant – they are black, young, and generally disadvantaged. Eleven percent of the Baltimore children were low birth weight. Prenatal care was associated with low birth weight, as those who had fewer than five prenatal visits were more likely to have a low-birth-weight infant. However, beginning prenatal care in the second or third trimester rather than the first trimester was not associated with low birth weight. Like other studies, socioeconomic differentials in birth weight were relatively small when we considered the amount of prenatal care (see Carlson, 1984).

As expected, low birth weight was associated with poor Apgar scores. But is there a connection between the mother's status and the child's birth weight and Apgar score? Whether the mother was on welfare, married, or in school at the time of the birth did not influence the likelihood of a low birth weight or a low Apgar score. Furthermore, those on welfare and not married were only slightly more likely to report infrequent prenatal visits (less than five). Thus, the mother's statuses are only weakly related to the child's well-being at birth. The high-quality care in Sinai Hospital, where all of our mothers received antenatal care, probably accounts for these weak associations (Baldwin and Cain, 1980; Mc-Cormick, 1985). Additionally, in samples of low-income women, health behaviors such as smoking seem to have higher associations with low birth weight than do maternal status measures (McCormick, 1985; McCormick et al., 1985).

Low-weight infants do more poorly on the Caldwell Preschool Inventory, suggesting that low birth weight may have long-term implications (see Newberger et al., 1976). But this disadvantage does not seem to be due to the maternal characteristics during pregnancy or at birth.

Mothers and their children at age 5

Much richer information exists on the situation of mothers and children at the 5-year follow-up. We know, for example, the mother's welfare, educational, marriage, and fertility history during the child's preschool years. Mothers also provided detailed reports on the children, and a battery of tests was administered to children in 1972. Many researchers argue that this early period, the preschool years, is crucial to later development – crucial because the child learns skills, develops social behavior, and acquires a sense of identity and worth. Some developmentalists go so far as to say that development is most plastic at this time and that children, once on a trajectory, are resistant to change. Further, the parental or family influence is believed to be especially conspicuous because the competing influences of peers and the school are still weak.

In the first phase of this study, Furstenberg (1976) showed that the adolescent mothers were not doing as well as their classmates who had children later, nor were their children doing as well as those with older parents. Clearly, then, early parenthood is disadvantageous for the mother and the young child. But great individual differences existed. Some mothers and children seemed to be doing quite well at this stage in their lives, others quite poorly. Here we explore the possible reasons for individual variability: Is the child's development strongly associated with crucial aspects of the mother's unfolding life course? The environmental situations examined are recent welfare experience (i.e., has the mother been on welfare in any year since the child was born?), current marital status (i.e., is the mother currently married?), educational status (i.e. has the mother been in school at least 2 years since the child was born?), and subsequent fertility (i.e., has the mother had an additional child?). The bivariate associations between these maternal status measurements and indicators of child welfare are presented in Table 5.1.

Table 5.1. *Bivariate associations between mother's status and child outcomes, time 4*

	Sample mean	(SD)	On welfare	Not married	Not in school	Has another child
Academic preparedness						
Preschool Inventory score	62.3	(27)	−10.1[a]	−8.1[a]	−4.3	−7.7[b]
Behavior problems						
Uncooperative	31.6	(18)	7.0[a]	1.8	−0.3	4.3[c]
Rude	28.0	(19)	8.6[a]	1.2	−0.1	2.8
Disobedient	28.6	(19)	6.3[b]	1.4	4.5	5.7[b]
(3-item index)[d]	(29.5)	(16)	(6.9)[a]	(.9)	(1.6)	(4.9)[b]
Personality/psychological reports						
Shy	33.7	(27)	5.5[c]	2.4	−8.0[b]	6.5[b]
Bored	13.4	(15)	3.5[c]	2.8	1.5	2.3
Sad	11.3	(13)	3.4[c]	1.2	−0.4	3.6[b]
(3-item index)[d]	(19.6)	(13)	(3.7)[b]	(−1.8)	(−1.8)	(4.7)[a]

Note: The bivariate association is measured by the difference in mean child scores across categories defined by mother's characteristics.
[a] Significant at .01 level.
[b] Significant at .05 level.
[c] Significant at .10 level.
[d] These are simple additive indexes: The mean score on the three items is taken as the index value.

The Preschool Inventory score is a measure of school readiness originally constructed for use with Head Start students (Caldwell, 1970). A score of 50 indicates that the student is as ready for school as the average disadvantaged student who was the target of the Head Start program. Observed scores ranged from 2 to 99 with a mean of 62.3. Both the wide variability and the higher-than-average mean score were expected. Our sample includes many 5-year-olds (the test was developed for 4-year-olds), and some of the children in this sample were economically ineligible for Head Start. Regardless of the higher-than-average mean, Table 5.1 indicates how much lower children score, on average, if their mother is on welfare, unmarried, not in school, or has a subsequent child. Specifically, those children with a mother on welfare scored on average 10.1 points lower than those whose mothers were not on welfare. Likewise, having an unmarried mother, having a mother who has not been in school for at least 2 years since the child's birth, and having a sibling decreased Preschool Inventory scores by 8.1, 4.3, and 7.7 points, respectively.

Another way to demonstrate the importance of the mother's statuses is to consider the set of maternal characteristics simultaneously. For example, let us return to two children described in Chapter 4, Randall and Claudina. Randall's Preschool Inventory score was in the high 30s, and Claudina's was in the high 60s. Randall's mother had additional children, was on welfare, and had dropped out of school, whereas Claudina's mother completed school, was not on welfare, had delayed childbearing, and was married. To see if these sharp differentials by mother's statuses characterized the full sample, we compared four advantageous and disadvantageous maternal characteristics.

Child A	*Child B*
Mother not married	Mother married
Mother on welfare	Mother not on welfare
Mother has three children	Mother has one child
Mother not in school more than 1 year	Mother in school 2 or more years since child's birth

If we compare child A, typified by Randall, with the most disadvantageous set of maternal characteristics, with child B, who, like Claudina, has the most favorable set, these children's preschool scores would differ by almost 30 (29.7) points – more than a standard deviation.[1] Thus, scores as different as Randall's and Claudina's could partially be attributed to different maternal characteristics.

Turning to other measures of children's well-being, when the child was approximately 5 years of age the mother was asked to rate the child on three behavior dimensions: cooperative/uncooperative, rude/polite, and disobedient/obedient, using a zero to 100 scale. Table 5.1 shows the mean score given by parents, 31.6 for uncooperative, for example. Also shown in this table are the shifts associated with the mother's status. Those on welfare, for instance, rate their children as being more uncooperative (by 7.0 points), more rude (8.6 points), and more disobedient (by 6.3 points). Differences this large are unlikely to be due to sampling variability. Having additional children has somewhat weaker, but otherwise similar, effects. Those mothers with at least one additional child rate their first child as more uncooperative, rude, and disobedient by 4.3, 2.8, and 5.7 points, respectively. Note that marital status and school attendance are not strongly or consistently related to these response items.

By combining these three maternal reports into a behavior problem index, we summarize the statistically significant and substantively important associations with maternal characteristics (see Table 5.1). Specifically, mothers on welfare and mothers with additional children report more behavioral problems. Average scores on the behavioral problems index are 6.9 and 4.9 points higher, respectively. Note that these behavioral reports come from mothers and are not observer ratings. Possibly some mothers (those on welfare or with low education, for example) may rate their children more negatively even though their children's

---

1 This estimate comes from regressing the Preschool Inventory score on all four maternal statuses simultaneously. A roughly 30-point difference results from comparing the expected preschool score of those with the most favorable and least favorable set of characteristics.

behavior does not warrant it. Unfortunately, we cannot determine the accuracy of these ratings, but even if a rating is influenced by maternal as well as child characteristics, a negative rating may indicate potential problems. From a labeling perspective, if a mother attributes a negative temperament to her toddler or preschooler, for example, then the child may be more likely to exhibit negative behavior in school (Buss and Plomin, 1984; Keogh, 1982; Lerner et al., 1982; see Becker, 1963, for a discussion of labeling).

Mothers also were asked to evaluate their child along three personality/temperament dimensions: outgoing/shy, eager to learn/bored, and happy/sad. Mothers again assigned their children a score between zero and 100. A summary index also was calculated, as for the preceding domain. The mean scores in the first column of Table 5.1 indicate that mothers on the average rated their children as somewhat shy, quite eager to learn, and not very unhappy. As with the behavioral measures, the mother's welfare status and her fertility were associated with these personality measures. Mothers on welfare or those who had an additional child rated their children as being more shy, bored, and unhappy.

To summarize, at this early stage of the life cycle, a close association exists between mother's and child's well-being. Maternal characteristics are most strongly related to school readiness. But the mother's status, at least her welfare and fertility experience, also is associated with behavior problems and personality characteristics. Mothers not on welfare and those who have avoided additional births have children who are better prepared for school, better behaved, and more outgoing and happy. At age 5 then, children whose mothers are doing better seem to be faring better themselves.

Mothers and adolescent children

Associations between mothers' characteristics and adolescents' well-being are presented in Tables 5.2 and 5.3. School performance is inferred from being below grade level. As we saw earlier, half of the adolescents had failed a grade. Those adolescents whose mothers were on welfare during the past 5 years were 2.67 times more likely to have failed a grade than others (see Table 5.2). Somewhat weaker associations were observed between other maternal environmental conditions and grade failure: Not being married, not having a high school degree, and having three or more children increase the likelihood of failing a grade by factors of 2.22, 2.44, and 1.78, respectively. If, as previously, we consider the most advantageous and unfavorable conditions simultaneously by contrasting child A (with the most disadvantageous set) and child B (with the most favorable set), child A is over 11 times more likely to have failed a grade than child B.[2]

Consistent with this prediction, Randall, the child discussed earlier who has

---

2 This estimate comes from an additive logistic regression equation that includes all four mothers' characteristics as covariates.

Table 5.2. *Bivariate associations between mother's status and grade failure and between mother's status and early intercourse, time 5*

	Sample mean[a]	On welfare	Not married	Not high school graduate	Has 3+ children
Academic performance, failed grade	.50	2.67[b]	2.22[b]	2.44[b]	1.78[c]
Early intercourse, intercourse by age 15	.69	1.64[c]	1.35	1.21	1.33

Note: The bivariate association is measured by the odds ratio. It measures the factor change in the likelihood of "grade failure" or "intercourse by age 15" across contrasts defined by mother's characteristics (e.g., on welfare time 5, yes or no; unmarried or married, etc.)
[a] The sample means reported here may differ slightly from those in Chapter 4 because of listwise deletion of missing values.
[b] Significant at .01 level.
[c] Significant at .05 level.

the most unfavorable set of conditions, has failed two grades and is barely doing C work. He is eager to leave school. Claudina, in contrast, whose mother is married, is a high school graduate, and has a secure economic status, is currently doing well in school and has college aspirations. Differences such as these between Randall and Claudina can be traced to the mother's background and her unfolding life course.

Turning to other measures of well-being, 69% of the adolescents report having intercourse by age 15 (see Table 5.2). Early intercourse is problematic because adolescents are often ill prepared to practice contraceptive vigilance, elevating the possibility of early pregnancy and premature parenthood. Thus, sexual experience can be a key link in the intergenerational transmission of poverty. Indeed, the fact that nearly 70% of the sample are sexually active by age 15 (almost all of the boys and roughly half of the girls) is consistent with this view. However, individual differences in the likelihood of intercourse by age 15 are associated with maternal characteristics. Those with mothers on welfare are over 60% more likely to have had intercourse, and having mothers who are unmarried, not in school, and have additional children all increase the likelihood of intercourse by 20–40%. These associations are not nearly as strong as the ones noted earlier for school failure, but nevertheless suggest an influence of maternal statuses on adolescent sexuality.

Parent and child reports of behavior problems are presented in Table 5.3. Roughly half (52%) of the mothers report receiving a note from school about the child's behavior. Forty-four percent of the children have been expelled from school, 15% have run away, 21% have stolen something of significant value,

Table 5.3. *Associations between mother's status and child behavior measures, time 5*

Behavior problems	Sample mean	On welfare	Not married	Not high school graduate	Has 3+ children
Parent report					
Note from school	.52	1.21	1.89[c]	1.34	1.15
Expelled from school	.44	1.41	1.32	1.35	1.15
Ever run away	.15	2.29[c]	1.06	1.52	1.70
Ever stolen	.21	2.12[c]	1.64	1.16	1.46
Ever stopped by police	.28	1.61[d]	2.44[b]	.98	.88
(5-item index)[a]	(.32)	(.09)[c]	(.10)[c]	(.04)	(.01)
Cheats	.54	1.23	1.64[c]	1.29	1.32
Misbehaves at home	.41	1.11	.70	1.21	1.36
Misbehaves at school	.34	.74	.99	.68	.80
Friends misbehave	.29	1.89[c]	1.45	1.28	1.41
(4-item index)[a]	(.40)	(.02)	(.03)	(.02)	(.02)
Child report					
Ever seriously hurt someone	.19	1.39	1.35	2.18[c]	1.15
Ever lied about something important	.58	1.52	1.27	.75	1.37
Ever stole something	.11	1.35	2.12	1.63	1.34
Ever stopped by police	.33	1.71[c]	1.75[c]	1.34	1.17
Ever damaged school property	.05	2.97[d]	1.64	4.49[c]	.34
(5-item index)[a]	(.25)	(.07)[c]	(.06)[c]	(.05)[c]	(.02)
Ever smoke cigarettes	.51	1.31	1.22	1.00	1.61
Ever drink	.60	.90	1.61[c]	.98	1.16
Ever get drunk	.28	1.40	1.37	1.91[c]	1.61
Ever smoke marijuana	.47	1.50	1.89[c]	.80	1.26
Ever use other drugs	.05	2.46	1.85	.36	.77
(5-item index)[a]	(.46)	(.06)[d]	(.08)[c]	(.01)	(.04)

Note: These factor changes (odds ratios) measure the difference in the likelihood of an event/report between those whose mothers have and do not have a given characteristic. Values greater than 1.0 indicate increases; values below 1.0 indicate reductions. See text for more details.
[a] These are simple additive indexes: The mean score on the relevant items is taken as the index value.
[b] Significant at .01 level.
[c] Significant at .05 level.
[d] Significant at .10 level.

and 28% have been stopped and questioned by the police. Mothers with recent welfare experience are approximately 20% more likely to report getting a note from school, 40% more likely to report the child has been expelled, over twice as likely to report that their child ran away or stole something of value, and 60%

more likely to report that the child had been stopped or questioned by police. Being unmarried is similarly related to these reports. In contrast, not graduating from high school and family size are, at best, weakly related to these reports. When we average these five items to form an index of delinquent behavior, only welfare and marital status are clearly associated with problem behavior. In contrast, marital status was not related to the behavior-problem measures at 5 years of age.

Parallel results for a series of other problems including whether the child sometimes cheats, misbehaves at home, misbehaves at school, and has bad friends were found (see Table 5.3). Except for the misbehave-at-school item, all values shown are greater than 1.0, indicating that the mother's welfare experience, being unmarried, not being a high school graduate, and having three or more children increase the likelihood of affirmative reports. However, the associations are generally weak. For instance, mothers on welfare are 1.23 times as likely (i.e., 23%) to report that their children sometimes cheat.

Childrens' reports of their own delinquent behavior also are presented in Table 5.3. Results are consistent with the parents' reports discussed earlier (and shown in Table 5.3). Specifically, having an unmarried mother or one with recent welfare experience increases the likelihood that a child will report that he or she has seriously hurt someone, lied about something important, stolen something of value, been stopped or questioned by police, or ever damaged school property. For instance, those whose mothers have recent welfare experience are almost three (2.97) times more likely to report damaging school property. Educational and fertility status have somewhat weaker associations. The associations for the five-item index mirror exactly those for the summary index from the mothers' report.

Finally, Table 5.3 shows the children's reports of substance abuse according to maternal characteristics. An index summing these items shows that substance abuse is associated with welfare and marital status, but not with education and fertility status. For instance, those whose mothers are on welfare are 1.5 times more likely to have smoked marijuana, and those whose mothers are unmarried are nearly 1.9 times more likely to have smoked it. In sum, having an unmarried mother or recent welfare experience raises the likelihood that a child will have smoked cigarettes, gotten drunk, smoked marijuana, and used other drugs.

Table 5.4 shows results from a similar analysis of adolescent personality problems as reported by mother and child. The absence of any strong or consistent associations between the mothers' characteristics and these items is striking. In adolescence, the child's emotional and psychological state does not seem to be strongly related to the status of the mother. Caution is certainly warranted here: Our measures of emotional and psychological well-being are rough at best. Firmer conclusions can be made only after our results have been replicated and

Table 5.4. *Factor changes in the likelihood of reporting selected psychological/personality problems by mother's status variables, time 5*

Psychological/ personality problems	Sample mean	On welfare	Not married	Not high school graduate	Has 3+ children
Parent report					
Moody	.84	2.11[b]	1.14	1.28	1.61
Feels unloved	.34	1.32	.94	.92	.86
Feels anxious	.46	1.72[b]	1.02	1.56[c]	1.38
Low esteem	.27	.81	.68	.80	.79
Unhappy	.44	1.08	1.13	1.18	1.23
(5-item index)[a]	(.47)	(.04)	(−.02)	(.01)	(.01)
Child report					
Feels lonely sometimes	.30	.90	.90	.51	.73
Feels nervous sometimes	.59	1.26	1.25	.90	1.30
Unhappy sometimes	.75	1.41	1.47	1.48	.98
Not highly satisfied with life	.57	1.19	1.58[b]	1.05	1.18
(4-item index)[a]	(.55)	(.04)	(.06)[b]	(−.02)	(.01)
Not satisfied with friends	.55	.78	1.12	1.04	1.18
Not satisfied with family	.29	.98	.75	1.03	1.09
Not satisfied with self	.33	.86	.76	1.24	1.26
Not satisfied with being girl/boy	.08	.79	1.82	.47	1.07
(4-item index)[a]	(.31)	(−.02)	(−.02)	(.01)	(.03)

Note: These factor changes (odds ratios) measure the difference in the likelihood of an event/report between those whose mothers have and do not have a given characteristic. Values greater than 1.0 indicate increases; values below 1.0 indicate reductions. See text for more details.
[a] These are simple additive indexes: The mean score on the relevant items is taken as the index value.
[b] Significant at .05 level.
[c] Significant at .10 level.

different measurements used. In short, we do not think this area of inquiry should be prematurely closed on the basis of these results. Yet we can find no evidence in our data of a relation between mother's social status and child's psychological well-being.

Consistency across mother's and child's life course

So far, the Baltimore data have been examined as if they were a series of cross-sectional surveys. We have not yet taken advantage of the longitudinal nature of the study to ask about change and consistency across time (C in Fig. 5.1). Yet the across-time associations are very important. Our life-course perspective em-

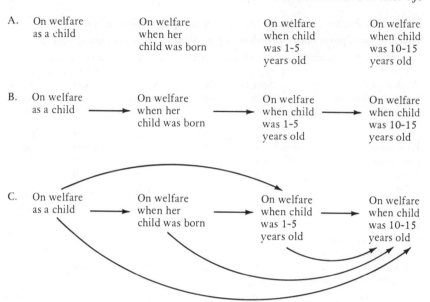

Figure 5.2. Three possible patterns the unfolding life course could take

phasizes that past experience influences present actions, and present actions influence future ones. If this is so, past welfare experience has implications for current economic status, for instance. We now document and describe life-course trajectories among the Baltimore adolescent mothers and their children. This separate description of mothers' and children's life courses is a necessary, preliminary step toward identifying how and where life courses intersect. The cross-sectional associations documented earlier could reflect contemporaneous effects or a rather stable life-course trajectory for mother and child. Can such stable trajectories be identified for mother and child? If so, for which mother's characteristics and for which child outcomes?

Mother's characteristics could be arranged in three distinct ways, as presented in Figure 5.2. Using welfare as an example, model A illustrates the possibility of no consistency over the life course; welfare status at any given point in time is unrelated to the individual's past welfare experience. This model, if accurate, would suggest that people are on welfare for relatively short periods of time and any individual, regardless of earlier welfare experience, is equally likely to be on welfare. However, some continuity in life experience is believed to exist and has been demonstrated in many life-course studies (Brim and Kagan, 1980; Elder, 1974; Valliant, 1977). Therefore, a more plausible scenario is that if a mother is on welfare at time 1, she should have an increased chance of being on welfare at time 5 (see model B, Fig. 5.2). At the same time, a change in trajectory at any point in time could alter the life course such that continuity disappears. For example, if a woman finishes school and obtains a stable job, she may be very unlikely to receive welfare in the future, even given a past welfare history. The most deterministic pattern, shown in model C, predicts that persons carry their welfare history with them. In other words, once on welfare, one tends to stay on welfare. In addition, those who escape economic dependency for a period of time are more likely than others to find themselves on welfare in the future.

These three possible patterns include a highly variable conception of development, in which life-course trajectories change frequently and do not build on subsequent events (model A); a highly deterministic one, in which change in trajectories is difficult if not impossible (model C); and a more flexible but continuous one, in which change is possible, under certain circumstances or through certain life events, even though in the absence of environmental alterations, life choices will continue on the current trajectory (model B). Our data suggest that the last scenario (model B, Fig. 5.2) is most applicable to our respondents' life courses (see Appendix F). There are life courses characterized by welfare dependency, nonmarriage, low education, and high fertility. Those whose life course takes such a trajectory are likely to remain on this path. But if individuals do alter this trajectory by getting a stable job, entering a stable marriage, acquiring educational credentials or curtailing subsequent fertility, they are no more likely than others to fall back within this trajectory. This more flexible, less deterministic view of development suggests that interventions aimed at altering the environments of the individual may help her escape economic dependence. We return to this point in the concluding section of this chapter.

Returning to the children of the Baltimore women, the same three possible patterns may be postulated to describe their development. Unfortunately, given that we have substantial data only in preschool and high school years, we cannot address whether children fall back into an unfavorable trajectory once they have escaped it. But we may look at continuities and discontinuities over time. Low birth weight, for instance, is negatively associated with preschool readiness, as is true in other studies as well (Escalona, 1982; Newberger et al., 1976). Thus, the mother's antenatal health and use of prenatal care can have long-lasting effects on the children's lives. Further, continuity is seen in academic performance from preschool to high school as well as in behavior and deviance problems. Clearly by age 5 then, continuity exists. Early experiences and competencies do influence later development. Assuring an adequate environment for young children, then, should pay dividends for later life chances.

The strength of these connections across the childhood life course is illustrated in Table 5.5. First, one standard deviation change in the Preschool Inventory (30 points) increases the likelihood of having failed a grade by roughly 90%.

Table 5.5. *Associations between time 4 and time 5 measures*

A 30-point (i.e., 1 standard deviation) decrease in the Preschool Inventory score almost doubles (increases by 1.9) the likelihood of having failed a grade.

Parents' time 4 reports on uncooperative, rude, and disobedient behaviors that place their child 1 standard deviation higher (i.e., 16 points higher on the 0–100 scale):
  Increase by 60% the likelihood of intercourse by age 15.
  On average, increase by 1.5 the mother's number of yes responses to the five questions on delinquent behavior (see Table 5.3 for list of items).
  Increase by roughly 1 the number of delinquent acts the child reports (see Table 5.3 for list of items).
  On average, increase by roughly 1.25 the mother's number of yes answers to questions on whether the child cheats, misbehaves at home, misbehaves at school, and has bad friends (see Table 5.3 for list of items).
  On average, only increase by .5 the number of yes answers to the five substance abuse questions (see Table 5.3 for list of items).

Parents' time 4 reports on the child's enthusiasm, shyness, and happiness (see Table 5.1) that place the child 1 standard deviation lower (approximately 13 points on the 0–100 point scale):
  On average, increase by .7 the number of mothers' yes responses to questions on whether child is moody, feels unloved, feels anxious, has low esteem, and is unhappy (see Table 5.4).
  Have negligible effects on the child's reports of happiness or satisfaction (see Table 5.4).

Note: See Appendix F for details regarding this analysis.

The preschool index of behavior problems is also consistently related to measures of delinquency in adolescence. Second, preschool behavior is associated with high school behavior only within domains. That is, the preschool measure of behavior problems is associated with adolescent misbehavior and delinquency, not with academic performance or temperament. Third, these strong associations are seen for academic success and misbehavior but not for personality and temperament. Perhaps our measures were situation or temporally specific: A person is happy or sad depending on the situation of the moment. Or, more likely, our measures were not tapping underlying temperament or personality dimensions; other studies have found associations between infancy and childhood for dimensions such as shyness and sociability (Bates, 1980; Bates, Freeland, and Lounsbury, 1979; Buss and Plomin, 1984; Plomin, 1983; Thomas and Chess, 1980; Thomas, Chess, and Birch, 1968), and for shyness between childhood and adolescence (Kagan and Moss, 1962).

The life course of mothers and children

The previous two analyses set the stage for the current one. Cross-sectional associations between mothers' characteristics and children's well-being in both the preschool years and in adolescence were found, as well as longitudinal associations in life courses for both mothers and children. We now ask, what are the precise connections between the unfolding life courses of the mothers and children? Are maternal influences primarily felt during the preschool years and maintained in adolescence because of strong life-course trajectories? Or do the mothers' more recent experiences have implications for their adolescents' well-being? To address these questions, four possibilities are postulated, as shown in Figure 5.3. The appropriate model may vary depending upon either the mother's characteristic or specific child outcome being considered.

Mother's status does not strongly influence the child's life course. Model A in Figure 5.3, states that no association exists between this dimension of the mother's experience and her child's behavior. We expect that certain kinds of maternal experiences do not consistently influence the child's behavior. For instance, many assume that the mother's employment experience, independent of her educational or occupational statuses, has important implications for the child's development. However, little evidence supports such a position.

Model B states that *the mother's influence operates only when the child is quite young* (Fig. 5.3). Stated differently, the mother's social circumstances set the trajectory for the child but do not alter its course once the child enters school and moves into adolescence. This model is certainly plausible because development is often believed to be most plastic in the early years and because the family environment is the primary system in which children are embedded. In our data set, an association between mother's status and preschool child outcomes may be due to environmental conditions throughout the first few years of life. Given this scenario, subsequent cross-sectional associations (in adolescence, for instance) result not from contemporaneous causes but from these early, persistent influences.

Model C indicates that *the mother's statuses have little influence early on but have more as the child grows older* (Fig. 5.3). Many developmentalists suggest that life-course trajectories are easier to change after the infancy years, as growth is less canalized over time (Bronfenbrenner, 1985; McCall, 1979, 1981; Scarr and Weinberg, 1978). Additionally, personal characteristic–environmental interactions are more likely as children become older since the children themselves may select or evoke different environmental contingencies. Many of our Baltimore mothers talked about choosing specific environments (i.e., the special school for teens) because they desired a high school diploma. Young children are not, in general, as easily able to select environments.

The final heuristic model (D) posits that *both early and later experiences of mothers influence their children.* In other words, the status of mother and child are closely intertwined. Mother's status influences the child at an early age, thereby setting a trajectory. But the mother's subsequent experience may alter this early development trajectory.

A. Mother's status does not strongly influence the child's life course.

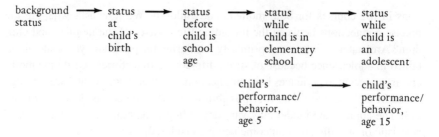

B. Mother's status influences child's life-course trajectory very early.

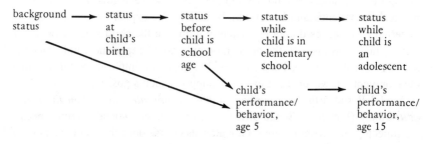

C. Mother's status influences child's life-course trajectory in adolescence.

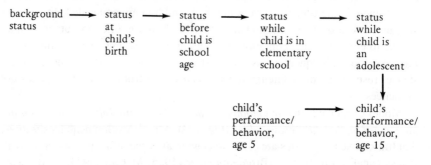

D. Mother's status influences child's life-course trajectory very early and in adolescence.

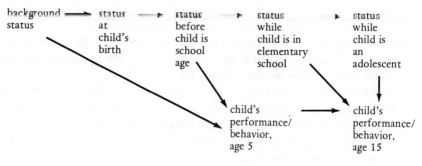

Figure 5.3. Possible connections between life course of mother and child

In general, our view of development as flexible within limits leads us to predict, on theoretical grounds, model D. Most of us might expect that mother's statuses would affect the child both in the preschool and adolescent years. However, it is not clear which specific aspects of the mother's life course – her welfare, marital, educational, and fertility experience – will be most salient. Which experiences have consequences for any particular child behavior? The discussion that follows summarizes the results of an analysis aimed at identifying potentially different influences of the mother's life-course decisions on particular child outcomes. Much of the detail of this analysis is presented in Appendix F.

Mother's economic status and child outcomes

The mother's economic status has pervasive effects on the child's academic performance, and the appropriate model, as expected, is D. If the mother was on welfare as a child and on welfare in the first years of the child's life, the child's score on the Preschool Inventory is sharply reduced (i.e., by an average of 21 points). The Preschool Inventory, measuring school readiness, is strongly associated with subsequent school performance (see Table 5.5). Welfare experience, operating through school readiness, increases by 50% the likelihood of failing a grade by time 5.

Net of this influence, if the mother was on welfare during the 5 years preceding the last survey round (i.e., when the child was entering adolescence), the likelihood of school failure almost tripled (i.e., increased by a factor of 2.9). This implies that recent welfare experience is considerably more important for current school performance than is preschool experience. These results indicate not only that preschool interventions will be beneficial but that older children must be aided by interventions as well, given their responsiveness to environmental conditions.

The early maternal influence (model B in Fig. 5.3) better describes the association between mother's welfare experience and behavior problems. Welfare experience affects preschool behavior and temperament, but the mother's status in subsequent years has no additional, independent effect. Welfare experience is associated with parents' reports that children are rude, disobedient, and uncooperative (i.e., items in the behavior index) at 5 years of age. Likewise, those mothers with welfare experience more often report that their kids are unhappy, bored, and shy (i.e., items in the personality problem index) at 5 years of age. Associations between mother's welfare status and adolescent problem behavior result from a trajectory set much earlier in the preschool years. In contrast, no association between mother's status and adolescent psychological reports was found despite a clear association during the preschool years. This occurs because there is no strong consistency in our measurement of psychological states across time.

The mother's economic status does affect the child, but the relation is complex. Being on welfare during the preschool years affects all aspects of the young child's behavior. Because of strong life-course trajectories, this early effect can still be seen in adolescence for school and behavior problems. In contrast, maternal economic status influences personality measures in early childhood but disappears by adolescence.

Mother's marital status and child outcomes

Marital status of the mother seems to have only weak effects on the preschool child's outcomes (see Table 5.1). But marital status is clearly associated with academic performance and behavior problems in adolescence (see Tables 5.2 and 5.3). This pattern of results is illustrative of model C, later maternal influences.

Why might marital status be unimportant early in the child's life but important later on? One answer might stress the flexible nature of the black family in helping teen mothers care for and rear their young children. Many women in our sample were dependent on their parents in the years immediately following the birth. This short-term dependence did not have a negative effect on the mother's eventual life success. Thus the lack of a spouse in these early years may have been offset by help from relatives. Also, women who marry at a young age and those who have premarital births and pregnancies have high risks of marital disruption (see Morgan and Rindfuss, 1985). Marriages contracted in the first 5 years of the study were likely to end in divorce (see Chapter 2). An unstable marriage does nothing to ease the problems that accompany early childbearing and indeed may exacerbate them. By contrast, few women were living with their parents 16 years after the birth of the study child, and few were accepting substantial help from relatives. Marriages still intact at this later time also were much more stable. Under these circumstances, marriage reduces the likelihood of welfare dependence and creates a stable family environment more conducive to strong academic performance and fewer behavior problems.

Mother's educational status and child outcomes

Mother's education provides another example of a model C pattern (later maternal influence). The Preschool Inventory is not influenced by the mother's early educational status. But net of Preschool Inventory score, having a mother who completed high school by the time the child was 16 decreases sharply the likelihood of grade failure. One explanation suggested at the outset is that those mothers who finish school under these less-than-ideal conditions (i.e., as adolescent parents) place a higher value on education. They therefore may socialize their children for educational achievement, be able to provide more help, and offer more educationally suitable role models. In contrast, maternal educational status does not have an observable influence on the child's behavioral or psychological measures.

Family size and child outcomes

All the child outcomes are influenced by the number of additional children the mother has prior to the child's fifth birthday (Table 5.1). Net of this effect, the mother's fertility in subsequent years is not strongly associated with child outcomes illustrative of the model B pattern (early maternal influence). Thus, it is the timing of subsequent fertility that seems most important. Rapid subsequent fertility reduces the time and resources spent on the first child. The importance of subsequent fertility for mother and child makes this an important point for policy intervention. In Chapter 3 we saw that teens who attended the Sinai Hospital Special Clinic program were more likely to use birth control and more likely to avoid a rapid repeat pregnancy. Controlling fertility is one path to recovery for the mothers. Results for the children suggest that the first child may benefit as well.

Summary

Work reported in this chapter is unique and ambitious because it attempts to link, across generations, the unfolding life courses of mother and child. As Chapter 4 documents, the mothers were not the only adult family members in the child's social network. Other relatives, especially grandmothers, husbands, and boyfriends, were important members. But the mother was a central figure in the child's life, and we expected that her life path would strongly influence the child's environment. We focused on four crucial aspects of the mother's unfolding life course: her economic, marital, educational, and fertility status. Each status has potential implications for the child. The central question, then, is whether these statuses influence the child and whether their impact is the same in early childhood and in adolescence.

In general, our analyses confirm clear connections between the life courses of mothers and children. Also generally, changes in the mother's life course at all ages affect some aspect of the child's behavior. Yet there is no simple or recurrent pattern of influence. No single model describes the interconnections between mother's and child's life courses. For some child outcomes (such as behavior problems) an aspect of the mother's life course (such as subsequent fertility) has an effect during the preschool years but not later on. In contrast, marital status is not related to preschool behavior problems but is clearly related to behavior problems and delinquency in adolescence. This complexity is an important finding with consequences for the life-course perspective and for subsequent research. As noted previously, earlier conceptions of development were characterized by the view that (1) early experience shapes an individual indelibly such that later change is difficult and not likely to be enduring; (2) development occurs largely independent of the social environment; and (3) development proceeds in a fairly standard sequence. Current views, informed by developmental research, challenge each of these points. Change occurs across the life span, developmental life courses are not entirely determined by early childhood experiences, and the social context can both expand and constrain the potential for change. Our results fit nicely within this revisionist perspective. Although it is now common to view development as dependent on the interaction between person and environmental characteristics, our research is unusual because of its focus on changing characteristics and how given characteristics might have different effects at different ages.

Our results are consistent with policy recommendations that call for support to young mothers with preschool children: Children are influenced by their mother's well-being at this formative time period. Both academic and behavioral life courses can be identified in the preschool years. Interventions that help mothers delay subsequent fertility seem a feasible and attractive option. Delayed fertility reduces the likelihood of economic dependency for the family and is associated with greater school readiness among children. Likewise, programs that help children prepare for school, like Head Start, make sense given the importance of school readiness for subsequent academic performance.

What our results say that is new, or at least said much less often, is that it is never too late for effective intervention. The life-course model that best fits these data is a flexible but continuous one. Change is possible under certain circumstances, or because of certain events; otherwise the life course will continue to unfold guided largely by its own momentum. In brief, there are life courses characterized by welfare dependency, nonmarriage, low education, and high fertility. Those whose life course takes such a trajectory are likely to remain on this path. But if they can escape, if they can alter this trajectory by getting a stable job, entering a stable marriage, acquiring educational credentials, or curtailing subsequent fertility, they are no more likely than others to fall back within this trajectory. Moreover, children benefit as their mother's life situation improves. For example, regardless of early welfare status, those mothers who are economically independent later on have children that are doing better – doing better in school and reporting less deviant behavior.

As a final comment and brief summary, note that statements made in this chapter are probabilistic, not deterministic. Living in an economically dependent family, for example, does not harm every child. But our results show that, "on average,'' behavior and academic performance are negatively affected by certain mother's characteristics: being on welfare, being unmarried, not finishing high school, and having an additional early birth. These environments are less conducive to strong academic performance and good behavior. What we have documented, then, are some interpretable regularities. The surprising diversity of adolescent mothers' later lives has clear implication for their children. The chance of these children ''making it'' is affected not only by the circumstances of their birth and their own abilities but also by the extent to which their mothers can overcome the disadvantage of early parenthood.

6   The life course of adolescent mothers: implications for public policy

The 17-year follow-up of the Baltimore adolescent mothers and their children is, to our knowledge, the only investigation to date that has traced the life course of adolescent parents from first pregnancy to later adulthood, looking at both child-bearers and their offspring. We have examined the long-term educational, familial, and economic careers of nearly 300 teenage mothers who were originally contacted at the time of their first pregnancy. The analysis provides a detailed account of changes in the life course of teenage mothers over a period of nearly two decades, identifying adaptations to early childbearing that predicted eventual success or failure. We then linked these maternal adaptations to the current well-being of the children.

Some of our results are of particular relevance to policymakers who must make difficult choices about when and how to intervene both in preventing the occurrence of adolescent childbearing and in lessening its costs. After reviewing what was learned about the adjustment of adolescent mothers and their children in later life, the question of how to enhance the efficacy of current intervention strategies aimed at reducing the adverse effects of early childbearing will be addressed.

The Baltimore study

The history of the Baltimore study and features of the research design were presented in Chapter 1. The sample is a predominantly black one residing in a large middle Atlantic city, and therefore the findings extend only to urban blacks. Although blacks contribute a disproportionate share of school-age births in the United States, they account for only a third of all births to mothers under age 18. How applicable our findings might be for the other two-thirds of teenage mothers is speculative at best. The participants in the Baltimore study were not selected at random but were recruited from a hospital clinic offering prenatal care to obstetric patients. However, since the majority of pregnant teenagers attended a clinic sometime prior to the birth of their child (i.e., over 90%; Singh, Torres, and Forrest, 1985), our sample may be fairly representative. Indeed, we found

130

that the women in the Baltimore study were broadly representative of black adolescent childbearers in the city generally.

Throughout the analyses of the maternal and child experiences, the results of our study are compared with data from several national surveys to determine the generalizability of the Baltimore findings. We were reassured in that most of the descriptive findings can be reproduced in parallel analysis of national surveys. Nevertheless, the Baltimore data are based on a single cohort that, like all others, has a unique historical experience. The women in our study came of age in the late 1960s, a time when public support was available. On the other hand, they may have been the last cohort of teenagers that believed early marriage was a viable long-term strategy for responding to premature parenthood. A substantial number left school in order to marry as soon as possible. Their daughters who become pregnant as adolescents will in all likelihood respond differently. Likewise, subsequent cohorts have greater access to abortion, which undoubtedly affects the number and characteristics of adolescent parents.

The life course of adolescent mothers

Based on the findings of the 5-year follow-up concluded in 1972, a certain amount of variation in the life course of the women in our study was anticipated. The oft-cited statement that "ninety percent of her life's script [is] written for her" when a girl has a child at the age of 16 appeared to be something of an exaggeration, based on what was known at the outset. However, we were unprepared for the extent of diversity that emerged when the results of the 17-year follow-up were examined.

Chapter 2 portrays how the variation within the sample increased in the 12 years between the previous and current interviews. In general, the situation of the young mothers was found to improve significantly over time. Between 1972 and 1984, 56% of the women in the study reported that they attended school at least part of 1 year. A sixth of the women completed high school during that period, a full third of all of those who had not graduated by the time of the 5-year follow-up. A substantial proportion of those women who had dropped out subsequently returned to get a high school diploma or GED. Moreover, many high school graduates continued or resumed their education in their twenties and even early thirties. Their commitment to further education continues today. Nearly a third of the women were in school for at least some time in the 5-year period just prior to the 1984 interview. By the 17-year follow-up, 30% of all the women in the study had received some postsecondary education, and 5% had completed college.

Their economic careers parallel their educational ones. Only 9% of the participants were not employed in any of the 5 years preceding the 1984 follow-up, and 60% had been employed all 5 of those years. At the time of the 1984 interview, more than two-thirds were currently employed, and three-fourths had worked in the past year. Most current jobholders had been regularly employed for a number of years and were earning between $10,000 and $20,000 annually. As might be expected from the high participation in the work force, two-thirds of the women had not received any public assistance in the preceding 5 years; only 13% were on welfare more or less continuously during that period. At the 17-year follow-up, about a quarter of the sample were currently receiving public assistance; some of these women also held part-time jobs and were only receiving supplementary payments.

The sample divides almost evenly into four distinct economic subgroups: those on welfare, the working poor with family incomes under $15,000 per year, those women with moderate incomes between $15,000 and $24,999, and the economically secure whose family income exceeded $25,000 in 1983, the last year for which we had complete information. In view of the conventional stereotype of teenage mothers, it is surprising that only a minority of the women, albeit a fairly significant one, are on welfare when they reach their early thirties. Perhaps even more unexpected is that a quarter of the women's current incomes placed them clearly in the middle class.

Lest too rosy a picture be painted of their economic circumstances, we must remember that the majority of those women doing well financially were currently married or living with a man. With few exceptions the single mothers did not earn enough from their own employment to place them in the top economic quartile. Virtually none of the married women was currently receiving welfare. Thus, marital and economic status, for those at the bottom and the top of the sample economically, were closely linked.

Almost four-fifths of the sample had been married, but only about a third were currently married in 1984 and just a quarter were still in first marriages. Although the women were only in their early thirties, two-thirds of first marriages had ended in separation or divorce, and just over half of those entering second unions had dissolved their marriages. Approximately the same proportion of women were currently married in 1984 as had been wed in 1972, when the 5-year follow-up was concluded.

Projecting from their behavior in 1972, the women seemed destined to exceed their desired family size by 1984. Surprisingly, however, many actually had fewer children than they either desired or expected in 1972. About one-fifth never had another birth and an additional two-fifths had only one more birth. Twenty-six percent had two births after the study child, and only 12% of the women had three or more subsequent births. *Close to two-thirds of all the births after the study child occurred within the first 5 years of the study.* This unexpected pattern of birth spacing suggests that with age, the women became acutely conscious of the costs of additional children and made strenuous efforts to curtail their fertility in their twenties and thirties.

The remarkable and unanticipated slowdown in the pace of family building was primarily achieved by voluntary sterilization. By 1984, 56% of the women in our sample had been medically sterilized, a figure that well exceeds the national average for black women in their early thirties. Over a third of the women with a single child, more than half with two children, and nearly three-fourths of those with three or more children were sterilized. At higher levels of parity, never- and previously married women were just as likely to be sterilized as were currently married women. The willingness to limit subsequent childbearing is an important determinant of long-term successful adaptation. Compared to their counterparts in national studies, the Baltimore women may have had better access to obstetric care, making sterilization more likely. This could well explain why they had a smaller family size on average than black teenage mothers of comparable age in the national surveys.

Although the adolescent mothers in this study fared much better in later life (in terms of jobs, welfare, and subsequent childbearing) than many observers would have predicted, they unquestionably remained at a disadvantage compared to women who postponed childbearing. The blacks in the Baltimore sample were compared to black women of similar age who had their first child *after* age 20 in several different national surveys. The results revealed that the Baltimore mothers were less likely to achieve educationally, more likely to be receiving welfare, and less likely to be currently married than the later childbearers in the national surveys. Differences were not seen in employment rates and family size, however.

In sum, many teenage parents seem to stage a recovery of sorts in later life. Most do not fit the popular image of the poorly educated, unemployed woman with a large number of children living on public assistance. Nonetheless, early childbearing exacts a price for many women. Premature parenthood diminishes the chance of economic mobility, in part by restricting educational and occupational opportunities, but also in large measure because it decreases the likelihood of marriage and marital stability. A strong implication of these results is that teenage childbearers do worse because they are much more likely in later life to become female heads of households, primarily or exclusively dependent on their own earning ability.

Explaining life-course trajectories

How can we account for the differences in the life-course trajectories of the adolescent mothers? Why do some women seem to recover from the burden of having a child early in life while others do not? Chapter 3 reviews the determi-

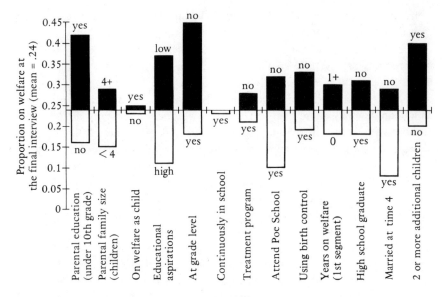

Figure 6.1. Predictors of economic dependence in 1984

nants of successful management of early childbearing. The analysis focused on two main adulthood outcomes, namely, whether the mother was currently on welfare, and whether she had limited her fertility to fewer than three children. Potential determinants included the young mother's personal attributes, the availability of social support, her involvement in two intervention programs, and different career decisions following the birth of her first child. Although by no means a complete inventory of the full range of potentially important influences on economic and fertility status in adulthood, this large and varied set of factors might be expected to affect these outcomes in later life.

To summarize the distinct contribution of each particular influence, we extrapolate from the results of the multivariate analysis by posing a series of hypothetical questions. Suppose, for example, that all mothers had received welfare for at least part of their childhood, what *proportion* would then be receiving public assistance in 1984? Such a question has more than heuristic value if a particular variable is subject to change by social intervention. The estimates of the unique contribution of major determinants of life-course trajectories, shown in Figures 6.1, 6.2, and 6.3, are based on the multivariate findings reported in Chapter 3. (See Appendix G for details about computation.)

Returning to the preceding hypothetical question, if all respondents had been on welfare as children, 25% would be receiving public assistance in 1984 compared to 24% if none of the mothers had been on welfare during childhood. Clearly, being on welfare as a child has negligible effects on the chance of re-

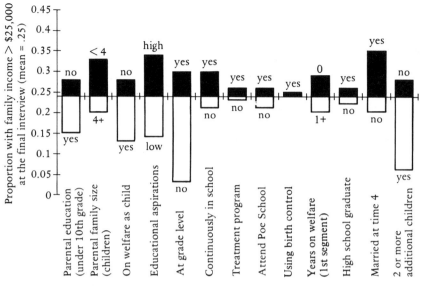

Figure 6.2. Predictors of economic security in 1984

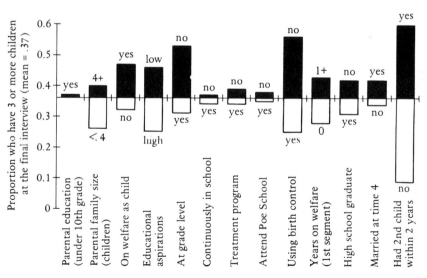

Figure 6.3. Predictors of large family size in 1984

ceiving assistance in 1984. Figures 6.1, 6.2, and 6.3 present, for the economic and fertility outcomes, respectively, parallel estimates. If all respondents had received welfare as children, 47% would have three or more children. If none had received such aid, only 32% would have this many children. (The model provides estimates of both the direct and indirect effects, i.e., the influence through intervening variables of each determinant.)

Several potential determinants did not have any sizable effect on the various outcomes and were not entered into the equation. Many of the background, attitude, and situation factors measured during the first 5 years after delivery did not influence economic status or family size in 1984. For example, a number of features of the family of origin such as parental marital status (i.e., whether the adolescent mother had both mother and father present), maternal employment, maternal age, and marital status at first birth were not directly linked to the outcomes examined in the 17-year follow-up. However, as can be seen in Figures 6.1–6.3, several family background variables are important. But clearly, the adaptation to parenthood was *not* primarily shaped by the young mother's family circumstances at the beginning of the study. Moreover, the quality of the adolescent's emotional relationship with her parents had no important effect on her long-term adjustment to early childbearing. Possibly our qualitative measures were not sensitive to nuances in family interaction, but none of the items tapping parent–child relations at pregnancy or in the first year after delivery were related to a successful adaptation in later life.

Residential arrangements following pregnancy also did not generally affect the outcomes examined, at least directly. Adolescents who lived with their parents immediately after the birth of their first child did not on average do better in later life than those who immediately left their parents. However, an earlier analysis of data from the first phase showed that a brief coresidence with parents could indirectly affect future prospects of success by improving an adolescent mother's chances of remaining in school and by preventing a hasty and ill-considered marriage.

Not only was initial family support not strongly linked to an adolescent mother's fate in later life, a number of personal attributes and attitudes, often thought to be related to the adjustment to early childbearing, had little impact on a woman's later economic fortunes or fertility level. For example, age at pregnancy was unrelated to economic success or ability to limit family size. Women who were under 16 when the pregnancy occurred were neither more nor less likely to end up on welfare or have three or more children in 1984 than women who were over 16. Similarly, an adolescent's initial response to the pregnancy did not predict her long-term life course. Whether she was happy, surprised, or distressed did not influence success in later life. Indeed, virtually none of the attitudes she or her parents expressed during the pregnancy or just after the birth of the child forecast how well she managed over the long term.

Now let us consider the determinants displayed in Figures 6.1–6.3 that did affect a young mother's economic status and fertility pattern in later life. Similar determinants of economic well-being and family size are seen, although the strength of their effect varies somewhat according to the outcome. Looking first at the factors predicting economic success, only a few stand out as really significant. As already mentioned, whether a woman was on welfare during childhood was one. Family size was another. Women who came from large families are distinctly less able to recover economically from premature parenthood compared to those from median and small families. The most potent legacy from the family of origin, however, was parental education. Relatively few parents of the adolescent mothers were high school graduates, and almost half never went beyond the 9th grade. Women from families in which neither parent had reached the 10th grade were much more likely to be on welfare than women whose parents had completed 10th grade. If all of the parents had at least attained a 10th-grade education, the proportion on welfare would have been .16 compared to .42 if none of the sample reached this level (see Fig. 6.1).

Both parental education and the size of the family of origin probably are associated with cognitive, motivational, and resource factors. Parents with limited education and more children are undoubtedly less capable of assisting in their pregnant daughters' schooling, less willing to reinforce their educational aims, and also may have less ability to provide the emotional and material support necessary for education. Indeed, parental education was linked to the educational performance and aspirations of the pregnant daughter. Each of these factors was a significant predictor of economic success in its own right, independent of the parent's educational level. Whether the adolescent was behind in school at the time of pregnancy was a powerful determinant of her economic position in later life. If all of the adolescents had been at grade level, the proportion on welfare is estimated to be .18, whereas if all of the adolescents had been held back at least one grade, the proportion would be .45. School aspirations have a more modest direct effect on economic success. However, their indirect effect is large, strongly influencing an adolescent's chances of remaining in school, of receiving special education, and of using birth control (see Chapter 3). Accordingly, if all adolescents had high educational ambitions, the estimated proportion on welfare as adults would have been .11; if all had low educational aspirations, the proportion would have been .37.

Avoiding school attrition is one of the essential keys to both economic independence and security. Adolescents who completed high school before the 5-year follow-up were half as likely to be receiving public assistance and twice as likely to be economically secure in 1984. A substantial number of the adolescents in our study attended the Edgar Allan Poe School, a special program for pregnant teenagers providing instruction, counseling, and child-care assistance during pregnancy and encouraging a return to regular classes following delivery.

The Poe School significantly reduced the proportion of women on welfare in adulthood. Had none of the students attended the Poe School, we estimate that the proportion on welfare would have been .32, in contrast to .11 if all had received the benefits of the special school. This difference is sizable, especially considering that the estimate is net of family background, motivation, and academic performance.

Economic success also may be traced to the young mothers' ability to restrict further childbearing. The probability of both receiving welfare and of achieving economic security was strongly influenced by the number of additional births occurring in the 5-year period after the birth of the study child. Women who had two or more additional children by the 5-year follow-up were almost four times more likely to be on welfare and 72% less likely to be economically secure at the 17-year follow-up. Also, adolescents who were using birth control 1 year after delivery were somewhat less likely to be economically disadvantaged in later life. Contraceptive use was, in turn, more likely among girls who returned to school, especially those who attended the Poe program. Thus, adolescents who continued their education were less likely to have rapid repeat pregnancies, and, of course, those who avoided repeat pregnancies were more likely to remain in school.

The teens who were enrolled in the Sinai Hospital comprehensive perinatal care program were more likely to avoid economic dependency in later life, in large part because they practiced birth control in the year following the delivery of their first child. By slowing down the process of family building, they managed to lower their risks of going on welfare. Had none of the adolescents been in the comprehensive program, the proportion on welfare would have risen to .28; had everyone received the treatment it would have been .21. Although this difference is not as great as some just reported, it does suggest that the perinatal program did reduce the number of chronic welfare recipients.

If teens had received both the comprehensive medical service and the Poe School program, the reduction of welfare would have been quite sizable. Our projections indicate that participants in both programs had a probability of .10 of being on welfare as compared to .34 among the teens who received neither of the services. Again, it is important to emphasize that these differences are net of parental education, motivation, and academic performance. Clearly, these results provide compelling evidence that services around the time of the first birth can make a difference in lowering the long-term risk of economic dependency.

In a more detailed examination of the impact of social services on the long-term prospects of the teen mothers (not reported in this monograph), we discovered that the two interventions were most beneficial for the most disadvantaged young mothers. This finding replicates the results in Project Redirection, a comprehensive service program for teen mothers. Young mothers from AFDC families profited more from participation in the program than those whose families were not on welfare (Polit, Kahn, and Stevens, 1985). In the Baltimore study, the Poe School and Sinai programs made a larger difference for women whose parents were less educated and economically dependent than those whose families of origin were better off. Social services possibly offset, at least in part, the disadvantages of weak family support.

On the other hand, the Baltimore study results do not suggest that social services improve a woman's chances of attaining economic security. Long-term economic success seems to be influenced by events and actions occurring much later in life. For example, an important route to economic security is marriage, or more precisely, stable marriage. Women who remained with their families for at least 3 years after their first child was born were less likely to experience economic prosperity, perhaps because they delayed marriage too long or had difficulty establishing economic independence. Women who remained with their families for lengthy spells were also more prone to staying on welfare, which in turn forecast economic disadvantage in adulthood.

Clearly, schooling plays some role in the achievement of economic well-being. However, a large part of this difference is accounted for by the fact that more ambitious and capable women remain in school. Specifically, adolescents who were at grade level had far better prospects of economic success in later life. None of those who had failed a grade achieved a high family income in 1984 compared to close to a third who had not been held back. The effect of educational ambition is not as marked, but it still is sizable. By contrast, continued schooling is only weakly linked to economic advantage when we hold constant the characteristics of individuals who remain in school.

Schooling and the programs that promote continued education appear to have more impact in reducing economic dependency than promoting economic advantage. What does affect a woman's chances of prosperity? We have already mentioned the importance of marriage and of establishing independence from the family of origin. Another major determinant of economic success is fertility limitation. Women who restricted their family size in the early years of the study were three and a half times more likely to be economically secure in 1984. Fertility control not only improved a woman's chances of avoiding welfare and being gainfully employed in later life, but it slightly improved her chances of remarriage. (Women who had fewer than three children in 1972 had a higher probability of entering or reentering marriage by 1984 though they were no more likely to remain married if they were married at the 5-year follow-up.)

The ability to limit family size was influenced by many of the same determinants of economic well-being (see Fig. 6.3). Women who were able to delay further childbearing for two or more years were much more likely to restrict their family size over the long term. If all women delayed additional childbearing for at least two years, only .09 would have had three or more children in 1984 as compared to .60 if none of the women had been able to postpone the birth of the second child.

Effective contraceptive use immediately after the first birth is a critical factor in controlling the pace of family building. A very crude measure of birth control use 1 year after delivery strongly predicts family size in 1984. As reported in Chapter 3, adolescents who were using contraception at this time were more educationally ambitious and had a better record of school performance. They also were significantly more likely to have attended the Poe School. Apparently, participation in the Poe School program helped to motivate the young mothers to remain in school and perhaps equipped them with the academic skills to continue their education. Women who continued their schooling were more likely to avoid a rapid repeat pregnancy.

The direct effect of the comprehensive service program offered by Sinai Hospital in postponing births was negligible. However, participants in the program were somewhat more likely to be using contraception at the 1-year follow-up and hence less likely to experience a rapid second birth. Thus the Sinai service made a contribution, albeit a very modest one, to reducing the risk of excess fertility, primarily by its immediate impact on improving birth control practice. Specifically, our analysis implies that a reduction of .05 (or about 15%) in the proportion of mothers with three or more children (.39 to .34) could have been achieved by supplying comprehensive perinatal and family-planning services to all of the adolescent mothers.

Being on public assistance may increase the chances of additional childbearing. Women who received welfare as children were more likely to have three or more children than women who were not on welfare early in life. And regardless of their experience during childhood, women who received welfare during the first phase of the study had a much higher probability of having larger families. Lack of precise data on the timing of welfare prevents us from concluding that receipt of public assistance encouraged additional childbearing. Certainly women who were unable to delay additional childbearing were more likely to receive public assistance and remain on welfare. Whether once on welfare they were less committed to preventing additional pregnancies is difficult to demonstrate with the data at hand. Those on welfare immediately after the birth of their first child do appear to be at somewhat greater risk of having more children in later life than women who avoided public assistance. Of those known to be on welfare in the year following delivery, 41% eventually had three or more children as compared to 28% of those who were not. This modest disparity suggests that receipt of welfare early in life is, at most, a weak incentive for subsequent childbearing.

The children of adolescent parents

The women in the Baltimore study, for the most part, displayed a remarkable commitment to their children by juggling school, work, and child-care responsibilities. And indeed, the majority succeeded in their efforts, as evidenced by the small number of chronic welfare dependents, the large number of high school graduates, and their relatively small families. However, their demanding life circumstances affected the environment in which their children were reared, so that the costs of teenage parenthood sometimes may have been borne by their offspring.

Children encountered a variety of conditions that shaped their development adversely: living in poverty, in single-parent households, with divorced mothers, with low or no paternal support, and with intermittent maternal separations. But again, great diversity in life experiences was evident; it was impossible to identify even three families with similar characteristics matching the three prototypic families featured in this book. This fact itself illustrates the breadth and complexity of life-course experiences of our families.

However, the childhoods of many of the Baltimore offspring were characterized by change in residential patterns, child care, and adult male support. About 10% were living with neither biological parent. And of those currently living with their mothers, almost a third had been separated from them for part of their childhood. Separations were sometimes due to disciplinary, marital, and custodial problems but more often were occasioned by educational or career objectives. Maternal separation in the infancy and preschool years has been shown to have negative consequences for eventual well-being of children (cf. Bowlby, 1969; Lamb et al., 1985; Rutter, 1979a). Whether maternal separations in later childhood have similar effects, it is clear that such transitions disrupt family and peer relationships.

Residing together, even continuously, is not necessarily an indication that the mother was the primary caregiver. Because so many mothers wanted to finish school and enter the job market, shared child-care arrangements were commonplace. Nearly two-fifths of the mothers were sharing care with other relatives (usually their mother) when their firstborns were toddlers. At the 5-year follow-up, almost half of the preschoolers had another adult spending as much time taking care of them as the mother. This pattern of shared caregiving responsibility was facilitated, in part, by maintaining residence with grandparents. Almost a quarter of the Baltimore children lived in their grandparents' homes when they were toddlers. By the preschool follow-up, however, only a tenth were in the grandparents' household. Even so, many young mothers continued to rely on their parents for major support in caregiving.

Shared caregiving was probably a good solution to the sometimes competing goals of furthering one's education and taking care of one's children. In fact, in single-parent families, the children who had a second adult involved in their care had higher preschool cognitive scores than those who did not. Early in the study, most of the mothers reported being satisfied with the child care arrangements they had worked out; mothers and children both seemed to profit from this solution. However, what was a "solution" to managing competing family and career sometimes developed into a problem in later years when mothers either insisted on assuming full responsibility against the grandparents' wishes or failed to do so when grandparents were inclined to relinquish their obligations. On balance, we discovered that long-term shared child-care arrangements conferred neither positive nor negative effects for children.

As we saw in Chapter 4, the impermanence of relationships with men implied the absence of paternal relatives for many of the Baltimore children and transient relatives for others. Only a sixth were living with their fathers by the 17-year follow-up. Another sixth saw their biological father weekly, however. In many cases, stepfathers and boyfriends took an active father role; one-third of the adolescents were living with a stepfather, and one-third of those not living with the biological father or a stepfather had someone who was "like a father" to them. Thus, while few children had an enduring relationship with their father, very few (7%) lived in a female-headed household for all of their first 16 years. Most had a father figure, or some combination of such figures, during their childhood. At the same time, only a minority of children experienced stable and continuous relations with a father figure.

In sum, the life-course decisions made by mothers often created family environments that were unsettling to their children: Most youth spent a portion of their childhood in a female-headed household, at or near the poverty level, being separated from their mother, in impermanent relationships with fathers and father surrogates, and with multiple child-care figures.

How these experiences translate into opportunities and limitations for the youth was a central feature of Chapters 4 and 5. Clearly, the Baltimore youth were not faring well as a group, although, as we have seen throughout the book, diversity was still the overriding feature. In the arenas of schooling, misbehavior, and sexual behavior, the Baltimore youth were at a disadvantage compared to the teenagers in the National Survey of Children whose mothers were older when they had their first child.

Restricting the findings to blacks, the offspring of the Baltimore women and those of early childbearers in the NSC look remarkably similar. Over half of the Baltimore youth have repeated a grade in school, close to half have been suspended or expelled in the past 5 years, two-fifths in the past year have had a school problem that has occasioned the visit of their parent, a sixth have run away, and a large proportion admit to using alcohol or drugs on a regular basis.

One area of behavior that deserves special notice is the tendency toward early childbearing among the adolescents. Although an extremely high proportion of the teens in the Baltimore study are sexually active, a much smaller proportion (7% of the males and 25% of the females) report pregnancies, and even fewer (1% of the males and 9% of the females) have had children by the 1984 interview. Males apparently are seriously underreporting paternity. In the 20-year follow-up currently under way, we are finding that approximately a third of the girls and a seventh of the boys have become parents. These figures may be a bit lower than many experts have predicted in the absence of data, but they are still quite substantial.

Interconnections between the maternal life course and child outcomes

By examining the occurrence, timing, and sequencing of multiple events in the mother's life course, we were able to explain some of the variability in economic status and fertility at the 17-year follow-up. Chapter 5 explores whether variability in children's outcomes can be explained by the timing and sequencing of particular maternal life events. The cross-sectional and longitudinal comparisons inform us of the role of environment on child growth and the continuity in developmental trajectories.

Continuity has been the central theme in developmental longitudinal research since the publication of *From Birth to Maturity* (Kagan and Moss, 1962) and perhaps since the advent of the testing movement (see Brim and Kagan, 1980). Continuity typically is believed to be domain specific, to be mediated by environmental events, to be fairly elusive in the infancy years, to become stronger in the preschool years, and to be stronger for cognitive than social development (exceptions to this statement include aggressive behavior and conduct problems; Rutter, 1979b). Since the Baltimore study selected information on the preschool and high school years, it is possible to determine the level of continuity from early childhood to adolescence. Moderate to high continuity for academic and behavior problems was seen, in keeping with other studies (Kellum, 1976). For example, a one standard deviation change in the Preschool Inventory increased the likelihood of having failed a grade by 90%. Cross-domain continuity was not found, nor was continuity evident in the personality domain (although our measures were relatively crude).

Clearly, then, once a trajectory was set, in terms of academic or behavior problems, it was likely to continue. But what of environmental effects? We know that maternal characteristics are related to preschool functioning, and our findings support this. For example, a child whose mother was not married, was on welfare, had two or more children, and was not in school at the 5-year follow-up had a Preschool Inventory score 30 points (one standard deviation) lower than a child whose mother did not have these four characteristics. And, as adolescents, having a mother with these four characteristics (replacing not being in school with not being a high school graduate and having two or more children with having three or more) increased the likelihood of grade failure 11 times over that of a child whose mother did not have these characteristics.

We present analyses similar to other cross-sectional and longitudinal studies (Garmezy and Rutter, 1983; Kagan and Moss, 1962; Kellam, Ensminger, and Turner, 1977; Rutter, 1979a). Our study is unique, however, in its attempt to interconnect the mothers' life course and their children's developmental trajectories. Many mothers altered their life-course trajectories over the 17 years. How did this affect their children's life chances? Four different models were tested, one in which the mother's life course did not affect child outcome, one in which the maternal status had an influence in the early years of life only, one in which the influence was in the adolescent years only, and one in which maternal influences occurred at both time points. Not surprisingly, perhaps, the most predictive model was contingent on the maternal characteristic and child behavior under examination. Thus, environmental effects are fairly specific, rather than diffuse, and are contingent on the age of the child and the behavioral domain under consideration. Take, for example, academic success. Maternal welfare status influences schooling in preschool and high school; though a trajectory for academic failure is set in motion by early welfare experiences, which limits preschool functioning, moving off welfare will reduce the likelihood of subsequent grade failure, even though grade repetition is related to low preschool scores. In contrast, current marital status and educational status influence school performance in the adolescent but not in the preschool years, suggesting that later maternal events, independent of earlier events, may influence school-related behavior. Finally, high fertility is a negative predictor of academic performance early but not late, suggesting that rapid subsequent fertility reduces time and resources spent on the first child. Later births have less of an effect on children, perhaps because of the primacy of maternal time demands in the first years of life.

Using behavior problems as the child outcome, a different set of trajectories is found. Early, not late, welfare experience influences behavior problems; the early effect is still seen in adolescence because of strong life-course trajectories in behavior problems. In contrast, marital status is associated with behavior problems in the adolescent but not in the preschool years, just as was found for academic problems. Perhaps family support is more available in the early years to young mothers, so that not having a father in the household is offset by the presence of other adult relatives (Kellam et al., 1977). Finally, maternal education has little effect at either age point.

In brief, then, clear connections between the life courses of mother and children exist, and environmental effects are seen on academic and behavior problems. *However, no single model describes the impact of maternal career contingencies on the course of children's development.* Although most life-span developmentalists will not be surprised by this finding, few studies have been able to examine developmental trajectories as a by-product of changes in the maternal life course.

Policy implications of the Baltimore study

We introduced this chapter by distinguishing between policies aimed at preventing teenage pregnancy and childbearing and policies designed to ameliorate the negative consequences of early childbearing for teenage mothers and their children. Because our study concerns the later life of adolescent mothers, much more can be said about the potential impact of ameliorative strategies than preventive ones. But by their very nature ameliorative programs do not address the underlying causes of teen childbearing. Typically, their goals are to make poverty conditions less onerous (as in the case of AFDC), although some alter the future mother's economic status through education and job training. At best, these efforts do not greatly reduce the incidence of teenage childbearing as they can only lower the rate of subsequent births. The most plausible ameliorative programs are, by necessity, expensive and time-consuming. Furthermore, some policy analysts believe that economic aid and services may have the unintended consequence of reducing barriers to early parenthood, making early childbearing a more attractive strategy for disadvantaged youths (see Fuchs, 1983; Rindfuss et al., in press). This point is hotly debated in the face of little evidence to support or refute it. At best, ameliorative strategies can back up prevention programs, offering what many would consider "Bandaid" solutions to teenage childbearing. For this reason, we believe that our recommendations must address prevention as well as amelioration. We begin on more secure ground by discussing the direct implications of the findings from the Baltimore study and then join these results with some more general observations about preventive approaches suggested by our work and the research of other investigators.

Ameliorative policies

Perhaps the most striking result of the 17-year follow-up is the tremendous diversity in the long-term adaptation to early childbearing. Adolescent mothers do not do as well in later life as women who postpone parenthood, but many manage to offset partially the burden of having a child in their teens. The invidious stereotype of the adolescent childbearer underestimates young mothers' chances of recovery, as we have seen in the Baltimore study. Ironically, part of the handicap of being a teenage mother may come from a widespread perception that failure is virtually inevitable – a belief that may become a self-fulfilling prophecy. As one of the few reluctant participants in our study wrote us after the interview:

Please do not contact me or my family again. I have beat the odds. . . . I no longer wish to participate in this study of Blacks who are supposed to end up on the welfare. I think in the future you should help people instead of asking questions. . . . Yes, I am a success and I will help others to become productive, independent and proud individuals.

The undifferentiated negative image of the teenage mother has several sources. Successful teenage mothers are not socially visible whereas unsuccessful ones are very conspicuous because of their reliance on social services. The three-quarters of our Baltimore women who are gainfully employed are far less likely to come to the attention of the helping professions than are the one-quarter currently on welfare. Because they serve a small minority of teenage mothers, service providers do not come into contact with the complete range of individuals who make up the pregnant teenage population – those working as well as those unemployed and the women who have steady sources of income as well as those on public assistance. In addition, service providers may not have ample opportunity to see the long-term benefits of their efforts. They see young mothers struggling during their teen years, not those who are more settled a decade later. This selective perspective leads many service providers to the inevitable conclusion that all or nearly all teenage mothers have severe problems in later life.

The perpetuation of a pejorative image of teenage motherhood predisposes service providers to treat all teenage parents more or less equivalently. On the basis of incomplete evidence, they are inclined to believe that teen parents are destined to drop out of school and become dependent on welfare. If teenage mothers are inadvertently treated as though their life course will follow this trajectory, self-fulfilling prophecies may be established. As the results of this study suggest, program planners and practitioners need to know that teenage mothers may require quite different kinds of assistance, that success may come to these parents after the teenage years, and that the timing and sequencing of services may be critical.

But what about the high-risk teen – the group for which discussions about the cycle of poverty are most relevant? Even though they are a small minority of teenage parents, mothers from disadvantaged families are distinctly more likely to experience severe problems in later life than teenage mothers who were relatively better off at the outset of the study. Identifying with more precision the highest risk group is important to policymakers and practitioners. First, programs can be tailored to the specific needs of this population. For example, one might offer help in the form of material resources and the reinforcing of educational goals since both are not always adequately provided in the home. Second, more intensive and comprehensive programs can be designed for and offered to this group. Contrary to some of their peers, for whom the provision of only one or perhaps two services might make a difference, the highest risk group may require a wide variety of services, given the relative paucity of assistance provided by families and their relatively greater need for aid. Third, more systematic recruitment efforts might be required to capture what often turns out to be a very elusive group of young women. Maintenance in service programs can also be a problem. It is often the clients most in need of services who drop out of programs due to low motivation, poor skills, and limited social support to persevere. Thus, strategies to enhance motivation and ultimately compliance must be developed, especially to assist teenage parents at highest risk of economic problems. This could involve providing a combination of short-range incentives such as cash stipends or day-care services and long-range incentives such as education scholarships or the promise of job placement.

Although teens whose families have been in poverty for decades or generations may be most difficult to serve, they also may yield the greatest benefits. High-risk teens probably receive a disproportionate share of the resources directed toward the adolescent parent, and any positive change could result in a substantial saving of public funds.

Even more important than the family background of the teenage parent are her own academic interests and abilities. As we saw in Chapter 3, the adolescents who were educationally ambitious and at grade level when they became pregnant had a far better chance of avoiding economic dependency and excess fertility in adulthood than those who had limited educational goals and were behind in school. Of course, some of the weaker students would have experienced disadvantage regardless of whether they had become parents early in life, but early childbearing seemed to push many of the marginal students out of school. The high rate of graduation among the classmates of the teenage mothers and the later childbearers in the national samples is persuasive evidence that early parenthood makes more problematic the life chances of the less motivated and able youth, especially those from disadvantaged backgrounds.

In addition, adolescents who are less academically competent may be at higher risk of early parenthood than those who are more competent or motivated. The patterns of early childbearing among the adolescents in our study are a case in point. Eighteen percent of the daughters who were at grade level had become pregnant by 1984 compared to 32% of those who had repeated a grade. There can be no doubt that academic competence and high educational aspirations reduce the risk of adolescent childbearing and, if it does occur, its negative long-term consequences.

Not surprisingly, then, programs designed to improve academic skills clearly enhanced the probability of later success, as demonstrated by the impressive effects of attendance at the Poe School, which made a direct and large contribution to economic independence and small family size. The program clearly attracted students with greater academic talents and educational ambitions, but its salutary effect seems not to be due merely to selective recruitment. Apparently, the Poe School was successful in aiding academically marginal as well as competent students. Whether the school had different strategies or components for teaching the more or less academically competent students is not known. However, ameliorative education programs are essential to reach students with low motivation or repeated school failure. Returning to a regular high school program may not be a wise course for the low-ability student, given her previous school history, her added burdens of child care, and her possible focus on nonacademic aspects of regular high school activities.

The Sinai Hospital perinatal program, which offered an array of health, social, and family-planning services to a randomly selected subgroup of our study participants, had only modest success in promoting economic independence and restricting subsequent unwanted births. That this program had any measurable impact at all was impressive in view of the fact that the pathways to later success were not generally affected by other indicators of prenatal and postnatal care.

Although hundreds of similar programs exist around the country for pregnant teens and young mothers, very few systematic evaluations have been carried out. The best of these studies has produced only weak support for the value of services. Typically, only modest and short-term effects are found for educational continuation and pregnancy-prevention programs (Burt et al., 1984; Hofferth, 1985; Klerman, 1979; Klerman and Jekel, 1973; Polit et al., 1985). Some of these studies may have underestimated the benefits of programs. The findings reported here reveal a greater effect than has been previously detected. Adolescent mothers who received both the Poe School program and the services at Sinai were substantially more likely to avoid welfare dependency and limit their family size in later life. And the most disadvantaged mothers appeared to have gained the most from the receipt of services during pregnancy. The evidence from this study indicates that more attention should be given to the question of how to intervene more effectively rather than whether to intervene.

Making existing services more effective is not a simple task. Recent surveys have not turned up a large number of imaginative schemes for improving comprehensive programs or replacing them with alternative specialized services. Little is known about the components of programs that make a difference or how particular subgroups use various forms of assistance. Assessments of ongoing services as well as carefully designed experiments of novel components are urgently needed. At the same time, we believe it is necessary for service providers to have a more realistic perception of their prospects of affecting the lives of teenage parents. No ameliorative program is going to be powerful enough to overcome the multiple burdens that some teenage parents face in restoring the damage done by an ill-timed birth. Nor will any program be able to serve all of its participants equally.

Some adolescents will not take advantage of assistance programs no matter how dedicated the staff. In any case, modest gains are to be expected given the educational deficits of many of the participants. Those working on the front lines need to recognize that programs are cost effective even if they only boost school graduation rates or cut repeat pregnancies by a modest differential.

These lessons are equally applicable to programs aimed at preventing first pregnancies. Elsewhere, we and others have described the many problems that teens face in using birth control (Furstenberg and Brooks-Gunn, 1986; Hayes, 1987). Irregular sexual activity, fears about the safety of the pill and IUD, high tolerance for risk taking, the desire to conceal sexual activity, and poor communication with sexual partners all contribute to increasing the difficulty of the effective practice of contraception. In order to counteract the resistance to regular birth control use, programs must cultivate contraceptive skills and motivation by customizing services for the high-risk teen. This may mean extensive counseling and aggressive follow-up (possibly including home visits by a public-health nurse) as well as more school-based health programs. Family-planning services might also benefit from promoting more active decision making, especially in terms of engaging in sexual activity. Many sexually active teens, even teen mothers, have difficulty resisting the entreaties of male partners. Instructing teens to exercise more conscious control over their sexual decisions is likely to improve their ability to use birth control in the long run. Postponing a first pregnancy is the most effective way of forestalling the second.

Given the difficulties teen parents have in using birth control and the importance of controlling family size for long-term favorable outcomes, the availability of abortion is one part of an overall strategy for limiting the effects of early childbearing. Few of the women in the Baltimore study expressed any enthusiasm for abortion, but many, as Chapter 2 shows, resorted to abortion when they were unable to practice contraception effectively. Thus not just for prevention of teen pregnancy, but as an ameliorative policy, abortion should be available and accessible (Hayes, 1987). Recent and current efforts by antiabortion lobbies to restrict access to abortion, or to ban it altogether, could place a major obstacle in the path of teenage parents' attempts at recovery.

Preventive programs

Preventive programs are heralded as our best hope for altering the transmission of intergenerational poverty as well as altering the life course of individual teenagers. Myriad programs have been implemented, many dedicated to altering current fertility trends. Regrettably, their effectiveness either is not evaluated or, worse, seems limited (Hayes, 1987). The reasons for this are of great concern to policymakers. Perhaps our understanding of the causes of teenage childbearing is at fault. As noted in Chapter 1, the timing of marriage and parenthood is determined by the interplay of individual decisions, based on personal and economic considerations, as well as prevailing social norms. Most programs attack the problem on an individual level, rather than on a societal level. Western societies always have had less restrictive norms about parenthood timing than, for example, Asian societies. The United States, in particular, stands out among Western nations in displaying great variability in parenthood timing and a traditionally high tolerance for early childbearing. But early childbearing has become increasingly frowned upon as fewer and fewer teens possess the economic and social resources deemed necessary to establish a family. Over the past several decades, early childbearing has gradually come to be regarded as less normative and as potentially harmful (Rindfuss et al., in press).

Accordingly, one of the most potent prevention strategies may involve public-health campaigns, generated by local leaders, to inform youth about the potential costs of early childbearing. Such programs have the potential to alter community perceptions of teen childbearing, as well as the cultural context in which fertility decisions are made. Major problems exist, however, in implementing public-health campaigns. Little is known about how to target high-risk groups, what strategies are most effective in different communities, and what types of community involvement are likely to have a high payoff. Recently, marketing techniques have been applied to the provision of social and health services and to the alteration of health-related behavior that may be applicable to pregnancy-prevention efforts (Brooks-Gunn et al., 1986; Manoff, 1985).

On a more informal basis, it may be necessary for community leaders to speak out against early childbearing, bolstering the will of communities to resist early childbearing. For example, only a few years ago, black leaders were often reluctant to speak out against early childbearing.[1] Today, through efforts sponsored by the Urban League and the Children's Defense Fund, leaders in many communities identify early childbearing as a serious problem for black youth – and rates of childbearing have been falling in the black community.

The importance of the social context can also be highlighted by putting the United States' experience in cross-cultural perspective. A recent study by the

---

1 Since the problem of teenage childbearing by single parenthood is more prevalent in black than white youth, it is not surprising that black leaders are in the forefront of the movement to advocate community responsibility for the problem. Given the fact that the proportion of out-of-wedlock teenage births is increasing rapidly in white adolescents, we may see a similar position taken in white communities in the near future.

Alan Guttmacher Institute (Jones et al., 1985) compares patterns of teenage pregnancy and sexuality in Western countries, specifically in America and Europe
over the past two decades. Rates of teenage pregnancy and childbearing are
substantially higher in the United States than in other Western (or industrialized)
countries. Moreover, while U.S. rates of early childbearing have remained in-
tractably high, figures in Western Europe have declined over the past decade.
These differences may not be attributed to differences in the onset of sexuality.
Countries such as Sweden, the Netherlands, or England have similar rates of
adolescent sexual activity to ours, even though their rates of pregnancy are much
lower than ours.

What are these countries doing that we are not? Simply put, they have focused
not on teenage sexuality as a problem but on teenage pregnancy as a social
problem. European nations have taken a much more forceful position in preparing teens to assume sexual responsibility. They provide excellent and comprehensive sex education and contraceptive services and do so enthusiastically. In
so doing, they produce responsible sexual behavior among teens – high rates of
contraception and low rates of abortion and childbearing. Americans probably
have not faced up to their obligation to educate young people to assume sexual
responsibility. The National Academy of Sciences (NAS) came to this conclusion after reviewing current programs and policies toward teenage childbearing.
The NAS recommends lowering barriers to contraceptive use by increasing access to clinics, promoting contraceptive use in the mass media, and encouraging
males to accept the condom (Hayes, 1987).

Clearly, however, lowering the barriers to contraceptive use will not be sufficient if youth do not believe it is beneficial to defer parenthood. The NAS panel
also recommends enhancing the life options of disadvantaged youth (see also
Dryfoos, 1983). Large numbers of American youth, especially among those who
are poor and/or members of some minority groups, feel, with some justification,
that their opportunity to succeed is limited. The probability of reduced life chances
leads many youth to engage in behavior that further compromises their chances
of success. Immediate gains in status through sexual conquests and early parenthood may appear to be attractive in the short run, especially when long-term
prospects of obtaining employment are low. Poor, especially poor minority, youths
may feel they have little to lose by premature parenthood. Furthermore, the costs
of early parenthood may be perceived as relatively low, especially given the lack
of sanctions in some communities. An extremely difficult part of altering these
normative standards involves reestablishing community controls while expand-
ing social opportunities.

It is often said about teenagers who become parents that they elect to have
children because they hold no hope for the future. But it is at least as likely that
adolescent childbearing results from a despair of the present. Half of the adoles-

cents in our study were not at grade level in 1984. From our earlier investigation and the results of other research, school failure appears to be an important risk factor in early childbearing (Brooks-Gunn and Furstenberg, 1986). Our results reported here make clear that mothers who were behind in school at the time of their pregnancy had dismal prospects of later recovery. Thus, programs that provide remedial training for children at risk of school failure could be one of the most effective ways of combating early childbearing as well as enhancing the adjustment of teens who do bear children.

Conclusion

The limited success of many programs, preventive and ameliorative alike, may come as a disappointment to service providers. But their disappointment is not fully justified. The Baltimore study shows that many teen mothers stage a recovery in adulthood: They return to school after dropping out, find employment after a stay on welfare, and curtail fertility after one or two additional births. The timing and sequencing of the life decisions that result in different life-course paths differ across individuals, but the direction of these paths is often not set until after the first child has entered school and the mother has entered adulthood. This study highlights the fact that events occurring early in the lives of adolescent mothers are not the only ones to affect their later adjustment to parenthood. From a policy perspective, the opportunities for recovery that occur during adulthood have barely been tapped. Teens who managed the transition to parenthood effectively did better in the long run, as we saw in Chapters 2 and 3. But it is equally clear that some women were late bloomers who altered their life courses when they reached adulthood. Several routes out of poverty in later life were identified. Marriage and voluntary sterilization were the most dramatic life-course transformers, but anecdotal evidence reported in case studies of some high achievers indicates that services offered in adulthood to disadvantaged mothers can make a profound difference. A substantial minority of mothers got low-level jobs in government or private organizations that provided channels of mobility. Many mothers obtained a GED only after they learned that high school graduation was necessary for career advancement. Some women used welfare support to complete high school and even college before they returned to the job market.

Marriage was an important path to economic security in this study (see also Duncan, 1984). In American society the breadwinner role still constitutes a father's primary familial contribution. Given rates of unemployment for young black urban males, which in some cases are over 50%, women may perceive few economic incentives to marry. Men are present in the Baltimore women's lives, but often in impermanent and transient ways. Greater economic opportunities to contribute to family welfare may solidify the position of males in the family. Ameliorative programs focusing on education, job training, and stable job opportunities for disadvantaged males may be as important as similar programs for teenage mothers that we advocate. Put more forcefully, the problem of teenage parenthood cannot be solved by simply directing services exclusively to females. Indeed, our failure to address the marginal position of males in disadvantaged communities may contribute to the perpetuation of teenage parenting.

In general, greater sensitivity to developmental differences within the population of teenage parents and at different points in the life span is needed. Many women took advantage of family-planning services only after their second child was born by which point sterilization became an increasingly acceptable alternative to further childbearing. Similarly, many young mothers may willingly give up public assistance when their children become older and no longer require day care. In short, not all teenage mothers will pursue the same strategy of recovery.

A more carefully designed developmental approach to service delivery may reduce the number of teenage mothers who are unable to escape from poverty. We may need to construct bridges of opportunity for adults who have not made use of ameliorative services offered to them earlier in life. Maintaining and augmenting programs of adult education, job training, and family-planning services may be highly cost effective approaches to dealing with the quarter of our sample who become chronic or near-chronic welfare dependents.

Finally, it is essential to build programs that reach the next generation, the offspring of the adolescent childbearers. Although it would be ill-advised to single out the children of teenage mothers for special services, programs for neighborhoods and schools where rates of early childbearing are especially high could be designed. Early childhood educational programs are particularly promising in that they may alter the developmental trajectory of academic failure and behavior problems set in the preschool periods. Federal programs such as Head Start are designed to serve the poorest segments of our communities and tend to have the greatest effects for the most disadvantaged (Lee, Brooks-Gunn, and Schnur, 1986; McKey et al., 1985). Such programs have the additional benefit of allowing the mothers to pursue educational or job training.

The prescriptions for action that we have offered are probably too broad and too numerous to satisfy some policymakers who are searching for a simple formula to reduce the enormous costs associated with early childbearing. Most of our recommendations will have only a modest impact on the problem. Without backing away from this incremental approach, we insist that any dramatic change in the incidence of early childbearing in the United States requires the kind of aggressive public-health campaign that the government has adopted to reduce smoking or drinking and driving.

It would be comforting to conclude that such a shift in public sentiment is now occurring and that we are finally witnessing a more active and enlightened policy toward preventing teen pregnancy. In fact, it is too early to tell which way the political winds are blowing; the moral divisions that surround the issue remain deep. The release of the report by the Panel on Adolescent Pregnancy and Childbearing of the NAS late in 1986 reignited a smoldering debate about our national policy toward teen pregnancy although it also revealed a groundswell of public support for greater involvement at both the federal and local level. If this public support dissipates and we remain stuck in our present policy of indecision, the piecemeal and often contradictory strategies of the 1970s and 1980s will continue into the next decade with the same kind of ineffectual results.

Appendixes

Appendix A: Life-history calendar

INSTITUTE FOR SURVEY RESEARCH—TEMPLE UNIVERSITY   BALTIMORE STUDY   #599-374-02

CASE #: _____   INTERVIEWER: _____   ID #: _____

CALENDAR

R'S AGE/	1966	1967	1968	1969	1970	1971	1972	1973	1974	1975	1976	1977	1978	1979	1980	1981	1982	1983	1984
MARRIAGES																			
RELATIONSHIPS																			
SEPARATIONS FROM CHILD																			
PREGNANCIES																			
SCHOOL																			
JOBS																			
WELFARE																			

Appendix B: Reliability

Reliability of demographic variables

Reliability reflects the extent to which subjects provide consistent responses to identical or similar questions posed at different times. Reinterviews in a panel study are an ideal way of assessing the reliability of data. The 17-year follow-up interviews with teenage mothers in Baltimore afford an opportunity to check the consistency of selected items from the 1984 interview with data collected in earlier interviews.

An analysis of reliability must focus on the comparability of both the questionnaire items themselves and the respondents' answers to these items. Ideally, questions from the different interviews are identical. If a question asks about a single event occurring at one point in time, reports of that event should not change retrospectively. Parallel questions will produce inconsistent data only because of respondent or interviewer error. Since interviewer discrepancies were usually corrected in the cleaning and coding process, our main concern in this appendix is respondent error.

Lower reliability may result from a respondent's error due to problems of recall, motivational factors, communication, or knowledge (Sudman and Bradburn, 1982). Recall is an important factor in any question about behavior; over time, a respondent will become less certain of the timing or detail of events. Some degree of uncertainty due to problems of recall should be expected and is evident in our most recent data. Motivation is an important cause of error in responding to questions that are threatening to a respondent. Questions about behaviors perceived to be "socially desirable" or "undesirable" are threatening and may elicit socially acceptable responses from the respondent. Respondents may over- or underreport, respectively, behaviors considered to be socially appropriate (voting, education, marriage) or inappropriate (crimes, welfare, and unemployment). Furthermore, while problems of recall may increase over time, panelists may be threatened less by events in their distant past than by more current events.

Because of random error, no measuring procedure is perfectly reliable. How-

158

Table B.1. *Reliability of demographic variables (standardized-item alphas)*

	Marriage		School		Welfare	
	Alpha	*N*	Alpha	*N*	Alpha	*N*
Time 1	.70	288	.77	277	—	—
Time 2	.68	277	.81	256	—	—
Time 3	.75	267	.90	234	—	—
Time 4	.72	250	.85	224	.70	246

ever, between parallel items, results should be reliable except for discrepancies resulting from respondent error. However, respondents may in fact respond inconsistently to identical questions. An estimate of reliability is obtained from Cronbach's standardized-item alpha, which is always less than or equal to the level of reliability between items. Alpha and reliability are equal when the questions are truly parallel. A reliability of at least .60 is considered acceptable.

Demographic variables: marriage, school, welfare

Included in the 17-year follow-up interview is a calendar of demographic events. Data are collected on various life events by calendar year spanning the years from 1966 to 1984. Information on several of these events, including marital status, graduation from high school, and receipt of welfare benefits, is selected and compared with data originally collected in the first four waves of the Baltimore study.

Results of our reliability analysis, as represented by Cronbach's alpha, are shown in Table B.1. Our estimates of reliability for marriage and school data are clearly acceptable at all interview times. Because marriage and graduation from high school are both salient and socially desirable life events, reporting error due to problems of recall or underreporting will tend to be low. Welfare data are also reliable because our questions about welfare benefits are not parallel; most recently, however, we have little information available for comparison with the calendar.

Inconsistencies may be explained to some extent by nonparallel questions that result in timing errors. The calendar asks about marriage by calendar year whereas the previous four interviews record current marital status by whether the respondent was married at the time of the interview. If the respondent was married at some point during the year in question but not at the time of the interview, there will be a discrepancy in the data due to timing (see Table B.2). Also, questions about school attendance are nonparallel because the calendar asks about events by calendar year while a year of schooling takes place over a period of 2 calendar

Table B.2. *Inconsistencies in Baltimore data (% of total N)*

	Positive→Negative[a]		Negative→Positive[b]		Total
	N	%	N	%	N
Marriage					
Time 1	17	6	20	7	288
Time 2	45	16	12	4	277
Time 3	36	13	12	4	267
Time 4	29	12	17	7	250
School					
Time 1	5	2	3	1	277
Time 2	12	5	20	8	256
Time 3	18	8	3	1	234
Time 4	27	12	4	2	224
Welfare					
Time 4	38	15	15	6	246

[a] Positive→Negative: time $1 \rightarrow$ time $4 = 1$ (yes); calendar $= 0$ (no).
[b] Negative→Positive: time $1 \rightarrow$ time $4 = 0$ (no); calendar $= 1$ (yes).

years (September to June). We have corrected this problem to some extent by eliminating cases where mothers were in the 12th grade at the original interview and reported graduation from high school for the same year on the calendar. Welfare questions were altogether nonparallel except at the 5-year follow-up, so measures of reliability for these questions were not included.

Inconsistencies due to problems of recall and motivation are apparent for all three demographic variables we examined. The welfare data that we do have indicate that respondents are more likely to "forget" having been on welfare than to "admit" receipt of welfare that they originally denied. Due to differences between calendar and school years, respondents would be more likely to report in retrospect that they graduated from high school in a given year when originally they did not report their graduation. However, because we have eliminated a number of the negative to positive inconsistencies, problems of recall appear to be more common. Marriage inconsistencies appear less obvious. Positive to negative inconsistencies are more common although marriage certainly does not have the same stigma attached to it that welfare does. Conceivably, the high degree of marriage dissolution among these teenage mothers lends itself to a denial of earlier marriage arrangements. Overall, despite the sensitivity of the material gathered and the length of time over which these women are asked to recall detail, we have obtained reliability measures that can be considered quite acceptable.

Appendix C: Analysis of sample attrition for bias

Several procedures were used to examine possible biases due to sample attrition. First, ten key indicators of the young mothers' status at the beginning of the study were inspected: (1) age, (2) race, (3) length of residence in Baltimore, (4) frequency of church attendance, (5) school performance, (6) the marital status of her parents, (7) her mother's education, (8) whether her mother was a teenage parent, (9) whether she was on welfare before she became pregnant, and (10) whether she participated in the comprehensive health program at Sinai Hospital. Four of these variables were unrelated to attrition in the bivariate tables and were dropped from the subsequent analysis – mother's education, the marital status of the parents, whether the adolescent mother had been on welfare as a child, and whether she had participated in the Sinai comprehensive care program.

The remaining six variables were examined in a logistic regression analysis to determine the predictive value of each of the variables controlling for all others. A separate multiple-classification analysis explored potential interactions among the separate predictors of attrition. The multivariate procedures considerably reduced the number of determinants. The most powerful predictor by far was residential stability. Adolescents who had lived in Baltimore for less than 4 years at the beginning of the study were a third less likely to participate in the 17-year follow-up. Presumably, these women were more likely to move elsewhere and therefore harder to trace.

Consistent with earlier results, whites were much less likely to remain in the study. Their higher dropout may be explained in several ways. Whites were undoubtedly more likely to give up their children for adoption and therefore less willing to remain in a study about early parenthood. Many whites, especially those who remained single, regarded premarital childbearing as a personal disgrace and were therefore more reluctant to cooperate in the research. The attrition rate of whites who were still single at the child's birth was 62%, virtually eliminating this subgroup from the sample. Thus, it would be extremely hazardous to generalize from the tiny sample of whites in the study, who clearly underrepresent white single mothers.

The only other determinant of attrition that appears to be significant in the multivariate analysis was frequency of church attendance. Women who attended church a few times a year or less were less likely to remain in the study. Again, this factor might have been related to residential mobility. Regular churchgoers also may be more conforming and willing to serve as subjects in a research project.

Appendix D: Description of data sets used for comparison of socioeconomic variables with Baltimore data set in Table 2.2

National Survey of Family Growth, cycle III (1982)

The National Survey of Family Growth (NSFG), cycle III, conducted in 1982, contains information about fertility and family formation gathered through in-home interviews with 7,969 women between the ages of 15 and 44. This sample was the result of a 5-stage area probability design, and is intended to represent all women ages 15 through 44 in the noninstitutional population of the conterminous United States. Due to the complexity of sample design and the intentional oversampling of certain population subgroups, the NSFG user documentation recommends that the weights included in the data set be used when estimating from the sample.

Subjects covered in the NSFG include reproductive knowledge and sex education, births and pregnancies, adoptions, contraceptive knowledge and use, sterility and subfecundity, births intended and expected, infertility services, family-planning services, child care, detailed information about pregnancies (prenatal care, outcome, and child health), marital history, and demographic characteristics.

The NSFG was commissioned by the National Center for Health Statistics. A listing of publications based on the NSFG and copies of the cycle III questionnaire can be obtained by writing to the Family Growth Survey Branch, Division of Vital Statistics, National Center for Health Statistics, 3700 East West Highway, Hyattsville, MD 20782. References: National Survey of Family Growth, cycle III (1982) (machine-readable data file), prepared by the National Center for Health Statistics, Hyattsville (1984); and National Survey of Family Growth, cycle III (1982) (public-use data-tape documentation), prepared by the National Center for Health Statistics, Hyattsville (1984).

Current Population Survey, June 1983: fertility and birth expectations

The Current Population Survey (CPS) is conducted monthly to provide data for official government statistics on employment and unemployment. Currently, a

163

probability sample of approximately 71,000 households out of the civilian, non-institutional population of the United States is selected to be interviewed once a month for 4 consecutive months in 1 year, and again for the 4 corresponding months a year later. In order to approximate the population more accurately and allow for nonrespondents, weights are used in calculations using the CPS data.

The CPS contains comprehensive data on labor force activity–employment status, hours worked, occupation, industry, and earnings, during the week prior to the survey for all persons 14 years old and over. A secondary purpose of the CPS is to gather data concerning the demographic structure of the population, and therefore information is also recorded about the age, sex, race, marital status, veteran status, household relationship, educational background, and ethnicity of individuals. Periodically, more detailed supplemental inquiries are included on health, education, income, and work experience. Each June, supplemental questions are asked of women 15–59 to obtain information on their childbearing and future birth expectations.

The CPS is conducted by the Bureau of the Census for the Bureau of Labor Statistics. The statistics gathered update the decennial census and are used by the government as indicators of the nation's economic situation and for planning and evaluating government programs. Published reports about CPS are available from the Superintendent of Documents, U.S. Government Printing Office, Washington, DC 20402. References: Current Population Survey, June 1983: Fertility and Birth Expectations (machine-readable data file), prepared by the Bureau of the Census, Washington DC (1984); and Current Population Survey, June 1983: Fertility and Birth Expectations (technical documentation), prepared by the Data User Services Division, Data Access and Use Staff, Bureau of the Census, Washington DC, 1984.

National Longitudinal Survey of Young Women, 1968–1982

The National Longitudinal Surveys (NLS) are a set of studies designed to examine the sources of variation in labor-market experience and behavior among four age and sex groups in the United States population: women 30–44, men 45–59, and men and women 14–24. The surveys began in 1966 and have been continued through 1984. In 1979, a new cohort was added, youth ages 14–21.

In the analysis presented in Table 2.2 the data from the Survey of Young Women aged 29–36 are used. The women were interviewed for the first time in 1968 and followed through 1982. The cohort is represented by a multistage probability sample of 5,533 women, designed to represent the civilian, noninstitutional population of the United States at the time of the initial survey. A weight is used to correct for noninterviews, oversampling of certain population subgroups, sample attrition, and chance variation from population distributions.

Included in the NLS is information about labor-market experience: current employment status, characteristics of current or more recent job, and work experience; human-capital and other socioeconomic variables: early formative influences, migration, education, training, health, marital and family characteristics, financial characteristics, job and work attitudes, educational and job aspirations, retrospective evaluation of labor-market experiences, socialpsychological measures; and environmental variables.

The NLS was conducted by the Center for Human Resource Research and the Bureau of the Census under contract with the Department of Labor. An annotated bibliography of reports using the NLS data is available from Center for Human Resource Research, Ohio State University, NLS User's Office, 5701 North High Street, Worthington, Ohio 43085.

References: National Longitudinal Survey of Young Women 29–36, 1968–1982 (machine-readable data file), prepared by Center for Human Resource Research, Columbus, Ohio (1983); and National Longitudinal Survey Handbook, prepared by the Center for Human Resource Research, Columbus, Ohio (1983).

The CPS and NLS data used in Table 2.2 were made available in part by the Inter-University Consortium for Political and Social Research. Neither the collector of the original data nor the Consortium bears any responsibility for the analyses or interpretations presented here.

National Survey of Children, 1976–1981

The National Survey of Children (NSC) was designed and sponsored by the Foundation for Child Development to determine the effects that social changes in America are having on children and to help guide programs and policies that affect children's lives. The study consists of two waves – the original study, conducted in 1976 when 2,258 children aged 7 to 11 and 1,747 of their parents were interviewed, and a follow-up cosponsored by the National Institute of Mental Health done in 1981, when a subsample of the original children and parents was reinterviewed. An additional objective of the 1981 survey was a more specific focus on the effects of marital disruption and remarriage on children's well-being.

The study population was defined as children living in households in the conterminous United States, who were born between September 1, 1964, and December 31, 1969. A multistage sampling technique was used to select the sample. Interviews were conducted with the child and the parent most capable of providing information about the child, usually the mother. In 1981, the subsample reinterviewed contained all families with a history of disruption or high conflict, and a sample of all other families originally in the study.

Topics covered in the National Survey of Children include background information from the parent regarding marriage and family, residence, patterns of socialization, childrearing practices, attitudes toward marriage and family life, health, and demographic characteristics; information about the child from both the parent and the child including schooling, socialization, health, behavior, parent–child relationship, attitudes about family life, life satisfaction, and favorite activities. Additionally, a teacher from the child's school supplied information about the child's classroom characteristics, behavior, and performance. New content was added in 1981 to reflect the focus on marital disruption and to take account of the older age of the children.

Information about the National Survey of Children can be obtained from Frank F. Furstenberg, Jr., Department of Sociology, University of Pennsylvania, Philadelphia, PA 19104. A machine-readable data file and codebook are available from the same address.

Appendix E: Methods and procedures used in Chapter 3

The analytic approach is described in Chapter 3. Basically, we allow earlier measured variables to affect subsequently measured ones as well as the ultimate outcome variable of interest.

Table E.1 shows the variables included in this analysis. All variables have two categories. Some variables are naturally dichotomous, such as "is the respondent using birth control at time 2?" Other variables are polytomous, such as number of subsequent children born. For the polytomous variables, we have examined various contrasts and have chosen one that captures the greater impact on the variables being examined, that makes the most sense substantively, and that produces a reasonable distribution between the two categories. Since we have dichotomized all variables, we do not have to model further the functional form of effects. This is a major advantage given the broad audience we are trying to reach – such discussions of functional form can become quite technical and the relevant tests can become quite involved. In addition, our sample is very small, thereby making fine distinctions between various functional forms difficult. Instead, our goal is to identify the important factors leading to variability in the subsequent life course. Subsequent research should replicate our work and extend the analysis to consider the functional form of effects.

We used a commonly used logistic-regression package to estimate the multivariate models in this chapter (i.e., the logistic-regression package in SAS; see Harrell, 1979). The models that produced the effects discussed in Chapter 3 are shown in Table E.2. The SAS procedure estimates additive effects on the log odds of an outcome. We have taken the antilog of these coefficients, so the model becomes a multiplicative one. We find factor changes in the odds of an outcome easier to communicate to the general reader than additive changes in the log odds.

There are four sets of variables defined by their measurement chronology. Tables E.1 and E.2 list them from more recently measured to more distantly measured.

Table E.2 shows 13 estimated multiplicative models. The dependent variable changes as one moves across columns. The first three models show the direct

167

Table E.1. *Definition of variables used in the analysis and their percentage distribution*

	% Yes
Outcome variables	
Welfare (received economic assistance in last year)	24
Economic security (report family income less than $25,000)	25
3+ children (report having 3 or more children)	37
Time 4 or 1st segment variables	
High additional childbearing, 1st segment (i.e., 2 or more additional children)[a]	17[a]
Not married at 5-year follow-up	.70
On welfare ≥ 2 years, 1st segment	52
Not high school graduate, time 4	53
Time 2 variables	
Continuously in school (throughout pregnancy and the year following the birth)	23
Attended Poe School	35
Assigned to the Sinai program	59
Not using birth control, time 2	35
Time 1 variables	
Below grade level (reported age and reported grade suggest a grade failure)	23
Low educational aspirations (respondent self-rating)	49
Background variables	
Low parental education (parent with most education less than 9 years)	30
Large parental family size (4 or more siblings)	66
On welfare as a child (reports that family received welfare while she was growing up)	25

Note: In subsequent analysis, the yes category is assigned a 1; no a zero.
[a]When estimating effects on fertility, a variable indicating whether a second birth occurred within 2 years is substituted. Of this sample, 54% had a second birth in 2 years.

effects of all independent variables on the primary outcome measures. The next four models show the effects of previously measured variables on the time 4 or first segment variables. Similarly, the next four models show the effects of previously measured variables on time 2 variables. Finally, the last two models show the effect of three background factors on variables measured at time 1. Effects on a given endogenous variable can be seen by looking down the appropriate column; effects of a given variable on a range of dependent variables can be seen by looking across rows.

In deciding which effects should be emphasized, we consider (1) the magnitude of the effect – is it large enough to be substantively important?; (2) whether the effect is statistically significant – what is the likelihood that the effect could be due to sampling variability?; and (3) whether the effect is substantively inter-

Table E.2. *Effects of variables measured earlier in the life course on subsequently measured variables*

	Outcome variables			Intermediate variables									
	Welfare	Economic security	3+ children	A	B	C	D	E	F	G	H	I	J
Time 4 or 1st segment variables													
(A) High additional childbearing, 1st segment	2.92[a]	.30[b]	8.92[a]										
(B) Not married at 5-year follow-up	3.19[a]	.45[a]	.69										
(C) On welfare ≥ 2 years, 1st segment	1.97	.61	1.90[b]										
(D) Not high school graduate, Time 4	1.97	.78	1.68										
Time 2 variables													
(E) Continuously in school	1.25	1.51	1.07	1.22	1.21	.65	.35[b]						
(F) Attended Poe School	.32[a]	.72	1.12	.83	.83	1.07	.98						
(G) Assigned to the Sinai Program	.58	.95	.87	.78	2.05[a]	1.34	1.67						
(H) Not using birth control, time 2	1.51	1.40	1.90[b]	3.59	.95	1.14	2.44[b]						
Time 1 variables													
(I) Below grade level	4.01[a]	.21[a]	1.80	.89	.50[b]	.58[b]	4.85[a]	.36[a]	.57[c]	1.27	.89		
(J) Low educational aspirations	1.68	.54[c]	1.60	3.10[a]	2.20[a]	2.29[a]	3.97[a]	.35[a]	.42[a]	1.32	1.68[c]		
Background variables													
(K) Low parental education	3.90[a]	.53[c]	1.07	.99	1.04	.63	1.29	.62	.72	1.12	1.16	1.07	1.36
(L) Large parental family size	1.38	.71	1.17	3.59[a]	1.27	.69	2.52[b]	.74	1.03	.76	1.30	1.20	1.47
(M) On welfare as a child	.71	.64	1.34	1.35	1.07	3.13[a]	1.96	1.28	1.40	.63	.96	1.58	1.39
Constant	.02	2.08	.04	.03	1.29	.77	.12	1.36	.99	1.37	.35	.22	.66
Overall odds	51/159	51/159	76/134	37/173	55/155	100/110	96/114	53/162	80/135	86/126	76/137	48/167	109/106
χ² Value	66.70	41.05	78.01	29.61	12.57	23.41	78.24	13.60	14.80	4.29	4.51	2.19	4.54

[a] Significant at .05 level.
[b] Significant at .10 level.
[c] Significant at .15 level.

pretable. Very strong effects are recognized regardless of whether they were expected. Weaker effects that fit our substantive expectations are also discussed. In short, we use statistical tests as a general guide, and as only one criterion of an important effect. Given this strategy, it is important that all estimated effects be shown here even if they are not discussed in the text. Effects we consider as uninterpretable or unimportant may be judged differently by others.

Appendix F: Description and details of multivariate analysis reported in Chapter 5

In the text we describe only the general results from our analysis of "consistency across the mother's and child's life" and "connections between the life course of mother and child." Here we discuss these results in greater detail and describe how we reached the general conclusions presented in Chapter 5. The final table in this appendix presents the items comprising the child maladjustment indexes and measures of their reliability. These indexes were used in Chapters 4 and 5.

Consistency across the mother's and child's life course

Figure 5.2 shows several possible arrangements of life-course events. Events can be unrelated, they can be related in a Markov process where only the most recently held status is relevant, or they can be related in a more complex way such that past experience, in addition to most recently held status, is relevant. We say that the second pattern, the Markov process, characterizes the mothers' statuses we examine: welfare status, marital status, educational status, and fertility status. Table F.1 shows the type analyses that led to this conclusion. This table presents a series of four logistic regressions where the column variable is regressed on the variables that comprise the rows. We have not transformed the coefficients to multiplicative adjustments but have left them as additive changes in the log odds of some outcome. We chose not to make this transformation in this appendix to allow easier comparison with OLS regression estimates in subsequent tables. Note that only coefficients on and above the main diagonal are estimated, because, as in other analyses in this monograph, we allow earlier experience in the life course to affect subsequent events. Thus, being on welfare at time 1 is affected only by welfare experience as a child; welfare experience in the first segment can be influenced by childhood welfare experience and the mother's own experience around the time of her first birth; etc. Our claim that the process has a Markov character is supported by the coefficients along the main diagonal. All are quite large, speaking both substantively and statistically. Again, these coefficients are additive changes in the log odds of being on welfare at a given life-cycle juncture.

Table F.1. *Effects of previous welfare experience on subsequent welfare experience*

Independent welfare variables	Time 1	On welfare		Time 5
		2+ years in 1st segment	5–9 years prior to time 5	
On welfare as child (% yes = 25)	.99[a]	.34	−.09	.45
On welfare time 1 (% yes = 39)	—	3.99[a]	.11	−.21
On welfare 1st segment (% yes = 51)	—	—	1.14[a]	.76
On welfare 5–9 years prior to Time 5 (% yes = 51)	—	—	—	2.47[a]
Constant	−.72	−1.24	−.52	2.63
χ^2	10.6	132.3	20.5	73.5
Number Y/N	92/145	121/116	123/114	83/154

Note: Estimated effects are additive changes in the log odds of being on welfare at a selected time. Dashes indicate the effect was not estimated, i.e., not entered in this equation.
[a]Statistically significant at .01 level.

Note that there are two other positive coefficients in the fourth equation estimated. The .76 increase in the log odds translates into a sizable effect substantively (e.g., roughly doubles the likelihood of welfare in the most recent period), the .45 somewhat less so (e.g., increases by roughly 50%). We caution against interpretation of individual coefficients since sampling variability with this small sample is considerable. Instead, we focus on the pattern of effects: strong effects on the main diagonal and weak and inconsistent effects above the diagonal. This same pattern of effects is found for educational, marital, and fertility statuses.

Also in this section (consistency across mother's and child's life course), we claim that recognizable paths can be observed for the children by time 4, when the children are roughly 5 years old. We note that well-being measures at time 4 are associated with time 5 measures only in the same domain. This supports our contention that life-course trajectories can be identified early on. For instance, the Preschool Inventory is strongly associated with subsequent academic performance, as measured by the likelihood of failing a grade, but not with other behavioral or psychological measures. Similarly, the mother's report of behavioral problems predicts adolescent behavior. Evidence for these claims can be found in Table F.2. In this table the dependent variables comprise the rows and the independent variables the columns. The first two equations are estimated

Table F.2. *Effects of time 4 child measures on time 5 measures*

	Time 4 measures of child welfare				
Time 5 outcomes	Academic preparedness (Preschool Inventory)	Behavior reports (mother)	Psychological reports (mother)	Constant	χ^2/R^2
1. Failed a grade (yes/no)	$-.61^a$	$-.20$	.06	1.96	20.55
2. Intercourse by age 15 (yes/no)	.25	$-.54^a$	$-.08$	3.25	11.06
3. Delinquency (parent)	$-.05$	$-.26^a$	.08	1.91	.07
4. Bad behavior (parent)	.00	$-.28^a$	.01	2.36	.08
5. Delinquency (child)	$-.04$	$-.12^b$	.01	1.72	.02
6. Substance use (child)	.11	$-.10$	.05	1.18	.02
7. Psychological problems (parent)	.06	$-.22^a$	.02	2.25	.05
8. Psychological problems (child)	.10	.09	.08	.07	.04
9. Satisfied with aspects of life (child)	$-.00$	.01	$-.07$	2.27	.00

Note: Outcome indexes 3–9 are created by summing several response items. See Chapter 5 or Table F.11 for items that are included.
^{a}Statistically significant at .01 level.
^{b}Statistically significant at .10 level.

using logistic regression; these dependent variables are dichotomous (failed a grade = 1, zero otherwise; had intercourse by age 15 = 1, zero otherwise). All of the time 4 measures of child well-being (defined in text) have been adjusted so that their standard deviation equals 1.0. The remaining seven dependent variables, also standardized to a 1.0 standard deviation, have been regressed on these same time 4 variables using OLS regression. See text and Table F.11 for items included in these indexes.

Turning to the results, only academic preparedness (the Preschool Inventory) is associated with subsequent grade failure. The log odds of failing a grade are lowered by .61 (i.e., by a factor of 1.84) if the child scores 1 standard deviation above the mean on the Preschool Inventory test. Likewise the mother's reports of the preschooler's behavior (i.e., higher scores indicate more cooperative, polite, and obedient behavior) are associated with the mother's and child's reports of behavior at time 5. Remember that these effects are negative because the time 4 variables are coded here so that the better behaved receive higher scores. In the case of the parent report of delinquent and other problem behavior, lying 1 standard deviation below the mean, for instance, increases time 5 scores by over .25 of a standard deviation.

Next, parental reports do not do a good job of predicting substance use. Also, the time 5 psychological reports seem not to be associated with earlier (time 4)

parental reports of shyness and happiness. This could reflect either poor measurement on these variables or a real lack of consistency across the life course.

Finally, while not shown here the respondents' sex is associated with the
items analyzed in Table F.2. However, the effects of time 4 measures of well-
being are attenuated only very slightly by including a control on sex. Moreover,
there are no statistically significant interactive effects of sex and time 4 well-
being measures. Thus, academic and behavioral life-course paths can be identified quite early for both boys and girls.

Connections between the life course of mother and child

The analytic model is discussed in some detail in the text. It consists of a two-
block design: (1) Background variables and the mother's early life-course experience can affect the child's readiness for school (behavior, or personality development) at time 4, roughly 5 years of age; and (2) all of these variables, plus
subsequent life-course events, are allowed to affect adolescent school performance (behavior, or personality). See Chapter 5 for further discussion.

Estimation of this model requires two equations, consistent with the two-
block design. We will present the results for mother's welfare experience in
detail, and discuss other results more quickly. Table F.3 shows the effects of
mother's early welfare experience on measures of child welfare at time 4. As
independent variables, we have three contrasts: those reporting they were on
welfare as children (scored 1; zero otherwise), those reporting they were on
welfare when the child was born (scored 1; zero otherwise), and those reporting
2 or more years of welfare use in the first 5 years of the study (scored 1; zero
otherwise). As previously noted, the measures of child well-being have been
standardized to a standard deviation of 1.0. OLS regression has been used to
estimate these relationships.

Note that being on welfare as a child and being on welfare for much of the
study's first segment have negative effects on all three measures of child well-
being. Being on welfare as a child, for example, lowers one's score on the
Preschool Inventory by .34 of a standard deviation. Similarly, this background
experience is associated with more negative reports from mothers regarding behavior (lowers by .39 of a standard deviation) and with mother's reports of the
child's happiness, shyness, and boredom (lowered by almost .50 of a standard
deviation). In short, early welfare experience clearly affects these measures of
child well-being.

The second part of the model involves estimating the effects of mother's welfare experience and these time 4 measures of well-being on the time 5 measures
of adolescent well-being. Table F.4 shows these results. Dependent variables
(i.e., measures of adolescent well-being) comprise the columns of this table and
the independent variables comprise the rows. The first two variables are dichot-

Table F.3. *Effects of mother's early welfare experience on child's time 4 measures of well-being*

Mother's early welfare experience	Time 4 measures of child welfare		
	Academic preparedness (Preschool Inventory)	Behavior reports	Psychological reports
On welfare as child	$-.34^b$	$-.39^b$	$-.48^a$
On welfare at time 1	.28	.25	$.51^a$
On welfare in 1st segment	$-.42^b$	$-.54^a$	$-.58^a$
Constant	2.40	4.68	6.26
R^2	.05	.08	.09

Note: OLS was used to estimate effects. Behavior and psychological measures are based on mother's reports (high values, fewer problems).
[a] Statistically significant at .01 level.
[b] Statistically significant at .05 level.

omous, and we estimate the effects using logistic regression. Estimated effects are the additive changes in the log odds of failing a grade (coded 1 if yes; zero otherwise) and the log odds of reporting intercourse prior to age 15 (coded 1 if yes; zero otherwise). The other dependent variables are indexes introduced in Chapter 5 and analyzed in Table F.2. These indexes are treated as interval-level variables and are standardized so that their standard deviations equal 1.0.

Looking first at model A and the measure of academic performance (first column of Table F.4), note (as in Table F.2) that academic preparedness decreases the risk of grade failure. Lying 1 standard deviation above the mean on this set of tests reduces the log likelihood of grade failure by .63. Consistent with results in Table F.2, we do not allow earlier (time 4) behavioral and personality measures to affect subsequent academic performance. We include five measures of welfare experience. The first three are the same variables identified in block one of the model (estimated in Table F.3). The last two identify mothers who had 2 or more years of welfare experience in the period 5–9 years prior to time 5 and 0–4 years prior to time 5. Which of these variables have an impact on the adolescent's academic performance *net of the time 4 measure of academic preparedness?* Two effects are statistically significant. First, those on welfare in the most recent period are much more likely to have failed a grade. Recent welfare experience raises the log odds on grade failure by 1.19, that is, raises the odds by over 3 times. Interestingly, the other significant effect is negative. Net of school readiness and subsequent welfare experience, those on welfare as children are *less likely* to have failed a grade.

Perhaps those with welfare experience as children are especially motivated to

Table F.4. *Effects of mother's welfare experience and earlier measures of child's well-being on time 5 measures of adolescent's well-being*

	Failed a grade		Intercourse by age 15		Delinquency (parent)		Behavior problems (parent)		Delinquency (child)		Substance use (child)		Psychological measures (parent)		Psychological measures (child)		Satisfied with aspects of life (child)	
	A	B	A	B	A	B	A	B	A	B	A	B	A	B	A	B	A	B
Measures of child welfare, time 4																		
Academic preparedness (Preschool Inventory)	−.63[a]	(−.52)[c]	—		—		—		—		—		—		—		—	
Behavior problems (mother)	—		−.42[b]	(−.46)[a]	−.23[a]	(−.25)[a]	−.31[a]	(−.30)[a]	−.15[b]	(−.14)[b]	−.05	(−.05)	—		—		—	
Personality/psychological problems (mother)	—		—		—		—		—		—		−.10	(−.10)	.15[b]	(.14)[b]	−.07	(−.08)
Mother's welfare history																		
On welfare as a child	−.95[a]		−.06		.03		−.24		−.24		−.08		−.13		.10		−.09	
On welfare time 1	.04		.18		.04		−.17		.05		.01		−.13		−.29		−.37	
On welfare 2+ years of 1st segment	.71		.77[c]		.24		.22		.04		.13		.17		.08		.18	
On welfare in 5–9 years preceding time 5	−.69		−.25		.06		−.10		.04		.16		.16		.01		.17	
On welfare 0–5 years preceding time 5	1.19[a]	(.90)[a]	−.14	(−.01)	.08	(.18)	−.01	(−.05)	.29[c]	(.31)[b]	.06	(.17)	.06	(.16)	.05	(.04)	.12	(.18)
Constant	1.28	(.87)	2.49	(2.90)	1.88	(2.15)	2.59	(2.50)	1.65	(1.60)	1.31	(1.45)	2.01	(2.07)	.20	(.26)	2.28	(2.33)
χ^2	38.19	(25.53)	15.66	(8.37)														
R^2	—		—		.10	(.08)	.11	(.09)	.05	(.05)	.02	(.01)	.03	(.02)	.03	(.02)	.04	(.02)

Note: Dashes indicate the effect was not estimated, i.e., not entered in this equation. Time 5 measures scored: higher values, more problems.

[a]Statistically significant at .01 level.
[b]Statistically significant at .05 level.
[c]Statistically significant at .10 level.

Table F.5. *Effects of mother's early marital experience on time 4 measures of child's well-being*

Mother's early marital experience	Time 4 measures of child welfare		
	Academic preparedness (Preschool Inventory)	Behavior reports	Psychological reports
Own mother experienced a marital disruption	.12	.01	−.01
Married at time 1	−.17	.04	.08
Married at time 4	.21	.10	−.20
Constant	2.15	4.36	6.08
R^2	.02	.00	.01

Note: Behavior and psychological measures are based on mother's reports (high values, fewer problems).

escape dependency. We do not mention this result in the text because it was unanticipated and because we do not find our explanation just offered very compelling. Sampling variability could explain this finding and our strategy is to interpret very cautiously unanticipated results.

Model B (for each dependent variable in Table F.4) includes only the time 4 measure of well-being and the most recent well-being measure. This model tests a more refined hypothesis. Instead of asking if the mother's welfare experience is important, we ask if a specific aspect of that experience has an influence. Since a woman's welfare experience has some continuity (see Table F.1), there is an association (e.g., multicolinearity) among these welfare variables.

Similarly, examination of other equations shows that welfare experience has little influence on the behavioral or psychological well-being measures. There is some evidence of an association between the mother's recent welfare experience and both the mother's report of the child's delinquent behavior and the child's report. Otherwise, mother's welfare experience does not predict well these outcomes.

Tables F.5, F.6, and F.7 show the effects of mother's early marital, educational, and fertility experience, respectively, on the time 4 measures of child well-being. Overall, effects are weaker than for welfare experience. Early marital experience seems to have no predictive power whatsoever. In terms of the mother's educational experience (Table F.6), her child's school readiness seems to be affected by low grandparents' education. This could reflect an impoverished home environment including fewer educational resources. In addition, if the mother was at grade level and remained in school following the pregnancy,

Table F.6. *Effects of mother's early educational experience on time 4 measures of child's well-being*

Mother's early education experience	Time 4 measures of child welfare		
	Academic preparedness (Preschool Inventory)	Behavior reports	Psychological reports
Parents' education low	−.52[a]	−.10	−.27[c]
At grade level, time 1	.28	.18	.39[b]
Attended school, 2+ years, 1st segment	.22	.19	−.21
Constant	2.10	4.23	5.85
R^2	.09	.01	.05

Note: Behavior and psychological measures are based on mother's reports (high values, fewer problems).
[a] Statistically significant at .01 level.
[b] Statistically significant at .05 level.
[c] Statistically significant at .10 level.

Table F.7. *Effects of mother's early fertility experience on time 4 measures of child's well-being*

Mother's early fertility experience	Time 4 measures of child welfare		
	Academic preparedness (Preschool Inventory)	Behavior reports	Psychological reports
Large parental family size	−.12	.05	−.01
2nd child within 2 years of the 1st	−.28[a]	−.14	−.32[b]
2+ additional children in 1st segment	.03	−.17	.21
Constant	2.43	4.48	6.19
R^2	.01	.01	.02

Note: Behavior and psychological measures are based on mother's reports (high value, fewer problems).
[a] Statistically significant at .10 level.
[b] Statistically significant at .05 level.

Table F.8. *Effects of mother's marital experience and earlier measures of child's well-being on time 5 measures of adolescent's well-being*

	Failed a grade		Intercourse by age 15		Delinquency (parent)		Behavior problems (parent)		Delinquency (child)		Substance use (child)		Psychological measures (parent)		Psychological measures (child)		Satisfied with aspects of life (child)	
	A	B	A	B	A	B	A	B	A	B	A	B	A	B	A	B	A	B
Measures of child welfare, time 4																		
Academic preparedness (Preschool Inventory)	-.60ᵃ	(-.60)ᵃ	—		—		—		—		—		—		—		—	
Behavior Problems (mother)	—		-.47ᵃ	(-.46)ᵃ	-.26ᵃ	(-.27)ᵃ	-.28ᵃ	(-.29)ᵃ	-.16ᵇ	(-.16)ᵇ	-.07	(-.07)ᵇ	—		—		—	
Personality/psychological problems (mother)	—		—		—		—		—		—		-.13	(-.11)	.13	(.13)ᵇ	-.10	(-.09)
Mother's marital history																		
Ever divorced	.22		.39		-.10		-.09		.05		.02		.06		-.03		-.06	
Married time 1	.12		.21		-.02		.10		.09		.15		.16		.02		.11	
Married time 4	-.26		.20		-.26ᶜ		-.24		-.27ᶜ		-.23		-.53ᵃ		-.06		-.40ᵃ	
Married time 5	-.85ᵇ	(-.89)ᵃ	-.20	(-.14)	-.16	(-.22)	.07	(.02)	-.25ᶜ	(.31)ᵇ	-.21	(-.25)ᵇ	.17	(-.06)	-.05	(-.06)	-.13	(-.22)
Constant	1.57	(1.62)	2.84	(2.95)	2.41	(2.34)	2.51	(2.46)	1.91	(1.90)	1.64	(1.64)	2.35	(2.16)	.35	(-.06)	2.71	(2.52)
χ^2	26.28	(25.21)	10.60	(8.56)	—													
R^2	—		—		.10	(.09)	.11	(.09)	.06	(.05)	.05	(.02)	.07	(.01)	.02	(.02)	.05	(.02)

Note: Dashes indicate the effect was not estimated, i.e., not entered in this equation. Time 5 measures scored: higher values, more problems.

ᵃStatistically significant at .01 level.
ᵇStatistically significant at .05 level.
ᶜStatistically significant at .10 level.

Table F.9. Effects of mother's education experience and earlier measures of child's well-being on time 5 measures of adolescent's well-being

	Failed a grade		Intercourse by age 15		Delinquency (parent)		Behavior problems (parent)		Delinquency (child)		Substance use (child)		Psychological measures (parent)		Psychological measures (child)		Satisfied with aspects of life (child)	
	A	B	A	B	A	B	A	B	A	B	A	B	A	B	A	B	A	B
Measures of child welfare, time 4																		
Academic preparedness (Preschool Inventory)	-.54[a]	(-.55)[a]	—				—		—		—		—		—		—	
Behavior problems (mother)	—		-.41[b]	(-.46)[a]	-.25[a]	(-.26)[a]	-.28[a]	(-.29)[a]	-.19[a]	(-.15)[b]	-.08	(-.06)	—		—		—	
Personality/psychological problems (mother)	—		—				—						-.14[b]	(-.11)[c]	.15[b]	(.13)	-.07	(-.09)
Mother's education history																		
Parents' education low	.19		-.31		.05		-.12		-.17		.05		-.01		-.22		.15	
At grade level, time 1	-.22		-.23		.28		.17		.09		.25		.26		-.28		-.15	
Attended school, 1st segment	-.13		.82[b]		.11		.23		.20		.20		.23		.11		.18	
Finished high school, preceding time 5	-.81[b]	(-.93)[a]	-.11	(.16)	-.30[b]	(-.15)	-.11	(-.00)	-.40[b]	(-.28)[c]	-.18	(-.05)	-.18	(-.05)	-.07	(-.01)	.07	(.03)
Constant	1.83	(1.89)	2.89	(2.81)	2.17	(2.35)	2.34	(2.47)	2.12	(1.96)	1.47	(1.59)	2.15	(2.18)	.37	(.26)	2.34	(2.43)
χ^2	25.25	(25.89)	10.90	(8.60)														
R^2	—		—		.10	(.08)	.10	(.09)	.08	(.04)	.03	(.01)	.04	(.01)	.02	(.02)	.03	(.01)

Note: Dashes indicate the effect was not estimated, i.e., not entered in this equation. Time 5 measures scored: higher values, more positive.

[a] Statistically significant at .01 level.
[b] Statistically significant at .05 level.
[c] Statistically significant at .10 level.

Table F.10. *Effects of mother's fertility experience and earlier measures of child's well-being on time 5 measures of adolescent's well-being*

	Failed a grade		Intercourse by age 15		Delinquency (parent)		Behavior problems (parent)		Delinquency (child)		Substance use (child)		Psychological measures (parent)		Psychological measures (child)		Satisfied with aspects of life (child)	
	A	B	A	B	A	B	A	B	A	B	A	B	A	B	A	B	A	B
Measures of child welfare, time 4																		
Academic preparedness (Preschool Inventory)	-.61[a]	(-.59)	—		—		—		—		—		—		—		—	
Behavior problems (mother)	—		-.48[a]	(-.46)[a]	-.27[a]	(-.26)	-.29[a]	(-.29)[a]	-.15[b]	(-.15)[b]	-.05	(-.05)	-.12[c]	(-.10)	.15[b]	(.15)[b]	-.09	(-.08)
Personality/psychological problems (mother)	—		—		—		—		—		—		—		—		—	
Mother's fertility history																		
Large parental family size	-.41		.44		-.08		-.08		-.25[c]		-.32[b]		-.19		.09		.03	
Additional child within 24 months	.24		-.34		-.27[c]		-.14		.15		-.01		-.15		-.23		-.19	
2+ additional children, 1st segment	.68		-.08		.31		.22		.30		.17		.17		-.06		-.02	
3+ children, time 5	.19	(.40)[b]	.15	(.03)	.02	(.08)	-.03	(.07)	-.17	(.12)[c]	.08	(.18)	.00	(.05)	.31[c]	(.11)	.15	(.00)
Constant	.93	(24.60)	2.87	(2.81)	2.41	(2.04)	2.57	(2.27)	1.85	(1.48)	1.67	(1.10)	2.42	(2.01)	.16	(-.06)	2.47	(2.37)
χ^2	28.35		10.95	(8.40)	—		—		—		—		—		—		—	
R^2	—		—		.10	(.08)	.10	(.10)	.05	(.04)	.03	(.03)	.03	(.01)	.03	(.03)	.02	(.01)

Note: Dashes indicate the effect was not estimated, i.e., not entered in this equation. Time 5 measures score: higher values, more problems.

[a] Statistically significant at .01 level.
[b] Statistically significant at .05 level.
[c] Statistically significant at .10 level.

Table F.11. *Measures of maladjustment*

Parent's report: time 5

Delinquency (alpha = .60)
1. Since January 1977, about the time of the first interview, has he/she had any behavior or discipline problems at school resulting in your receiving a note or being asked to come in and talk with the teacher or principal?
2. Has (child) been suspended, excluded, or expelled from school since January 1977?
3. Since January 1977, has (he/she) run away from home?
4. Since January 1977, has (child) stolen anything, regardless of its value?
5. How many times, if any, has (child) been stopped or questioned by the police or juvenile officers?

Problem behavior (alpha = .69)
Tell me whether each (of the following) statement(s) has been . . . true of (child) during the past three months:
1. Cheats or tells lies.
2. Is disobedient at home.
3. Is disobedient at school.
4. Hangs around with kids who get into trouble.

Distress (alpha = .69)
Tell me whether each (of the following) statement(s) has been . . . true of (child) during the past three months.
1. Has sudden changes in mood or feelings.
2. Feels or complains that no one loves (him/her).
3. Is too fearful or anxious.
4. Feels worthless or inferior.
5. Is unhappy, sad, or distressed.

Delinquency (alpha = .52)
1. How many times, if ever, have you been stopped or questioned by the police or juvenile officers about something they thought you did wrong?
In the last year, about how many times have you:
2. Hurt someone badly enough to need bandages or a doctor?
3. Lied to your parent(s) about something important?
4. Taken something from a store without paying for it?
5. Damaged school property on purpose?

Dissatisfaction (alpha = .71)
Are you satisfied, somewhat satisfied, or not too satisfied with:
1. Your friends?
2. Your family?
3. Yourself?
4. Being a (boy/girl)?
5. Being an American?

Distress (alpha = .46)
1. Do you feel lonely and wish you had more friends?
2. Do you have days when you are nervous, tense, or on edge?
3. Do you have days when you are unhappy, sad, or depressed?
4. All things considered, (how) is your life going?

Table F.11. *(cont.)*

	Score
Parent's report: time 4	

Parents describe their children in different ways. Suppose you were giving (child) a score on the way (he/she) behaves. On this card is a list of things that describe children – and for each one I'd like you to give me a score from zero to 100. For instance, the first one is uncooperative or cooperative. If (he/she) is totally uncooperative, you would give a score of zero. If (he/she) were the opposite – perfectly cooperative – you would give a score of 100. Or you may give (him/her) a score anywhere between zero and 100. Where would (he/she) actually belong?

		Score
Behavior Problems (alpha = .76)		
a.	Uncooperative/cooperative	_____
f.	Rude/polite	_____
i.	Disobedient/obedient	_____
Personality/psychological reports (alpha = .42)		
b.	Shy/outgoing	_____
g.	Bored/eager to learn	_____
h.	Sad/happy	_____

then her child scored somewhat better on the Preschool Inventory. Finally, the only aspect of early fertility experience that is associated with the child's time 4 well-being is a short second birth interval (Table F.7). Those mothers who had another child within 24 months of the first had children who scored over .25 of a standard deviation below other children. Negative coefficients can also be seen for the remaining two dependent variables. In short, we find less evidence that the mother's early marriage, educational, and fertility experience is relevant for these measures of child well-being. But there is some evidence that a rapid second birth has pervasive effects and that the mother's educational history, if more favorable, increases her child's performance on the Preschool Inventory test.

Tables F.8, F.9, and F.10 show the effects of time 5 measures of well-being and mother's marital, educational, and fertility experience. These tables parallel Table F.4. In brief, recent marital, educational, and fertility experiences affect academic performance. There is also some evidence that being married at time 5 reduces the amount of delinquency and substance use. This latter finding is consistent with the notion that a two-parent family can provide better supervision of adolescents.

Construction and reliability of maladjustment indexes

The time 5 measure of academic performance is a single-item measure. Mothers were asked if the study child had ever failed a grade. Likewise, the "intercourse by age 15" measure is based on a single report from the adolescents. The remaining seven outcome measures are indexes constructed from multiple items asked of mothers or the children. The items comprising these scales and a measure of reliability are given in Table F.11.

Appendix G: Procedure for computing summary statistics in Chapter 6

The analysis in Chapter 3 was designed to show the causal paths by which independent variables influenced the outcomes of interest. In some cases a variable's influence was almost totally direct e.g.; there were no significant indirect effects. Other variables had weak direct effects but several strong indirect effects operating through other variables included in the model. Here we are interested in the relative magnitude of effects, both direct and indirect. Which variable has the greatest effect on these outcomes? To answer this question, we evaluated the change in the proportion on welfare (the proportion economically secure or having three or more children) that resulted from altering the characteristics of the population. For instance, given the observed proportion whose parents had low education, what proportion do we expect to be on welfare? If we now assume everyone's parents have low education and then in turn assume no one's parents have low education, we have a series of proportions that indicate the predicted impact of this variable. Such proportions are graphically presented in Chapter 6 for variables included in the analysis.

We chose to show the estimated effects in proportions because we felt they would be more meaningful to a broader audience than changes in odds or log odds. Since our prediction equation estimates individual likelihoods and not sample proportions, we transformed each coefficient by multiplying it by $[P * (1-P)]$, where P is the mean of the dependent variable (see Hanushek and Jackson, 1977). The transformed coefficient shows the change in the proportion of the dependent variable that would result from a one-unit change in the independent variable – an interpretation identical to a regression coefficient. Since all variables in our analysis are dichotomies scored zero or 1, the coefficient shows the proportionate change in the dependent variable that results from assuming everyone has the characteristic versus no one having the characteristic (e.g., change in independent variable's sample mean from 1 to zero).

This computation is straightforward for direct effects but less so for indirect effects. To illustrate, $Y = a + b_1 X_1 + b_2 X_2 + \ldots b_i X_i$, represents the equation estimating direct effects on the dependent variable. After transforming the coefficients as described earlier, the direct effects of X_1 to X_i equal b_1 to b_i,

Table G.1. *Combined direct and indirect effects of background and life-course variables on welfare and fertility outcomes*

	On welfare			Economic security			3 or more children		
	Yes	Mean	No	Yes	Mean	No	Yes	Mean	No
Measured at time 1									
Parental education low	.42	.24	.16	.15	.24	.28	.37	.36	.35
Parental family size large	.29	.24	.15	.20	.24	.33	.40	.36	.32
On welfare as child	.25	.24	.23	.13	.24	.28	.47	.36	.32
Below grade level	.45	.24	.18	.03	.24	.30	.53	.36	.31
Low educational aspirations	.37	.24	.11	.14	.24	.34	.46	.36	.25
Measured at time 2									
Not using birth control	.33	.24	.19	.24	.24	.25	.56	.36	.25
Not in treatment program	.21	.24	.28	.23	.24	.26	.39	.36	.34
Continuously in school	.24	.24	.23	.30	.24	.21	.37	.36	.35
Attend Poe School	.10	.24	.32	.26	.24	.21	.37	.36	.35
Measured at time 4 or across the first 5 years									
On welfare 1st segment	.30	.24	.18	.20	.24	.29	.43	.36	.28
3+ children at time 4[a]	.40	.24	.20	.06	.24	.28	.60	.36	.09
Not high school grad at time 4	.31	.24	.18	.22	.24	.26	.42	.36	.31
Not married at time 4	.29	.24	.08	.20	.24	.35	.34	.36	.42

[a] When analyzing number of children (i.e., three or more children), a variable measuring the interval between the first and second birth is substituted (i.e., had second child within 24 months of the first).

respectively. But suppose that X_1 can affect Y by altering the level of X_2 in addition to its direct effect represented by b_1. Our estimation equation now becomes $Y = a + b_1 X_1 + b_2 (I) + \ldots . b_i X_i$, where I is the regression of X_2 on X_1 ($X_2 = a_I + B_I X_1$). Given the direct-effects equation with the indirect effects equation imbedded in it ($Y = a + b_1 X_1 + b_2 [a_I + B_I X_I] + \ldots . b_i X$), we can estimate the magnitude of change resulting from moving everyone from category zero to category 1 of variable X_1. Moreover, we can decompose this effect into direct and indirect components by first considering only the direct effect and then considering only the indirect effect.

Clearly, this procedure becomes cumbersome when the direct effects and indirect effects are all those shown in Table E.2. But the work is made much easier by a microcomputer and a spread-sheet application such as Lotus 1–2–3. Table G.1 shows combined direct and indirect effects, for our three dependent variables, computed in this way. These effects are plotted in Figures 6.1–6.3.

Bibliography

Adelson, J. (Ed.). 1980. *Handbook of Adolescent Psychology*. New York: Wiley.

Alan Guttmacher Institute. 1976. *Eleven Million Teenagers*. New York: Alan Guttmacher Institute.

Alan Guttmacher Institute. 1981. *Teenage Pregnancy: The Problem That Hasn't Gone Away*. New York: Alan Guttmacher Institute.

Apgar, V. 1953. "A Proposal for a New Method of Evaluation of the Newborn Infant." *Current Researches in Anesthesia and Analgesia*, 32:260–267.

Apgar, V., and L. James. 1962. "Further Observations on the Newborn Scoring System." *American Journal of Diseases of Children*, 104:419–428.

Bachrach, C. A. 1984. "Contraceptive Practice among American Women, 1973–1982." *Family Planning Perspectives* 16:253–259.

Baldwin, W. S. 1976. "Adolescent Pregnancy and Childbearing – Growing Concerns for Americans." *Population Bulletin*, 31:2. Washington, DC: Population Reference Bureau.

Baldwin, W., and V. S. Cain. 1980. "The Children of Teenage Parents." *Family Planning Perspectives*, 12:34–43.

Baldwin, W., and V. S. Cain. 1981. "The Children of Teenage Parents." In F. F. Furstenberg, Jr., R. Lincoln, and J. Menken (Eds.), *Teenage Sexuality, Pregnancy and Childbearing*. Philadelphia: University of Pennsylvania Press.

Baltes, P. B., and O. G. Brim, Jr. (Eds.). 1978–1981. *Life-Span Development and Behavior*. Vols. 1–4. New York: Academic Press.

Baltes, P. B., and J. R. Nesselroade. 1973. "The Developmental Analysis of Individual Differences on Multiple Measures." In J. R. Nesselroade and H. W. Reese (Eds.), *Life-Span Developmental Psychology: Methodological Issues*. New York: Academic Press.

Bane, M. J. 1986. "Household Composition and Poverty." In Sheldon H. Danzinger and Daniel H. Weinberg (Eds.), *Fighting Poverty*. Cambridge, MA: Harvard University Press.

Bane, M. J., and D. T. Ellwood. 1983. "The Dynamics of Dependence: The Routes to Self-Sufficiency." Report prepared for Assistant Secretary for Planning and Evaluation, Department of Health and Human Services. Cambridge, MA: Harvard University Press.

Bane, M. J., and D. T. Ellwood. 1984. "Single Mothers and Their Living Arrangements." Paper prepared for the U.S. Department of Health and Human Services under Contract HHS-100–82–0038.

Bates, J. E. 1980. "The Concept of Difficult Temperament." *Merrill-Palmer Quarterly*, 26:299–319.

Bates, J. E., C. B. Freeland, and M. L. Lounsbury. 1979. "Measurement of Infant Difficulty." *Child Development*, 50:794–803.

Becker, H. S., 1963. *Outsiders: Studies in the Sociology of Deviance*. New York: Free Press.

Beckwith, L., and S. E. Cohen. 1984. "Home Environment and Cognitive Competence in Preterm Children during the First Five Years." In A. W. Gottfried (Ed.), *Home Environment and Early Cognitive Development: Longitudinal Research*. New York: Academic Press.

187

Bergner, L., and M. W. Susser. 1970. "Low Birth Weight and Prenatal Nutrition: An Interpretative Review." *Pediatrics*, 46:946–966.

Bierman, B. R., and R. Streett. 1982. "Adolescent Girls as Mothers: Problems in Parenting." In I. R. Stuart and C. F. Wells (Eds.), *Pregnancy in Adolescence: Needs, Problems, and Management*. New York: Van Nostrand Reinhold.

Blake, J. 1981a. "The Only Child in America: Prejudice versus Performance." *Population and Development Review*, 7:43–54.

Blake, J. 1981b. "Family Size and the Quality of Children." *Demography*, 18:421–442.

Blau, P. M., and O. D. Duncan. 1967. *The American Occupational Structure*. New York: Wiley.

Bloom, B. S. 1961. *Stability and Change in Human Characteristics*. New York: Wiley.

Bongaarts, J., and R. G. Potter. 1983. *Fertility, Biology and Behavior*. New York: Academic Press.

Bowlby, J. 1969. *Achievement and Loss*. Vol. 1. New York: Basic.

Bradley, R., and B. Caldwell. 1976. "Early Home Environment and Changes in Mental Test Performance in Children 6–36 Months." *Developmental Psychology*, 12:93–97.

Brim, O. G., and J. Kagan (Eds.). 1980. *Constancy and Change in Human Development*. Cambridge, MA: Harvard University Press.

Bronfenbrenner, U. 1979. *The Ecology of Human Development*. Cambridge, MA: Harvard University Press.

Bronfenbrenner, U. 1985. "Interacting Systems in Human Development: Research Paradigms, Present and Future." Paper presented to the Society for Research in Child Development Study Group, Cornell University, Ithaca, NY.

Brooks-Gunn, J. 1984. "The Psychological Significance of Different Pubertal Events to Young Girls." *Journal of Early Adolescence*, 4:315–327.

Brooks-Gunn, J. In press. "Transitions to Early Adolescence: Developmental Issues." In M. Gunnar (Ed.), *Minnesota Symposium in Child Psychology*, vol. 21. Hillsdale, NJ: Erlbaum.

Brooks-Gunn, J., and F. F. Furstenberg, Jr. 1985. "Antecedents and Consequences of Parenting: The Case of Adolescent Motherhood." In A. D. Fogel and G. F. Melson (Eds.), *The Origins of Nurturance*. Hillsdale, NJ: Erlbaum.

Brooks-Gunn, J., and F. F. Furstenberg, Jr. 1986. "The Children of Adolescent Mothers: Physical, Academic and Psychological Outcomes." *Developmental Review*, 6:224–251.

Brooks-Gunn, J., and F. F. Furstenberg, Jr. 1987. "Continuity and Change in the Context of Poverty: Adolescent Mothers and Their Children." In J. J. Gallagher (Ed.), *The Malleability of Children*. Baltimore: Brookes.

Brooks-Gunn, J., and D. Ruble. 1982. "The Development of Menstrual-Related Beliefs and Behaviors during Early Adolescence." *Child Development*, 53:1567–1577.

Bumpass, L. L., R. R. Rindfuss, and R. B. Janosik. 1978. "Age and Marital Status at First Birth and the Pace of Subsequent Fertility." *Demography*, 15:75–86.

Burt, M., M. Kimmich, J. Goldmuntz, and F. Sonenstein. 1984. "Helping Pregnant Adolescents: Outcomes and Costs of Service Delivery." Final report to Office of Adolescent Pregnancy Programs, NIH. Washington, DC: Urban Institute.

Buss, A. H., and R. Plomin. 1984. *Temperament: Early Developing Personality Traits*. Hillsdale, NJ: Erlbaum.

Cambell, A. A. 1968. "The Role of Family Planning in the Reduction of Poverty." *Journal of Marriage and the Family*, 30:2:236–245.

Card, J. J., and L. L. Wise. 1978. "Teenage Mothers and Teenage Fathers: The Impact of Early Childbearing on the Parents' Personal and Professional Lives." *Family Planning Perspectives* 10:199–205.

Carlson, E. D. 1984. "Social Determinants of Low Birth Weight in a High Risk Population." *Demography*, 21:207–215.

Cherlin, A. J. 1981. *Marriage, Divorce, Remarriage*. Cambridge, MA: Harvard University Press.

Chilman, C. S. 1983. *Adolescent Sexuality in a Changing American Society: Social and Psycho-*

logical Perspectives for the Human Services Professions, 2nd ed. New York: Wiley.

Clark, S. D., Jr., L. S. Zabin, and J. B. Hardy. 1984. "Sex, Contraception and Parenthood: Experience and Attitudes among Urban Black Young Men." *Family Planning Perspectives,* 16:77–82.

Clarke-Stewart, K. A. 1977. *Childcare in the Family.* New York: Academic Press.

Clewell, B. C., Brooks-Gunn, J., and Benasich, A. A. 1986. "Child-Focused Programs for Teenage Parents: Anticipated and Unanticipated Benefits." Unpublished manuscript.

Coleman, J. S., et al. 1966. *Equality of Educational Opportunity.* Washington, DC: U.S. Government Printing Office.

Collaborative Perinatal Study. 1984. *Adolescent Pregnancy and Childbearing: Rates, Trends, and Research Findings.* Washington, DC: National Institute of Child and Human Development.

Committee to Study the Prevention of Low Birthweight (Institute of Medicine) 1985. *Preventing Low Birthweight.* Washington, DC: National Academy Press.

Congressional Budget Office, Congress of the U.S. 1978. *Childcare and Preschool Options.* Washington, DC: U.S. Government Printing Office.

Coombs, L. C., R. Freedman, and J. Friedman. 1970. "Premarital Pregnancy and Status before and after Marriage." *American Journal of Sociology,* 75:800–820.

Cooperative Tests and Services. 1970. *The Preschool Inventory Handbook.* Rev. ed. Princeton, NJ: Educational Testing Service.

Crandall, V. C. 1969. "Sex Differences in Expectancy of Intellectual and Academic Reinforcement." In C. P. Smith (Ed.), *Achievement: Related Motives in Children.* New York: Russell Sage Foundation.

Cutright, P. 1971. "Illegitimacy: Myths, Causes and Cures." *Family Planning Perspectives*, 3:25–48.

Cutright, P. 1972. "Illegitimacy in the United States, 1920–1968." In C. W. Westoff and R. Parke (Eds.), *Demographic and Social Aspects of Population Growth.* Washington, DC: U.S. Government Printing Office.

Darity, W. A., and S. L. Meyers, Jr. 1984. "Does Welfare Dependency Cause Female Headship? The Case of the Black Family." *Journal of Marriage and the Family,* 46:765–779.

Davis, K., and J. Blake. 1956. "Social Structure and Fertility: An Analytic Framework" *Economic Development and Cultural Change,* 4:211–235.

Demos, J., and S. S. Boocock (Eds.). 1978. *Turning Points: Historical and Sociological Essays on the Family.* Supplement to *American Journal of Sociology,* vol. 84. Chicago: University of Chicago Press.

Deaux, K., and T. Emswiller. 1974. "Explanations of Successful Performance on Sex-Linked Tasks: What's Skill for the Male Is Luck for the Female." *Journal of Personality and Social Psychology,* 29:80–85.

Deaux, K., L. White, and E. Farris. 1975. "Skill vs. Luck: Field and Laboratory Studies of Male and Female Preferences." *Journal of Personality and Social Psychology,* 32:629–636.

Dryfoos, J. G. 1983. "Review of Interventions in the Field of Prevention of Adolescent Pregnancy." Preliminary report to the Rockefeller Foundation, New York.

Duncan, C. J. 1984. *Years of Poverty, Years of Plenty: The Changing Fortunes of American Workers and Families.* Ann Arbor, MI: Institute for Social Research.

Elder, G. H., Jr. 1974. *Children of the Great Depression.* Chicago: University of Chicago Press.

Elder, G. H., Jr. 1984a. "Families, Kin, and the Life Course: A Sociological Perspective." In Ross Parke (Ed.), *The Family.* Chicago: University of Chicago Press.

Elder, G. H., Jr. 1984b. "Perspectives on the Life Course." In G. H. Elder, Jr. (Ed.), *Life Course Dynamics: From 1968 to the 1980s.* Ithaca, NY: Cornell University Press.

Escalona, S. K. 1982. "Babies at Double Hazard: Early Development of Infants at Biologic and Social Risk." *Pediatrics,* 70:670.

Featherman, D. L., and R. M. Hauser. 1976a. "Changes in the Socioeconomic Stratification of the Races, 1962–1973." *American Journal of Sociology,* 82:621–649.

Featherman, D. L., and R. M. Hauser. 1976b. "Sexual Inequalities and Socioeconomic Achievement in the U.S., 1962–1973." *American Sociological Review*, 41:462–483.

Featherman, D. L., and R. M. Hauser. 1978. *Opportunity and Change*. New York: Academic Press.

Freedman, D., A. Thornton, D. Camburn, D. Alwin, and L. Young-DeMarco. 1986. "The Life History Calendar: A Technique for Collecting Retrospective Data." Unpublished manuscript, Survey Research Center, University of Michigan.

Fuchs, V. R. 1983. *How We Live: An Economic Perspective on Americans from Birth to Death*. Cambridge, MA: Harvard University Press.

Fuchs, V. R. 1986. "Sex Differences in Economic Well-Being." *Science*, 232:459–464.

Furstenberg, F. F., Jr. 1976. *Unplanned Parenthood: The Social Consequences of Teenage Childbearing*. New York: Free Press.

Furstenberg, F. F., Jr. 1981. "Implicating the Family: Teenage Parenthood and Kinship Involvement." In T. Ooms (Ed.), *Teenage Pregnancy in a Family Context: Implications for Policy*. Philadelphia, PA: Temple University Press.

Furstenberg, F. F., Jr., and P. A. Allison. 1985. "How Marital Dissolution Affects Children: Variations by Age and Sex." Paper presented to Society for Research in Child Development, Toronto.

Furstenberg, F. F., Jr., and J. Brooks-Gunn. 1985. "Antecedents and Consequences of Teenage Parenthood: Young Mothers, Fathers, and Their Children." Grant proposal to the Robert Wood Johnson Foundation, October.

Furstenberg, F. F., Jr., and J. Brooks-Gunn. 1986. "Teenage Childbearing: Causes, Consequences, and Remedies." In L. H. Aiken and D. Mechanic (Eds.), *Applications of Social Science to Clinical Medicine and Health Policy*. New Brunswick, NJ: Rutgers University Press.

Furstenberg, F. F., Jr., and A. G. Crawford. 1978. "Family Support: Helping Teenage Mothers to Cope." *Family Planning Perspectives*, 10:322–333.

Furstenberg, F. F., Jr., R. Lincoln, and J. Menken (Eds.). 1981. *Teenage Sexuality, Pregnancy and Childbearing*. Philadelphia: University of Pennsylvania Press.

Furstenberg, F. F., Jr., C. W. Nord, J. L. Peterson, and N. Zill. 1983. "The Life Course of Children of Divorce: Marital Disruption and Parental Conflict." *American Sociological Review*, 48:656–668.

Garfinkel, I., and S. McLanahan. 1985. "The Feminization of Poverty: Nature, Causes and a Partial Cure." Paper presented at the meetings of the Population Association of America, Boston, MA.

Garmezy, N., and M. Rutter. 1983. *Stress, Coping and Development in Children*. New York: McGraw-Hill.

Gollin, E. S. (Ed.). 1981. *Developmental Plasticity: Behavioral and Biological Aspects of Variations in Development*. New York: Academic Press.

Grady, W. R., and N. S. Landale. 1985. "Marital Status at First Birth and the Timing of Second Birth among Adolescent Mothers." Presented at the Annual Meetings of the Population Association of America, San Francisco. (Authors are at Battelle in Seattle and Department of Sociology, University of Washington, respectively.)

Griffith, J., H. Koo, and C. M. Suchindran. 1985. "Childbearing and Family in Remarriage." *Demography*, 22:73–88.

Haggstrom, G. W., D. E. Kanouse, and P. A. Morrison. 1983. "Accounting for the Educational Shortfalls of Young Mothers." Unpublished manuscript, Rand, Santa Monica, CA.

Hamburg, B. A. 1981. "Teenagers as Parents: Developmental Issues in School-Age Pregnancy." In E. Purcell (Ed.), *Psychopathology of Children and Youth: A Cross-Cultural Perspective*. New York: Josiah Macy, Jr., Foundation.

Hanushek, E. A., and J. E. Jackson. 1977. *Statistical Methods for Social Scientists*. New York: Academic Press.

Hareven, T. K. 1978. *Transitions; The Family and the Life Course in Historical Perspective*. New York: Academic Press.

Harrell, Frank. 1980. "The Logistic Procedure." In P. S. Reinhardt (Ed.), *SAS Supplemental Library User's Guide*, 1980 ed. Cary, NC: SAS Institute.

Harvey, D., J. Prince, J. Bunton, C. Parkingson, and C. Campbell. 1982. "Abilities of Children Who Were Small for Gestational-Age Babies." *Pediatrics*, 69: 296.

Hayes, C. D. (Ed.). 1987. *Risking the Future*. Vol. 1. Washington, DC: National Academy Press.

Hecht, P. K., and P. Cutright. 1979. "Racial Differences in Infant Mortality Rates: United States, 1969." *Social Forces*, 57:1180–1193.

Henshaw, S. K., and K. O'Reilly. 1983. "Characteristics of Abortion Patients in the United States, 1979 and 1980." *Family Planning Perspectives*, 15:5–16.

Hofferth, S. L. 1986. "Updating Children's Life Course." *Journal of Marriage and the Family*, 47:93–115.

Hofferth, S. L., and C. D. Hayes. (Eds.). 1987. *Risking the Future*. Vol. 2. Washington, DC: National Academy Press.

Hofferth, S. L., and K. A. Moore. 1979. "Early Childbearing and Later Economic Well-Being." *American Sociological Review*, 44:784–815.

Hogan, D. P. 1978. "The Variable Order of Events in the Life Course." *American Sociological Review*, 43:573–586.

Hogan, D. P. 1980. "The Transition to Adulthood as a Career Contingency." *American Sociological Review*, 45:261–276.

Howard, M. 1968. "The Webster School: A District of Columbia Program for Pregnant Girls." Children's Bureau Research Report, no. 2. Washington, DC: HEW, Social and Rehabilitation Service.

Hunt, J. McV. 1961. *Intelligence and Experience*. New York: Ronald.

Jencks, C., M. Smith, H. Acland, M. J. Bane, C. Cohen, H. Gintis, B. Heyns, and S. Michelson. 1972. *Inequality: A Reassessment of Family and Schooling in America*. New York: Basic.

Jencks, C., M. Smith, H. Acland, M. J. Bane, C. Cohen, H. Gintis, B. Heyns, and S. Michelson. 1979. *Who Gets Ahead?* New York: Basic.

Jones, E. F., J. D. Forrest, N. Goldman, S. K. Henshaw, R. Lincoln, J. I. Rosoff, C. F. Westoff, and D. Wulf. 1985. "Teenage Pregnancy in Developed Countries: Determinants and Policy Implications." *Family Planning Perspectives*, 17:53–63.

Kagan, J., and H. A. Moss. 1962. *From Birth to Maturity: The Fels Study on Psychological Development*. New York: Wiley.

Kellam, S. G., M. E. Ensminger, and R. J. Turner. 1977. "Family Structure and the Mental Health of Children." *Archives of General Psychiatry*, 34:1012.

Kellam, S. G., C. H. Brown, B. R. Rubin, and M. E. Ensminger. 1983. "Paths Leading to Teenage Psychiatric Symptoms and Substance Use: Developmental Epidemiological Studies in Woodlawn." In S. B. Guze, F. J. Earls, and J. E. Barnett (Eds.), *Childhood Psychopathology and Development*. New York: Raven Press.

Keogh, B. 1982. "Children's Temperament and Teachers' Decisions." In R. Porter and G. Collins (Eds.), *Temperamental Differences in Infants and Young Children*. London: Pitman.

Klerman, L. V. 1979. "Evaluating Service Programs for School-Age Parents: Design Problems and Evaluations." *Health Professionals*, 2:55–70.

Klerman, L. V., and J. F. Jekel. 1973. *School-Age Mothers: Problems, Programs, and Policy*. Hamden, CT: Linnet.

Lamb, M. E., R. A. Thompson, W. Gardner, and E. L. Charnov. 1985. *Infant-Mother Attachment: The Origins and Developmental Significance of Individual Difference in Strange Situation Behavior*. Hillsdale, NJ: Erlbaum.

Lee, V., Brooks-Gunn, J., and Schnur, E. (1986). "Does Head Start Close the Gap? A Comparison of Children Attending Head Start, No Preschool, and Other Preschool Programs." Unpublished manuscript.

Leibowitz, A., M. Eisen, and W. K. Chow. 1986. "An Economic Model of Teenage Pregnancy Decision-Making." *Demography*, 23:67–79.

Lerner, R. M. 1984. *On the Nature of Human Plasticity*. Cambridge: Cambridge University Press.

Lerner, R. M., M. Palermo, A. Spiro, and J. Nesselroade. 1982. "Assessing the Dimensions of Temperament Survey (DOTS)." *Child Development*, 53:149–160.

McAnarney, E. R., and C. Schreider. 1984. *Identifying Social and Psychological Antecedents of Adolescent Pregnancy: The Contribution of Research to Concepts of Prevention*. New York: William T. Grant Foundation.

McCall, R. B. 1979. "The Development of Intellectual Functioning in Infancy and the Prediction of Later IQ." In J. Osofsky (Ed.), *Handbook of Infant Development*. New York: Wiley.

McCall, R. B. 1981. "Nature-Nurture and the Two Realms of Development: A Proposed Integration with Respect to Mental Development." *Child Development*, 52:1–12.

McCarthy, J., and J. Menken. 1979. "Marriage, Remarriage, Marital Disruption and Age at First Birth." *Family Planning Perspectives*, 11:21–30.

McCormick, M. C. 1985. "The Contribution of Low Birth Weight to Infant Mortality and Childhood Morbidity." *New England Journal of Medicine*, 312:82–90.

McCormick, M. C., J. Brooks-Gunn, T. Shorter, J. H. Holmes, C. Wallace, and M. C. Heagarty. 1985. "The Use of Outreach Workers to Increase Prenatal Care among Low-Income Women." Paper presented at the Ambulatory Pediatric Association Meeting, Washington, D.C.

McCormick, M. C., J. Brooks-Gunn, C. Wallace, T. Shorter, J. Holmes, and M. C. Heagarty. In press. "The Planning of Pregnancy among Low-Income Women in Central Harlem." *American Journal of Obstetrics and Gynecology*.

McKey, R. H., L. Condelli, H. Granson, B. Barrett, C. McConkey, and M. Plantz. 1985. *The Impact of Head Start on Children, Families and Communities*. Final report of the Head Start Evaluation, Synthesis and Utilization Project. Washington, DC: CSR, Inc.

McLanahan, S. 1985. "Family Structure and the Reproduction of Poverty." *American Journal of Sociology*, 90:873–901.

Manoff, R. K. 1985. *Social Marketing; A New Imperative for Public Health*. New York: Praeger.

Marini, M. M. 1981a. "Effects of the Timing of Marriage and First Birth on Fertility." *Journal of Marriage and the Family*, 43:27–46.

Marini, M. M. 1981b. "Measuring the Effects of the Timing of Marriage and First Birth." *Journal of Marriage and the Family*, 43:19–26.

Masnick, G., and M. J. Bane. 1980. *The Nation's Families: 1960–1990*. Boston: Auburn House.

Millman, S. R., and G. E. Hendershot. 1980. "Early Fertility and Lifetime Fertility." *Family Planning Perspectives*, 12:139–149.

Modell, J., F. F. Furstenberg, Jr., and T. Hershberg. 1976. "Social Change and Transitions to Adulthood in Historical Perspective." *Journal of Family History*, 1:7–32.

Modell, J., F. F. Furstenberg, Jr., and D. Strong. 1978. "The Timing of Marriage in the Transition to Adulthood: Continuity and Change, 1860–1975." In J. Demos and S. S. Boocock (Eds.), *Turning Points: Historical and Sociological Essays on the Family*. Chicago: University of Chicago Press.

Moore, K. A., and M. R. Burt. 1982. *Private Crisis, Public Cost: Policy Perspectives on Teenage Childbearing*. Washington, DC: Urban Institute Press.

Moore, K. A., and L. Waite. 1981. "Marital Dissolution, Early Motherhood and Early Marriage." *Social Forces*, 60:20–40.

Moore, K. A., M. C. Simms, and C. L. Betsey. 1986. *Choice and Circumstance: Racial Differences in Adolescent Sexuality and Fertility*. Draft project report, Urban Institute, Washington, DC.

Morgan, S. P., and R. R. Rindfuss. 1985. "Marital Disruption: Structural and Temporal Dimensions." *American Journal of Sociology*, 90:1055–1077.

Mott, F. L. 1983. *Fertility-Related Data in the 1982 National Longitudinal Survey of Work Expe-*

rience of Youth: An Evaluation of Data Quality and Some Preliminary Analytical Results. Columbus, Ohio: Ohio State University, Center for Human Resource Research.

Mott, F. L., and N. L. Maxwell. 1981. "School-Age Mothers: 1968 and 1979." *Family Planning Perspectives*, 13:287–292.

Namboodiri, N. K. 1972. "Some Observations on the Economic Framework for Fertility Analysis." *Population Studies*, 26:185–206.

National Center for Health Statistics. 1983. "Advance Report of Final Natality Statistics, 1981." *Monthly Vital Statistics Report*, 32:9. Hyattsville, MD: Public Health Service.

National Center for Health Statistics. 1985. "Advance Report of Final Natality Statistics, 1983." *Monthly Vital Statistics Report*, 34:6, supp. Hyattsville, MD: Public Health Service.

National Center for Health Statistics. 1986. "Advance Report of Final Natality Statistics, 1984." *Monthly Vital Statistics Report*, 35:4. Hyattsville, MD: Public Health Service.

Newberger, E. H., C. Newberger Moore, and J. B. Richmond. 1976. "Child Health in America: Toward a Rational Public Policy." *Milbank Memorial Fund Quarterly*, 54:249–298.

Norton, A. J., and J. E. Moorman. 1986. "Marriage and Divorce Patterns of U.S. Women in the 1980s." Paper presented at the Population Association of America Meetings, San Francisco, April 3–5.

O'Connell, M., and K. A. Moore. 1980. "The Legitimacy Status of First Births to U.S. Women Aged 15–24, 1939–1978." *Family Planning Perspectives*, 16:157–162.

O'Connell, M., and C. C. Rogers. 1984. "Out-of-Wedlock Births, Premarital Pregnancies and Their Effect on Family Formation and Dissolution." *Family Planning Perspectives*, 16:157–162.

Petchesky, R. P. 1984. *Abortion and Woman's Choice; The State, Sexuality, and Reproductive Freedom* (ch. 6: "Abortion and Heterosexual Culture: The Teenage Question"). New York: Longman.

Petersen, A. C., and W. E. Craighead. 1985. "Emotional and Personality Development in Normal Adolescents and Young Adults." In G. Klerman (Ed.), *Preventive Aspects of Suicide and Affective Disorders among Adolescents and Young Adults*. New York: Guilford.

Plomin, R. 1983. "Childhood Temperament." *Advances in Clinical Child Psychology*, 6:45–92.

Polit, D., J. Kahn, and D. Stevens. 1985. *Project Redirection: Conclusions on a Program for Pregnant and Parenting Teens*. New York: Manpower Demonstration Research.

Rainwater, L. 1970. *Behind Ghetto Walls: Black Families in a Federal Slum*. Chicago: Aldine.

Rainwater, L., and W. L. Yancey. 1967. *The Moynihan Report and the Politics of Controversy*. Cambridge, MA: MIT Press.

Riley, M. W., M. Johnson, and A. Foner. 1972. *Aging and Society: A Sociology of Age Stratification*. New York: Russell Sage Foundation.

Rindfuss, R. R., C. St. John, and L. L. Bumpass. 1984. "Education and the Timing of Motherhood: Disentangling Causation." *Journal of Marriage and the Family*, 46:981–984.

Rindfuss, R. R., S. P. Morgan, and C. G. Swicegood. In press. *The Transition to Parenthood*. Berkeley: University of California Press.

Rock, D. A., R. B. Ekstrom, M. E. Guertz, and J. Pollack. 1985. *Determinants of Achievement Gain in High School, 1980 to 1982*. Washington, DC: National Center for Education Statistics.

Rodriquez, G., J. Hobcraft, J. McDonald, J. Jenken, and J. Trussell. 1984. "A Comparative Analysis of the Determinants of Birth Intervals." *WFS Comparative Studies*, no. 30. Voorburg, Netherlands: International Statistical Institute.

Ross, H. L., and I. V. Sawhill. 1975. *Time of Transition: The Growth of Families Headed by Women*. Washington, DC: Urban Institute.

Ross, S. 1979. *The Youth Values Project*. Washington, DC: Population Institute.

Rutter, M. 1979a. "Maternal Deprivation, 1972–1978: New Findings, New Concepts, New Approaches." *Child Development*, 50:283–305.

Rutter, M. 1979b. *Changing Youth in a Changing Society.* Cambridge, MA: Harvard University Press.

Ryder, N. B. 1965. "The Cohort as a Concept in the Study of Social Change." *American Sociological Review,* 30:843–861.

Scarr, S. 1985. "Constructing Psychology: Making Facts and Fables for Our Times." *American Psychologist,* 40:499–512.

Scarr, S., and R. A. Weinberg. 1978. "The Influence of Family Background on Intellectual Attainment." *American Sociological Review,* 43:674–692.

Schnur, E. S., and J. Brooks-Gunn. 1986. "Who Attends Head Start?" In collaboration with V. Shipman. Unpublished manuscript, Educational Testing Service, Princeton, NJ.

Schultz, D. A. 1969. *Coming Up Black: Patterns of Ghetto Socialization.* Englewood Cliffs, NJ: Prentice-Hall.

Sewell, W. H., and V. P. Shah. 1968. "Parents' Education and Children's Educational Aspirations and Achievements." *American Sociological Review,* 33:191–209.

Singh, S., A. Torres, and J. D. Forrest. 1985. "The Need for Prenatal Care in the United States: Evidence from the 1980 National Natality Survey." *Family Planning Perspectives,* 17:118–124.

Sklar, J., and B. Berkov. 1974. "Abortion, Illegitimacy and the American Birth Rate." *Science,* 185:909.

Sonenstein, F. L. 1986. "Risking Paternity: Sex and Contraception among Adolescent Males." In A. B. Ester and M. E. Lamb (Eds.), *Adolescent Fatherhood.* Hillsdale, NJ: Erlbaum.

Stewart, A. L. 1981. "Outcomes for Infants of Very Low Birthweight; Survey of World Literature." *Lancet,* 1:1038.

St. John, C. 1982. "Race Differences in Age at First Birth and the Pace of Subsequent Fertility: Implications for the Minority Group Status Hypothesis." *Demography,* 19:301–314.

Sudman, S., and N. M. Bradburn. 1982. *Asking Questions: A Practical Guide to Questionnaire Design.* San Francisco: Jossey-Bass.

Taffel, S. 1980. "Factors Associated with Low Birth Weight, U.S. 1976." *Vital and Health Statistics,* ser. 21, no. 37. Rockville, MD: National Center for Health Statistics.

Tanfer, K., and M. C. Horn. 1985. "Contraceptive Use, Pregnancy and Fertility Patterns among Single American Women in Their 20s." *Family Planning Perspectives,* 17:10–19.

Teachman, J. D. 1985. "The Declining Significance of First-Birth Timing." *Demography,* 22:185–198.

Thomas, A., and S. Chess. 1980. *The Dynamics of Psychological Development.* New York: Brunner/Mazel.

Thomas, A., S. Chess, and H. Birch. 1968. *Temperament and Behavior Disorders in Children.* New York: New York University Press.

Thornton, A., and D. Freedman. 1983. "The Changing American Family." *Population Reference Bureau,* 38:3–44.

Trussell, J. 1985. "Teenage Pregnancy." Working paper, Office of Population Research, Princeton University, Princeton, NJ.

Trussell, J., and J. Menken. 1978. "Early Childbearing and Subsequent Fertility." *Family Planninig Perspectives,* 10:209–218.

U.S. Department of Commerce, Bureau of the Census. 1984. "Childspacing among Birth Cohorts of American Women: 1905 to 1959." *Current Population Reports,* ser. P-20, no. 385. Washington, DC: U.S. Government Printing Office.

U.S. Department of Commerce, Bureau of the Census. 1985. "Marital Status and Living Arrangements: March 1984." *Current Population Reports,* ser. P-20, no. 399. Washington, DC: U.S. Government Printing Office.

Vaillant, G. E. 1977. *Adaptation to Life: How the Best and the Brightest Came of Age.* Boston: Little, Brown.

Vinovskis, M. A. 1981. ''An 'Epidemic' of Adolescent Pregnancy? Some Historical Considerations.'' *Journal of Family History* (Summer): 205–230.

Wachs, T. D., and G. Gruen. 1982. *Early Experience and Human Development*. New York: Plenum.

Wattenberg, B. J. (Ed.). 1976. *The Statistical History of the United States: From Colonial Times to the Present*. New York: Basic.

Weiner, G., and T. Milton. 1972. ''Demographic Correlates of Low Birth Weight.'' *American Journal of Epidemiology*, 91:260–272.

Westoff, C. F., G. Calot, and A. D. Foster. 1983. ''Teenage Fertility in Developed Nations: 1971–1980.'' *Family Planning Perspectives*, 15:105–110.

Wilensky, H. L. ''Orderly Careers and Social Participation.'' *American Sociological Review*, August.

Wilson, W. J., and K. M. Neckerman. 1985. ''Poverty and Family Structure: The Widening Gap between Evidence and Public Policy Issues.'' Unpublished conference paper, Institute for Research on Poverty, University of Wisconsin.

Zabin, L. S., J. B. Hardy, R. Streett, and T. M. King. 1984. ''A School-, Hospital- and University-Based Adolescent Pregnancy Prevention Program: A Cooperative Design for Service and Research.'' *Journal of Reproductive Medicine*, 29:421–426.

Zabin, L. S., M. B. Hirsh, E. A. Smith, and J. B. Hardy. 1984. ''Adolescent Sexual Attitudes and Behavior: Are They Consistent?'' *Family Planning Perspectives*, 16:181–185.

Zajonc, R. B. 1976. ''Family Configuration and Intelligence.'' *Science*, 192:227–236.

Zelnick, M., and J. F. Kantner. 1980. ''Sexual Activity, Contraceptive Use and Pregnancy among Metropolitan-Area Teenagers: 1971–1979.'' *Family Planning Perspectives*, 12:231–237.

Zelnick, M., J. F. Kantner, and K. Ford. 1981. *Sex and Pregnancy in Adolescence*. Sage Library of Social Research, vol. 133. Beverly Hills: Sage Publications.

Zelnick, M., and F. K. Shah. 1983. ''First Intercourse among Young Americans.'' *Family Planning Perspectives*, 15:64–70.

Zigler, E. F., and E. W. Gordon. 1982. *Day Care: Scientific and Social Policy Issues*. Boston, MA: Auburn House.

Zigler, E. F., and S. Muenchow. 1984. ''How to Influence Social Policy Affecting Children and Families.'' *American Psychologist*, 39:415–420.

Zigler, E. F., and J. Valentine (Eds.). 1979. *Project Head Start: A Legacy of the War on Poverty*. New York: Free Press.

Index

abortion, 4, 5, 38, 71, 151; availability of, 18, 36–7, 39, 131, 149; legalization of, 4, 48, 70–1, 89; rates of, 36–7, 37f
academic ability, 50–1, 62, 108
academic achievement: children of teenage mothers, 104; *see also* school performance
academic domain, 110, 111; *see also* schooling
academic problems: low birth weight and, 89
academic success (children of teenage mothers), 109, 115–16, 116t, 121, 122, 125, 126, 128, 129, 144; *see also* school performance
additional childbearing, 36t, 64, 72; birth control use and, 65–6; consequences of, 71; and economic status, 55–6, 57, 61, 138; *see also* pregnancy(ies), repeat
adolescence, 9
adolescent fertility: outside marriage, 6; public policy and, 19–20; by race, 2–3t
adolescent motherhood: as experienced by children, 77–105
adolescent mothers: characteristics of, 54–7; costs to, 133; goal of, for their children, 104–5; life connections with children, 122–7, 124f; and newborns, 111–12; profile of, 19, 21–47; *see also* life course
adolescent outcomes: children of teenage mothers, 78, 81, 110, 115–19, 122, 125, 126, 128, 144
adolescent parenthood: reassessment of, 1–20
adolescents: and social services, 146–7, 149
adoption, 89
adult education, 153; *see also* post-high school education
adulthood: conditions affecting adaptation of early childbearers in, 9, 19, 48–76; pathways to success in, 48–76; teenage mothers' experiences in, 18–19, 21–47, 48–76
AFDC, 40, 138–9, 145
age: at first birth, 1; at first intercourse, 54; at marriage, 1, 4–5; at pregnancy, 54, 102–3, 136
age-appropriate behavior, 5

age-parity cohort (Baltimore study), 48–9
Alan Guttmacher Institute, 5, 151
ameliorative policy programs, 145–9, 152, 153
antisocial acts: children of teenage mothers, 78, 97–8; *see also* juvenile delinquency
Apgar score, 90, 111–12
attitudes: and economic status, 54, 60; about family size, 60–1; and life course, 136; toward pregnancy, 54, 89; about welfare, 61

baby boom, 1
Baltimore: City Health Department, 17
Baltimore study, 10–21, 130–1, 152; analysis of sample attrition for bias, 161–2; data sets used for comparison, 163–6; design of, 12t; five-year follow-up, 11, 13, 16, 21, 25, 30, 34, 35, 40, 47, 53, 78, 84, 87, 112–15, 131; generalizability of, 18, 19, 131; initial phase, 11; methods and procedures, 167–70; multivariate analysis, 171–83; origins of, 11–13; policy implications of, 145–52; procedure for computing summary statistics, 184–6; reliability of demographic variables in, 15–16, 158–60; representativeness of, 16–18, 130–1; 17-year follow-up, 13–20, 22, 33, 35, 46–7, 48, 50–1, 57, 61, 70–4, 78, 87–8, 107, 130, 132, 143, 145–6; strategy for data analysis, 49–50
Bane, M. J., 40
behavior/misbehavior: children of teenage mothers, 15, 93, 94t, 96–8, 99t, 104, 109, 114–15, 116–18, 117t, 121, 122, 125–6, 127–8, 129, 142–3, 144, 145, 172–3; low birth weight and, 89
behavioral domain, 110, 111
birth control, 36, 39; attitudes toward, 54
birth control information: given by mothers, 101–2, 103–4
birth control use, 137; barriers to, 151; by children of teenage mothers, 95, 101–2, 116; and economic status, 54, 55–6, 65–6, 66f, 68, 138, 140; and family size, 73; and fer-

197